KB100491

TOEFL® MAP
ACTUAL TEST

New TOEFL® Edition

Reading 2

DARAKWON

TOEFL® MAP
ACTUAL TEST
Reading 2

Publisher Chung Kyudo
Editors Cho Sangik, Zong Ziin
Authors Michael A. Putlack, Stephen Poirier
Designers Park Narae, Chung Kyuok

First published in April 2022
By Darakwon, Inc.
Darakwon Bldg., 211, Munbal-ro, Paju-si, Gyeonggi-do 10881
Republic of Korea
Tel: 82-2-736-2031 (Ext. 250)
Fax: 82-2-732-2037

ISBN 978-89-277-8009-0 14740
978-89-277-8007-6 14740 (set)

www.darakwon.co.kr

Photo Credits
Shutterstock.com

Components Main Book / Translation Book
8 7 6 5 4 3 2 23 24 25 26 27

TOEFL® MAP
ACTUAL TEST

New TOEFL® Edition

Reading 2

INTRODUCTION

Studying for the TOEFL® iBT is no easy task and is not one that is to be undertaken lightly. It requires a great deal of effort as well as dedication on the part of the student. It is our hope that, by using *TOEFL Map Actual Test Reading* as either a textbook or a study guide, the task of studying for the TOEFL® iBT will become somewhat easier for the student and less of a burden.

Students who wish to excel on the TOEFL® iBT must attain a solid grasp of the four important skills in the English language: reading, listening, speaking, and writing. The Darakwon *TOEFL Map* series covers all four of these skills in separate books. There are three different levels in all four topics. In addition, there are *TOEFL Map Actual Test* books that contain a number of actual tests that students can use to prepare themselves for the TOEFL® iBT. This book, *TOEFL Map Actual Test Reading*, covers the reading aspect of the test by providing reading passages in the TOEFL® iBT actual test format.

TOEFL Map Actual Test Reading has been designed for use both in a classroom setting and as a study guide for individual learners. It contains a total of seven full-length reading actual tests. Each test contains a varying number of reading passages. Every passage is the same length as those found on the TOEFL® iBT. The passages also have the same numbers and types of questions that appear on actual TOEFL® iBT reading section passages. In addition, the changes that were made to the TOEFL® iBT in August 2019 have been incorporated into this book. By studying these passages, learners should be able to prepare themselves to take and, more importantly, to excel on the TOEFL® iBT.

TOEFL Map Actual Test Reading has a great amount of information and should prove to be invaluable as a study guide for learners who are preparing for the TOEFL® iBT. However, while this book is comprehensive, it is up to each person to do the actual work. In order for *TOEFL Map Actual Test Reading* to be of any use, the individual learner must dedicate him or herself to studying the information found within its pages. While we have strived to make this book as user friendly and as full of crucial information as possible, ultimately, it is up to each person to make the best of the material in the book. We wish you luck in your study of both English and the TOEFL® iBT, and we hope that you are able to use *TOEFL Map Actual Test Reading* to improve your abilities in both of them.

Michael A. Putlack
Stephen Poirier

TABLE OF CONTENTS

HOW IS THIS BOOK DIFFERENT

CONTAINS PASSAGES MOST RECENTLY PRESENTED

- Has 24 passages in total
- Reconstructs the most frequently asked questions after analyzing real TOEFL® iBT questions
- Reflects the changes made to the TOEFL® iBT in August 2019

CONSISTS OF VARIOUS TOPICS

- Deals with academic topics such as the humanities, sciences, and arts

PROVIDES AN EXPLANATION FOR EVERY QUESTION

- Shows the question types and provides detailed explanations
- Presents tips for getting a higher score

PRESENTS TRANSLATIONS OF THE READING PASSAGES

- Contains translations for all passages

OFFERS FREE MP3 FILES

- Provides MP3 files for free at www.darakwon.co.kr
- Includes QR codes for listening to the MP3 files instantly

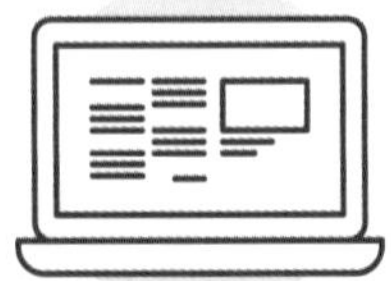

HOW TO USE THIS BOOK

QUESTION

This book contains every type of question that appears on the TOEFL® iBT. The difficulty level of the questions is the same as those on the actual TOEFL® iBT.

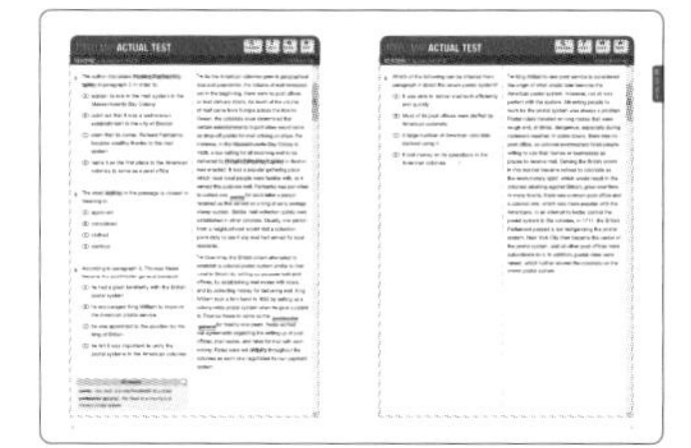

EXPLANATION

Every question has its own detailed explanation, so readers can learn why some answer choices are correct while others are not.

TRANSLATION

In case some Korean readers cannot fully understand the script, a translation section has been attached to the book. This section can help readers grasp the meanings of certain passages.

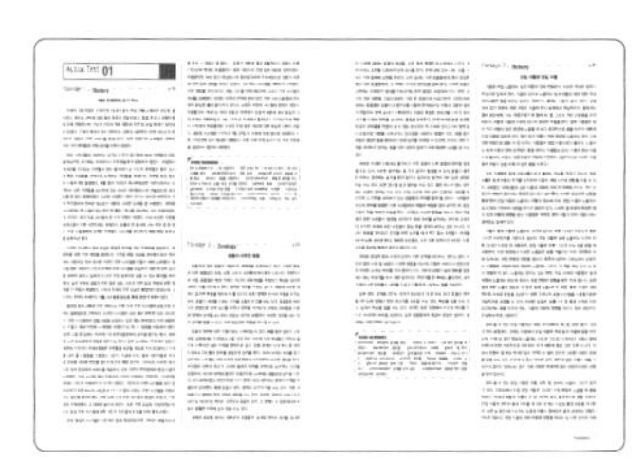

WORD REMINDER

Words and expressions that frequently appear on the actual TOEFL® iBT are listed in this section. In addition, readers can learn key words related to specific topics.

ABOUT THE TOEFL® iBT

TOEFL® iBT Test Sections

Section	Tasks	Time Limit	Questions
Reading	Read 3-4 passages from academic texts and answer questions.	54 – 72 minutes	30 – 40 questions
Listening	Listen to lectures, classroom discussions, and conversations and then answer questions.	41 – 57 minutes	28 – 39 questions
Break 10 minutes			
Speaking	Express an opinion on a familiar topic and also speak based on reading and listening tasks.	17 minutes	4 tasks
Writing	Write essay responses based on reading and listening tasks and support an opinion in writing.	50 minutes	2 tasks

TOEFL® iBT Test Contents

The TOEFL® iBT test is a test given in English on an Internet-based format. The TOEFL® iBT has four sections: reading, listening, speaking, and writing. The test requires approximately three and a half hours to take.

Combining All Four Skills: Reading, Listening, Speaking, and Writing

During the test, learners must use more than one of the four basic skills at the same time. For instance, learners may have to:

- listen to a question and then speak a response
- read and listen and then speak a response to a question
- read and listen and then write a response to a question

What Is the TOEFL® iBT Test?

The TOEFL® iBT test measures how well learners understand university-level English. The test requires students to use a combination of their reading, listening, speaking, and writing skills to do various academic tasks.

Which Learners Take the TOEFL® iBT Test?

Around one million people take the TOEFL® iBT test every year. The English abilities of most people taking the test are anywhere from intermediate to advanced. The following types of people most commonly take the TOEFL® iBT test:

- students who will study at institutes of higher learning
- students who wish to gain admission to English education programs
- individuals who are applying for scholarships or certificates
- learners who want to determine the level of their English ability
- students and other individuals who are applying for visas

Who Accepts TOEFL® iBT Test Scores?

In more than 130 countries around the world, over 8,000 colleges, universities, agencies, and other institutions accept TOEFL® iBT scores. In addition, the following places utilize TOEFL® iBT scores:

- immigration departments that use the scores when issuing visas
- medical and licensing agencies that award various certificates
- individuals who are trying to determine the level of their English ability

ABOUT THE READING QUESTION TYPES

Type 1 Vocabulary Questions

Vocabulary questions require the test taker to understand specific words or phrases that are used in the passage. These questions ask the test taker to choose another word or phrase that is the most similar in meaning to the highlighted text. The vocabulary words that are highlighted are often important words, so knowing their meanings is often critical for understanding the entire passage. The highlighted words typically have several meanings, so test takers need to be careful to avoid selecting an answer choice simply because it is the word's or phrase's most common meaning.

Type 2 Reference Questions

Reference questions require the test taker to understand the relationship between words and their referents in the passage. These questions most frequently ask the test taker to identify the antecedent of a pronoun. In many cases, the pronouns are words like *he*, *she*, or *they* or *its*, *his*, *hers*, or *theirs*. However, in other cases, relative pronouns like *which* or demonstrative pronouns like *this* or *that* may be asked about instead. This type of question seldom appears on the test anymore.

Type 3 Factual Information Questions

Factual Information questions require the test taker to understand and to be able to recognize facts that are mentioned in the passage. These questions may cover any facts or information that is explicitly covered in the passage. These may appear in the form of details, definitions, explanations, or other kinds of data. The facts which the questions ask about are typically found only in one part of the passage—perhaps in a sentence or two—and do not require a comprehensive understanding of the passage as a whole.

Type 4 Negative Factual Information Questions

Negative Factual Information questions require the test taker to understand and to be able to recognize facts that are mentioned in the passage. These questions may be about any facts or information that is explicitly covered in the passage. However, these questions ask the test taker to identify the incorrect information in the answer choices. Three of the four answer choices will therefore have correct information that can be found in the passage. The answer the test taker must choose will either have incorrect information or information that is not found in the passage.

Type 5 Sentence Simplification Questions

Sentence Simplification questions require the test taker to select a sentence that best restates one that has been highlighted in the passage. These questions ask the test taker to note the main points in the sentence and to make sure that they are mentioned in the rewritten sentence. These sentences use words, phrases, and grammar that are different from the highlighted sentence. They also sometimes do not appear in a passage. When they are asked, there is only one Sentence Simplification question per passage.

Type 6 Inference Questions

Inference questions require the test taker to understand the argument that the passage is attempting to make. These questions ask the test taker to consider the information that is presented and then to come to a logical conclusion about it. The answers to these questions are never explicitly stated in the passage. Instead, the test taker is asked to infer what the author means. These questions often deal with cause and effect or comparisons between two different things, ideas, events, or people.

Type 7 Rhetorical Purpose Questions

Rhetorical Purpose questions require the test taker to understand why the author mentioned or wrote about something in the passage. These questions ask the test taker to consider the reasoning behind the information that is being presented in the passage. For these questions, the function—not the meaning—of the material is the most important aspect to be aware of. The questions often focus on the relationship between the information mentioned or covered either in paragraphs or individual sentences in the passage and the purpose or intention of the information that is given.

Type 8 Insert Text Questions

Insert Text questions require the test taker to determine where in the passage another sentence should be placed. These questions ask the test taker to consider various aspects, including grammar, logic, connecting words, and flow, when deciding where the new sentence best belongs. Recently, there is almost always one Insert Text question per passage. This question always appears just before the last question.

Type 9 Prose Summary Questions

Prose Summary questions require the test taker to understand the main point of the passage and then to select sentences which emphasize the main point. These questions present a sentence which is essentially a thesis statement for the entire passage. The sentence synthesizes the main points of the passage. The test taker must then choose three out of six sentences which most closely describe points mentioned in the introductory sentence. This means that three of the choices are minor points, have incorrect information, or contain information that does not appear in the passage, so they are all therefore incorrect. These are always the last question asked about a Reading passage. Recently, they appear on the test very frequently.

Type 10 Fill in a Table Questions

Fill in a Table questions require the test taker to have a comprehensive understanding of the entire passage. These questions typically break the passage down into two—or sometimes three—main points or themes. The test taker must then read a number of sentences or phrases and determine which of the points or themes the sentences or phrases refer to. These questions often ask the test taker to consider cause and effect, to compare and contrast, or to understand various theories or ideas covered. These are always the last question asked about a Reading passage, but they have become less common recently.

TOEFL® MAP

ACTUAL TEST

Reading 2

CONTINUE

Reading Section Directions

This section measures your ability to understand academic passages in English. You will have **54 minutes** to read and answer questions about **3 passages**. A clock at the top of the screen will show you how much time is remaining.

Most questions are worth 1 point but the last question for each passage is worth more than 1 point. The directions for the last question indicate how many points you may receive.

Some passages include a word or phrase that is **underlined** in blue. Click on the word or phrase to see a definition or an explanation.

When you want to move to the next question, click on **Next**. You may skip questions and go back to them later. If you want to return to previous questions, click on **Back**. You can click on **Reivew** at any time, and the review screen will show you which questions you have answered and which you have not answered. From this review screen, you may go directly to any question you have already seen in the Reading section.

Click on **Continue** to go on.

The Early History of the American Post Office

During colonial American times in the seventeenth and eighteenth centuries, the main means of communication was the written word. Letters were sent by ship or over land, were often carried by friends or travelers, and were subject to delays and possible loss due to distance and the forces of nature. There was no organized government mail service until the late seventeenth century, and early attempts to improve the service typically fell prey to a wide variety of problems.

As the American colonies grew in geographical size and population, the volume of mail increased, yet in the beginning, there were no post offices or mail delivery riders. As much of the volume of mail came from Europe across the Atlantic Ocean, the colonists soon determined that certain establishments in port cities would serve as drop-off points for mail arriving on ships. For instance, in the Massachusetts Bay Colony in 1639, a law calling for all incoming mail to be delivered to Richard Fairbanks's tavern in Boston was enacted. It was a popular gathering place which most local people were familiar with, so it served this purpose well. Fairbanks was permitted to collect one **penny** for each letter a person received as this served as a kind of early postage stamp system. Similar mail collection points were established in other colonies. Usually, one person from a neighborhood would visit a collection point daily to see if any mail had arrived for local residents.

Over time, the British crown attempted to establish a colonial postal system similar to that used in Britain by setting up purpose-built post offices, by establishing mail routes with riders, and by collecting money for delivering mail. King William took a firm hand in 1692 by setting up a colony-wide postal system when he gave a patent to Thomas Neale to serve as the **postmaster general** for twenty-one years. Neale worked out agreements regarding the setting up of post offices, mail routes, and rates for mail with each colony. Rates were not uniform throughout the colonies as each one negotiated its own payment system.

King William's new post service is considered the origin of what would later become the American postal system. However, not all was perfect with the system. Attracting people to work for the postal system was always a problem. Postal riders traveled on long routes that were rough and, at times, dangerous, especially during inclement weather. In some towns, there was no post office, so colonial postmasters hired people willing to use their homes or businesses as places to receive mail. Serving the British crown in this manner became odious to colonists as the revolutionary spirit, which would result in the colonies rebelling against Britain, grew over time. In many towns, there was a crown post office and a colonial one, which was more popular with the Americans. In an attempt to better control the postal system in the colonies, in 1711, the British Parliament passed a law reorganizing the postal system. New York City then became the center of the postal system, and all other post offices were subordinate to it. In addition, postal rates were raised, which further soured the colonists on the crown postal system.

The crown system grew along with the colonies but was never very efficient as letters took weeks—and sometimes months—to be delivered. Then, in 1753, Benjamin Franklin was appointed deputy postmaster general for the northern colonies. Franklin had experience as a postal official, having served as postmaster for Philadelphia, Pennsylvania, for sixteen years. He immediately began to reform the system. He improved mail routes, cut down on delivery times, and eliminated the postal system's debt. However, rumblings throughout the colonies about payments made to the crown through the postal service still plagued the system. Franklin himself was removed from office in 1774 when his association with the growing rebellion movement made the crown sour on him. When the American Revolution began in 1775, Franklin was the obvious choice to serve as the American postmaster general. A new system was enacted by the American Congress on July 25, 1775. Then, in 1792, President George Washington signed a law establishing the United States Post Office Department, which later became the United States Postal Service.

Glossary

penny: one cent; one one-hundredth of a dollar

postmaster general: the head of a country's or colony's postal system

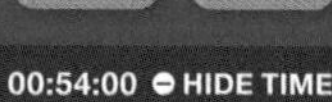

1 The phrase fell prey to in the passage is closest in meaning to

Ⓐ was discovered by

Ⓑ resulted in

Ⓒ were harmed by

Ⓓ appeared with

2 Which of the sentences below best expresses the essential information in the highlighted sentence in the passage? *Incorrect* answer choices change the meaning in important ways or leave out essential information.

Ⓐ Most of the mail between the colonies and Europe traveled across the Atlantic Ocean, so the colonists had the mail delivered to certain drop-off points in cities.

Ⓑ The colonists used various places in port cities as places where mail could be delivered since most of it was sent from Europe across the Atlantic Ocean.

Ⓒ Colonists could visit various establishments in port cities when they wanted to see if they had any mail sent to them across the Atlantic Ocean from Europe.

Ⓓ It took time for mail to arrive across the Atlantic Ocean from Europe, so the colonists set up places to receive mail in certain port cities in the colonies.

Glossary

penny: one cent; one one-hundredth of a dollar

The Early History of the American Post Office

During colonial American times in the seventeenth and eighteenth centuries, the main means of communication was the written word. Letters were sent by ship or over land, were often carried by friends or travelers, and were subject to delays and possible loss due to distance and the forces of nature. There was no organized government mail service until the late seventeenth century, and early attempts to improve the service typically fell prey to a wide variety of problems.

As the American colonies grew in geographical size and population, the volume of mail increased, yet in the beginning, there were no post offices or mail delivery riders. As much of the volume of mail came from Europe across the Atlantic Ocean, the colonists soon determined that certain establishments in port cities would serve as drop-off points for mail arriving on ships. For instance, in the Massachusetts Bay Colony in 1639, a law calling for all incoming mail to be delivered to Richard Fairbanks's tavern in Boston was enacted. It was a popular gathering place which most local people were familiar with, so it served this purpose well. Fairbanks was permitted to collect one **penny** for each letter a person received as this served as a king of early postage stamp system. Similar mail collection points were established in other colonies. Usually, one person from a neighborhood would visit a collection point daily to see if any mail had arrived for local residents.

3 The author discusses Richard Fairbanks's tavern in paragraph 2 in order to

Ⓐ explain its role in the mail system in the Massachusetts Bay Colony

Ⓑ point out that it was a well-known establishment in the city of Boston

Ⓒ claim that its owner, Richard Fairbanks, became wealthy thanks to the mail system

Ⓓ name it as the first place in the American colonies to serve as a post office

4 The word uniform in the passage is closest in meaning to

Ⓐ approved

Ⓑ considered

Ⓒ clothed

Ⓓ identical

5 According to paragraph 3, Thomas Neale became the postmaster general because

Ⓐ he had a great familiarity with the British postal system

Ⓑ he encouraged King William to improve the American postal service

Ⓒ he was appointed to the position by the king of Britain

Ⓓ he felt it was important to unify the postal systems in the American colonies

Glossary

penny: one cent; one one-hundredth of a dollar
postmaster general: the head of a country's or colony's postal system

2→ As the American colonies grew in geographical size and population, the volume of mail increased, yet in the beginning, there were no post offices or mail delivery riders. As much of the volume of mail came from Europe across the Atlantic Ocean, the colonists soon determined that certain establishments in port cities would serve as drop-off points for mail arriving on ships. For instance, in the Massachusetts Bay Colony in 1639, a law calling for all incoming mail to be delivered to Richard Fairbanks's tavern in Boston was enacted. It was a popular gathering place which most local people were familiar with, so it served this purpose well. Fairbanks was permitted to collect one **penny** for each letter a person received as this served as a king of early postage stamp system. Similar mail collection points were established in other colonies. Usually, one person from a neighborhood would visit a collection point daily to see if any mail had arrived for local residents.

3→ Over time, the British crown attempted to establish a colonial postal system similar to that used in Britain by setting up purpose-built post offices, by establishing mail routes with riders, and by collecting money for delivering mail. King William took a firm hand in 1692 by setting up a colony-wide postal system when he gave a patent to Thomas Neale to serve as the **postmaster general** for twenty-one years. Neale worked out agreements regarding the setting up of post offices, mail routes, and rates for mail with each colony. Rates were not uniform throughout the colonies as each one negotiated its own payment system.

6 Which of the following can be inferred from paragraph 4 about the crown postal system?

Ⓐ It was able to deliver mail both efficiently and quickly.

Ⓑ Most of its post offices were staffed by American colonists.

Ⓒ A large number of American colonists disliked using it.

Ⓓ It lost money on its operations in the American colonies.

4→ King William's new post service is considered the origin of what would later become the American postal system. However, not all was perfect with the system. Attracting people to work for the postal system was always a problem. Postal riders traveled on long routes that were rough and, at times, dangerous, especially during inclement weather. In some towns, there was no post office, so colonial postmasters hired people willing to use their homes or businesses as places to receive mail. Serving the British crown in this manner became odious to colonists as the revolutionary spirit, which would result in the colonies rebelling against Britain, grew over time. In many towns, there was a crown post office and a colonial one, which was more popular with the Americans. In an attempt to better control the postal system in the colonies, in 1711, the British Parliament passed a law reorganizing the postal system. New York City then became the center of the postal system, and all other post offices were subordinate to it. In addition, postal rates were raised, which further soured the colonists on the crown postal system.

7 In paragraph 5, why does the author mention President George Washington?

Ⓐ To describe the reforms that he made to the United States Post Office Department

Ⓑ To explain the role that he played during the fighting in the American Revolution

Ⓒ To argue that he was more important to the American postal system than Benjamin Franklin

Ⓓ To credit him with establishing what would become the United States Postal Service

8 According to paragraph 5, which of the following is true of Benjamin Franklin?

Ⓐ He worked for both the British and the American postal systems in America.

Ⓑ He helped the post office make deliveries faster but increased its debt.

Ⓒ He worked for the crown postal system even during the American Revolution.

Ⓓ He became the postmaster general for all of the American colonies in 1753.

5→ The crown system grew along with the colonies but was never very efficient as letters took weeks—and sometimes months—to be delivered. Then, in 1753, Benjamin Franklin was appointed deputy postmaster general for the northern colonies. Franklin had experience as a postal official, having served as postmaster for Philadelphia, Pennsylvania, for sixteen years. He immediately began to reform the system. He improved mail routes, cut down on delivery times, and eliminated the postal system's debt. However, rumblings throughout the colonies about payments made to the crown through the postal service still plagued the system. Franklin himself was removed from office in 1774 when his association with the growing rebellion movement made the crown sour on him. When the American Revolution began in 1775, Franklin was the obvious choice to serve as the American postmaster general. A new system was enacted by the American Congress on July 25, 1775. Then, in 1792, President George Washington signed a law establishing the United States Post Office Department, which later became the United States Postal Service.

9 Look at the four squares [■] that indicate where the following sentence could be added to the passage.

Some of them were also subjected to attacks by hostile Native Americans while others were robbed by bandits at times.

Where would the sentence best fit?

Click on a square [■] to add the sentence to the passage.

King William's new post service is considered the origin of what would later become the American postal system. However, not all was perfect with the system. Attracting people to work for the postal system was always a problem. **1** Postal riders traveled on long routes that were rough and, at times, dangerous, especially during inclement weather. **2** In some towns, there was no post office, so colonial postmasters hired people willing to use their homes or businesses as places to receive mail. **3** Serving the British crown in this manner became odious to colonists as the revolutionary spirit, which would result in the colonies rebelling against Britain, grew over time. **4** In many towns, there was a crown post office and a colonial one, which was more popular with the Americans. In an attempt to better control the postal system in the colonies, in 1711, the British Parliament passed a law reorganizing the postal system. New York City then became the center of the postal system, and all other post offices were subordinate to it. In addition, postal rates were raised, which further soured the colonists on the crown postal system.

10 Directions: An introductory sentence for a brief summary of the passage is provided below. Complete the summary by selecting the THREE answer choices that express the most important ideas of the passage. Some sentences do not belong because they express ideas that are not presented in the passage or are minor ideas in the passage. **This question is worth 2 points.**

Drag your answer choices to the spaces where they belong.
To remove an answer choice, click on it. To review the passage, click on **View Text**.

Developments in the postal system in the American colonies led to the eventual establishment of the United States Postal Service.

-
-
-

Answer Choices

1 Many American colonists became upset with the British, so they forced some crown post offices to close down.

2 The British crown set up a postal system, and men such as Thomas Neale worked hard to improve its service.

3 Mail often got lost or was delivered late because of problems with transportation during colonial times in America.

4 Benjamin Franklin worked in the postal system and was later appointed postmaster general during the American Revolution.

5 Some people's homes were used as post offices because the towns in which they lived lacked an office.

6 Mail collection points were set up in some port cities, and people could visit them both to send and receive mail.

Animal Territorial Behavior

In the animal kingdom, some species can be fiercely territorial. This behavior is more common with insects, birds, and mammals than other creatures. These animals typically stake a claim to an area and then protect it, sometimes to the death. Their territories are where they obtain their food sources, so without these lands, they would perish. Their territories may also serve as breeding grounds and may contain shelters where the animals raise their young. Animals mark and protect their land in numerous ways, including using body secretions to indicate the boundaries of their territories. Crossing these may invite attack and possibly result in death for any perpetrators.

An animal's territory may consist of any type of terrain. In Yellowstone National Park, for instance, wolf packs consisting of between five to twenty-five members claim large regions of hilly, forested land and attack any wolves from rival packs that enter their territory. Lions, which live in groups called prides, act similarly while living on the **savannahs** of Africa. Hippopotamuses claim stretches of land by riverbanks and lakeshores and attack any living things, including humans, that enter their territory and are deemed threats. Walruses are equally fierce in defending the parts of beaches they consider their own. For some animals, their territory may be small; it may only comprise the area around a minute anthill or beehive. In other cases, such as with wolves and the big cats of Africa and Asia, a territory may encompass a vast area of land covering many kilometers.

Most territorial animals mark the boundaries of their land with scents. These scents come from the animals' feces, urine, or special secretion-producing glands. Dogs and wolves employ urine to mark their territory. They spray it on trees, bushes, and other objects in their land. The scent of the urine indicates to other animals, particularly those of their own species, that the area has been claimed. The urine of these animals has a chemical substance which permits the scent to remain active for a long time. Meanwhile, members of the cat family, from tiny domestic cats to the largest tigers, rub their faces or **flanks** against objects, which imparts their scents onto them and thereby marks their territory. Deer have special glands they use to secrete substances indicating their territory. Other types of territorial markers include displays of color and warning sounds. Birds, for instance, may flap their wings to warn off intruders and also make particular sounds to let other birds know an area is occupied.

Sometimes, despite these indicators, an animal may cross into another's territory. In these instances, several results may ensue. If the animal stays for a short time, it may depart unmolested or even unnoticed. The animal may also flee after being warned, or if it does not leave, a fight may occur. If the animal appears intent on remaining in the area, it will attract the attention of the animals that claimed it. Wolves swiftly challenge and attack other wolves that cross into their territory and battle invaders to the death. Lions engage in similar behavior, particularly when unattached males attack a pride in search of females. Yet the pride males do not always fight to the death; if they sense they are losing, they may flee and allow the unattached males to take over. The vanquished males then roam by themselves until they defeat another pride's males, something which rarely happens.

Occasionally, males and females of the same species occupy different territories. Male and female cheetahs and leopards do this as they travel in small groups which are solely male or female. When cheetahs and leopards cross into another's territory, they do so for the purpose of mating. After having done that, they part, and the females raise the young and teach them to hunt after they are born.

In some cases, the costs of defending a territory can outweigh the benefits. Animals may expend a massive amount of energy while defending their territory. They may suffer injuries and even be killed. However, in the game of survival, defending their food sources and protecting their homes and groups are equally important to animals. Ultimately, only the strongest survive.

Glossary

savannah: a plain with grasses and few trees that receives seasonal rainfall

flank: the side of an animal's body

11 According to paragraph 1, what is the most important reason that animals mark their territories?

Ⓐ To enable them to have safe places to raise their young

Ⓑ To give them areas where they can sleep and hide from predators

Ⓒ To provide them with places where they can mate and reproduce

Ⓓ To guarantee them a food supply to prevent them from starving

12 According to paragraph 2, which of the following is NOT true of the territory that animals claim as their own?

Ⓐ The region that lions claim may cover a relatively large amount of land.

Ⓑ The size of the territory that animals claim depends on the animals themselves.

Ⓒ The territory that wolves claim may be forested land or grassy plains.

Ⓓ Hippopotamuses react violently when their territory is encroached.

Glossary

savannah: a plain with grasses and few trees that receives seasonal rainfall

Animal Territorial Behavior

[1]→ In the animal kingdom, some species can be fiercely territorial. This behavior is more common with insects, birds, and mammals than other creatures. These animals typically stake a claim to an area and then protect it, sometimes to the death. Their territories are where they obtain their food sources, so without these lands, they would perish. Their territories may also serve as breeding grounds and may contain shelters where the animals raise their young. Animals mark and protect their land in numerous ways, including using body secretions to indicate the boundaries of their territories. Crossing these may invite attack and possibly result in death for any perpetrators.

[2]→ An animal's territory may consist of any type of terrain. In Yellowstone National Park, for instance, wolf packs consisting of between five to twenty-five members claim large regions of hilly, forested land and attack any wolves from rival packs that enter their territory. Lions, which live in groups called prides, act similarly while living on the **savannahs** of Africa. Hippopotamuses claim stretches of land by riverbanks and lakeshores and attack any living things, including humans, that enter their territory and are deemed threats. Walruses are equally fierce in defending the parts of beaches they consider their own. For some animals, their territory may be small; it may only comprise the area around a minute anthill or beehive. In other cases, such as with wolves and the big cats of Africa and Asia, a territory may encompass a vast area of land covering many kilometers.

13 The word imparts in the passage is closest in meaning to

Ⓐ conveys

Ⓑ deflects

Ⓒ transfigures

Ⓓ removes

14 According to paragraph 3, cats mark their territory by

Ⓐ secreting substances from glands located in their bodies

Ⓑ rubbing some parts of their bodies onto various objects

Ⓒ urinating on the boundaries of the land that they claim as their own

Ⓓ making unique sounds that are meant to drive off other animals

Glossary

flank: the side of an animal's body

3→ Most territorial animals mark the boundaries of their land with scents. These scents come from the animals' feces, urine, or special secretion-producing glands. Dogs and wolves employ urine to mark their territory. They spray it on trees, bushes, and other objects in their land. The scent of the urine indicates to other animals, particularly those of their own species, that the area has been claimed. The urine of these animals has a chemical substance which permits the scent to remain active for a long time. Meanwhile, members of the cat family, from tiny domestic cats to the largest tigers, rub their faces or **flanks** against objects, which imparts their scents onto them and thereby marks their territory. Deer have special glands they use to secrete substances indicating their territory. Other types of territorial markers include displays of color and warning sounds. Birds, for instance, may flap their wings to warn off intruders and also make particular sounds to let other birds know an area is occupied.

15 The word unmolested in the passage is closest in meaning to

Ⓐ unopposed

Ⓑ undecided

Ⓒ unsupported

Ⓓ unattached

16 According to paragraph 4, which of the following is true of lions?

Ⓐ They fight other lions trying to take over their pride to the death.

Ⓑ It is common for lions to defeat the other males in a pride.

Ⓒ Male lions may attack a pride in order to kill the cubs in it.

Ⓓ Lions that are losing a fight may run away to save themselves.

4→ Sometimes, despite these indicators, an animal may cross into another's territory. In these instances, several results may ensue. If the animal stays for a short time, it may depart unmolested or even unnoticed. The animal may also flee after being warned, or if it does not leave, a fight may occur. If the animal appears intent on remaining in the area, it will attract the attention of the animals that claimed it. Wolves swiftly challenge and attack other wolves that cross into their territory and battle invaders to the death. Lions engage in similar behavior, particularly when unattached males attack a pride in search of females. Yet the pride males do not always fight to the death; if they sense they are losing, they may flee and allow the unattached males to take over. The vanquished males then roam by themselves until they defeat another pride's males, something which rarely happens.

[5] → Occasionally, males and females of the same species occupy different territories. Male and female cheetahs and leopards do this as they travel in small groups which are solely male or female. When cheetahs and leopards cross into another's territory, they do so for the purpose of mating. After having done that, they part, and the females raise the young and teach them to hunt after they are born.

[6] → In some cases, the costs of defending a territory can outweigh the benefits. Animals may expend a massive amount of energy while defending their territory. They may suffer injuries and even be killed. However, in the game of survival, defending their food sources and protecting their homes and groups are equally important to animals. Ultimately, only the strongest survive.

17 The author discusses cheetahs and leopards in paragraph 5 in order to

Ⓐ describe how female cheetahs and leopards raise and train their young

Ⓑ focus on the similarities in how they live and how lions and tigers live

Ⓒ mention that the males and females of these species live separately

Ⓓ give the reason that these animals almost always live in small groups

18 In paragraph 6, the author implies that animals

Ⓐ do not always benefit from defending their territories from other animals

Ⓑ often seek to increase the sizes of their territories by attacking others

Ⓒ have to consume a lot of food if they constantly fight with invaders

Ⓓ will always fight to the death to protect their young from attacking animals

PREVIEW

HELP

BACK

NEXT

19 Look at the four squares [■] that indicate where the following sentence could be added to the passage.

Similarly, some rabbits have glands near their chins from which they can release secretions.

Where would the sentence best fit?

Click on a square [■] to add the sentence to the passage.

Most territorial animals mark the boundaries of their land with scents. These scents come from the animals' feces, urine, or special secretion-producing glands. Dogs and wolves employ urine to mark their territory. They spray it on trees, bushes, and other objects in their land. The scent of the urine indicates to other animals, particularly those of their own species, that the area has been claimed. [1] The urine of these animals has a chemical substance which permits the scent to remain active for a long time. [2] Meanwhile, members of the cat family, from tiny domestic cats to the largest tigers, rub their faces or **flanks** against objects, which imparts their scents onto them and thereby marks their territory. [3] Deer have special glands they use to secrete substances indicating their territory. [4] Other types of territorial markers include displays of color and warning sounds. Birds, for instance, may flap their wings to warn off intruders and also make particular sounds to let other birds know an area is occupied.

Glossary

flank: the side of an animal's body

20 Directions: An introductory sentence for a brief summary of the passage is provided below. Complete the summary by selecting the THREE answer choices that express the most important ideas of the passage. Some sentences do not belong because they express ideas that are not presented in the passage or are minor ideas in the passage. **This question is worth 2 points.**

Drag your answer choices to the spaces where they belong.
To remove an answer choice, click on it. To review the passage, click on **View Text**.

Many animals claim land as their own and will fight other animals in order to protect their territories.

-
-
-

Answer Choices

1. When one animal goes into another's territory, the two of them often fight.
2. Ants and bees are two types of animals that claim small areas of land for their own.
3. Many lions live together in groups of males, females, and cubs called prides.
4. The majority of wolves prefer to live in packs that roam forested areas of land.
5. Animals may use urine, bodily secretions, and displays of color to mark their territories.
6. Hippopotamuses, wolves, and walruses all fight animals that invade their areas.

Short-Day and Long-Day Plants

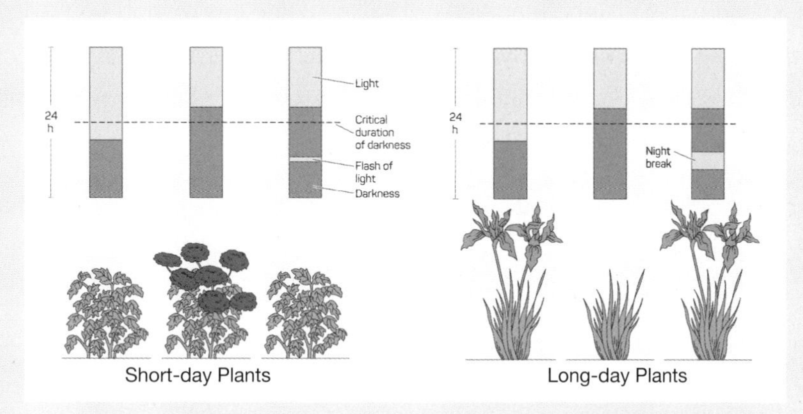

The conditions for flowering of short-day and long-day plants

Plants respond to the amounts of light and darkness which they are exposed to every day. This phenomenon is known as photoperiodism. The primary response mechanism in plants to the amount of light and darkness exposure is flowering, which is the ability to produce flower blossoms. The process of flowering is key to a plant's ability to propagate since flowers contain a plant's reproductive organs. Flowers produce nectar that, along with their color and aroma, attracts birds, bees, and other insects, which play a role in the pollination of the plant. Some plants flower more efficiently when they are exposed to less light and more darkness and are accordingly known as short-day plants. Other plants have a better flowering response when exposed to more light and less darkness and are therefore named long-day plants. There are also some plants capable of flowering regardless of the amount of light or darkness they receive. These are called day-neutral plants, and their flowering response is based on their age.

All plants have pigments in their leaves called **phytochromes**, which can detect periods of light and darkness and thus influence when a plant flowers. For a long time, botanists believed that it was the amount of daylight and sunlight absorption which had the most influence on the flowering of all kinds of plants. However, it has now been established through extensive experimentation that short-day plants flower depending upon their level of darkness exposure while long-day plants flower based upon the amount of light they are exposed to. Due to this, plants influenced by certain amounts of light and darkness are also sometimes known by the terms long-night plants and short-night plants.

The length of time that a plant is exposed to light and darkness is based on a rate of more or fewer than twelve hours per day. Short-day plants flower when exposed to fewer than twelve hours of light per day whereas long-day plants flower when they receive more than twelve hours of light per day. In natural settings, this amount of exposure is typically influenced by the seasonal changes induced by the tilt of Earth's axis. Plants growing at high latitudes to the north and the south have shorter daylight exposure during some seasons and greater daylight exposure in others while plants close to the equator experience only minor seasonal changes in their levels of exposure to light and darkness. Light exposure can also be adjusted artificially by the use of high-energy lighting systems for greater light exposure or extensive coverings to simulate darkness. These methods are regularly employed in commercial greenhouses to influence the flowering of plants that normally would not bloom under natural conditions at certain times of the year.

Some common short-day plants include chrysanthemums, poinsettias, rice, soybeans, onions, strawberries, and cotton. At high latitudes, short-day plants mostly flower in spring and autumn, which is when daylight exposure is fewer than twelve hours. Flowering takes place at night but is not always certain since a continuous period of darkness is required. Therefore, any flashes of light, such as lightning during a thunderstorm, may interrupt the process. On the other hand, if there is a period of darkness during the day, such as when the sun is concealed by thick clouds or a solar eclipse, the flowering process is influenced in neither a positive nor negative manner.

Some common long-day plants are asters, lettuce, wheat, poppies, spinach, and potatoes. At high latitudes, these long-day plants flower when they are exposed to more than twelve hours of sunlight. Therefore, they flower more efficiently during the long daylight hours of late spring and summer. Unlike with short-day plants, flashes of light during hours of darkness actually stimulate flower growth. Additionally, if a period of daylight is interrupted by a period of darkness, there is no influence on flower growth. Another factor which influences the flowering response of long-day plants is the presence of **gibberellic acid**. It is a natural hormone which is found in most plants and prompts the accelerated growth of plant cells. In long-day plants, gibberellic acid plays an active role in flowering, but in short-day plants, it has no influence whatsoever on when plants flower.

Glossary

phytochrome: a pigment in plants that is connected to the absorption of light

gibberellic acid: a type of hormone found in both plants and fungi

21 The word propagate in the passage is closest in meaning to

Ⓐ evolve

Ⓑ grow

Ⓒ blossom

Ⓓ spread

22 According to paragraph 2, which of the following is true of long-day plants?

Ⓐ When they produce flowers depends upon the amount of light that they receive.

Ⓑ Their leaves do not have as many phytochromes as those of short-day plants.

Ⓒ Many biologists prefer to refer to them by the name short-night plants.

Ⓓ They are capable of absorbing large amounts of sunlight during daylight hours.

Glossary

phytochrome: a pigment in plants that is connected to the absorption of light

Short-Day and Long-Day Plants

Plants respond to the amounts of light and darkness which they are exposed to every day. This phenomenon is known as photoperiodism. The primary response mechanism in plants to the amount of light and darkness exposure is flowering, which is the ability to produce flower blossoms. The process of flowering is key to a plant's ability to propagate since flowers contain a plant's reproductive organs. Flowers produce nectar that, along with their color and aroma, attracts birds, bees, and other insects, which play a role in the pollination of the plant. Some plants flower more efficiently when they are exposed to less light and more darkness and are accordingly known as short-day plants. Other plants have a better flowering response when exposed to more light and less darkness and are therefore named long-day plants. There are also some plants capable of flowering regardless of the amount of light or darkness they receive. These are called day-neutral plants, and their flowering response is based on their age.

[2]→ All plants have pigments in their leaves called **phytochromes**, which can detect periods of light and darkness and thus influence when a plant flowers. For a long time, botanists believed that it was the amount of daylight and sunlight absorption which had the most influence on the flowering of all kinds of plants. However, it has now been established through extensive experimentation that short-day plants flower depending upon their level of darkness exposure while long-day plants flower based upon the amount of light they are exposed to. Due to this, plants influenced by certain amounts of light and darkness are also sometimes known by the terms long-night plants and short-night plants.

23 Which of the sentences below best expresses the essential information in the highlighted sentence in the passage? *Incorrect* answer choices change the meaning in important ways or leave out essential information.

Ⓐ Short-day plants tend to grow better at high latitudes due to the changes in the seasons whereas long-day plants do better at the equator, where there are not many seasonal changes.

Ⓑ It is possible for most plants to grow at the equator since they get regular amounts of light and darkness, but some plants cannot grow at high latitudes during certain times of the year.

Ⓒ The seasons determine how much light plants growing at high altitudes receive, but plants growing near the equator mostly receive a constant amount of light and darkness.

Ⓓ The types of plants that grow at high latitudes and at the equator vary because there are seasonal changes at high latitudes but constant weather in areas close to the equator.

24 In paragraph 3, the author implies that greenhouses

Ⓐ allow farmers to produce greater amounts of crops all throughout the year

Ⓑ enable people to grow plants during seasons when they do not normally grow

Ⓒ are better for growing short-day plants than they are for growing long-day plants

Ⓓ can only be used effectively at certain latitudes in most places around the world

[3]→ The length of time that a plant is exposed to light and darkness is based on a rate of more or fewer than twelve hours per day. Short-day plants flower when exposed to fewer than twelve hours of light per day whereas long-day plants flower when they receive more than twelve hours of light per day. In natural settings, this amount of exposure is typically influenced by the seasonal changes induced by the tilt of Earth's axis. Plants growing at high latitudes to the north and the south have shorter daylight exposure during some seasons and greater daylight exposure in others while plants close to the equator experience only minor seasonal changes in their levels of exposure to light and darkness. Light exposure can also be adjusted artificially by the use of high-energy lighting systems for greater light exposure or extensive coverings to simulate darkness. These methods are regularly employed in commercial greenhouses to influence the flowering of plants that normally would not bloom under natural conditions at certain times of the year.

25 The word concealed in the passage is closest in meaning to

Ⓐ revealed

Ⓑ approached

Ⓒ covered

Ⓓ hindered

26 In paragraph 4, the author's description of short-day plants includes all of the following EXCEPT:

Ⓐ The number of hours of darkness per day they require for their seeds to germinate

Ⓑ The manner in which some types of light can affect how well they flower

Ⓒ The names of some of the plants which are commonly considered to be short-day plants

Ⓓ The way that long periods of darkness can affect the flowering process for them

4→ Some common short-day plants include chrysanthemums, poinsettias, rice, soybeans, onions, strawberries, and cotton. At high latitudes, short-day plants mostly flower in spring and autumn, which is when daylight exposure is fewer than twelve hours. Flowering takes place at night but is not always certain since a continuous period of darkness is required. Therefore, any flashes of light, such as lightning during a thunderstorm, may interrupt the process. On the other hand, if there is a period of darkness during the day, such as when the sun is concealed by thick clouds or a solar eclipse, the flowering process is influenced in neither a positive nor negative manner.

27 In paragraph 5, the author uses asters, lettuce, wheat, poppies, spinach, and potatoes as examples of

Ⓐ the most popular crops that are known to be long-day plants

Ⓑ crops that can only be grown at high latitudes and not near the equator

Ⓒ plants that flower better when exposed to large amounts of sunlight

Ⓓ types of plants that cannot be affected at all by gibberellic acid

28 According to paragraph 5, gibberellic acid affects long-day plants by

Ⓐ acting in a manner that can assist the cells in plants in growing well

Ⓑ helping plants grow at night even though they do not get any sunlight then

Ⓒ reducing the amount of sunlight that they need to be exposed to on a daily basis

Ⓓ producing large numbers of flowers when plants create more of the acid

Glossary

gibberellic acid: a type of hormone found in both plants and fungi

5→ Some common long-day plants are asters, lettuce, wheat, poppies, spinach, and potatoes. At high latitudes, these long-day plants flower when they are exposed to more than twelve hours of sunlight. Therefore, they flower more efficiently during the long daylight hours of late spring and summer. Unlike with short-day plants, flashes of light during hours of darkness actually stimulate flower growth. Additionally, if a period of daylight is interrupted by a period of darkness, there is no influence on flower growth. Another factor which influences the flowering response of long-day plants is the presence of **gibberellic acid**. It is a natural hormone which is found in most plants and prompts the accelerated growth of plant cells. In long-day plants, gibberellic acid plays an active role in flowering, but in short-day plants, it has no influence whatsoever on when plants flower.

29 Look at the four squares [■] that indicate where the following sentence could be added to the passage.

As a general rule, these plants produce a larger number of flowers as they become older.

Where would the sentence best fit?

Click on a square [■] to add the sentence to the passage.

Plants respond to the amounts of light and darkness which they are exposed to every day. This phenomenon is known as photoperiodism. The primary response mechanism in plants to the amount of light and darkness exposure is flowering, which is the ability to produce flower blossoms. The process of flowering is key to a plant's ability to propagate since flowers contain a plant's reproductive organs. Flowers produce nectar that, along with their color and aroma, attracts birds, bees, and other insects, which play a role in the pollination of the plant. Some plants flower more efficiently when they are exposed to less light and more darkness and are accordingly known as short-day plants. [1] Other plants have a better flowering response when exposed to more light and less darkness and are therefore named long-day plants. [2] There are also some plants capable of flowering regardless of the amount of light or darkness they receive. [3] These are called day-neutral plants, and their flowering response is based on their age. [4]

30 **Directions:** Select the appropriate statements from the answer choices and match them to the type of plant to which they relate. TWO of the answer choices will NOT be used. **This question is worth 3 points.**

Drag your answer choices to the spaces where they belong.
To remove an answer choice, click on it. To review the passage, click on **View Text**.

Answer Choices

1. Typically flowers in spring and autumn when growing at high latitudes
2. Can grow better when exposed to light during times of darkness
3. Makes the most flowers during the late spring and summer months
4. Is not affected by the presence or absence of gibberellic acid
5. Produces flowers when it receives sunlight for less than half of a day
6. Is capable of growing equally well at high latitudes and at the equator
7. Grows very well in greenhouses during the summer and winter months

TYPE OF PLANT

Short-Day Plant

•
•
•

Long-Day Plant

•
•

TOEFL® MAP

ACTUAL TEST

Reading 2

02

CONTINUE

Reading Section Directions

This section measures your ability to understand academic passages in English. You will have **72 minutes** to read and answer questions about **4 passages**. A clock at the top of the screen will show you how much time is remaining.

Most questions are worth 1 point but the last question for each passage is worth more than 1 point. The directions for the last question indicate how many points you may receive.

Some passages include a word or phrase that is **underlined** in blue. Click on the word or phrase to see a definition or an explanation.

When you want to move to the next question, click on **Next**. You may skip questions and go back to them later. If you want to return to previous questions, click on **Back**. You can click on **Reivew** at any time, and the review screen will show you which questions you have answered and which you have not answered. From this review screen, you may go directly to any question you have already seen in the Reading section.

Click on **Continue** to go on.

The Nitrogen Cycle

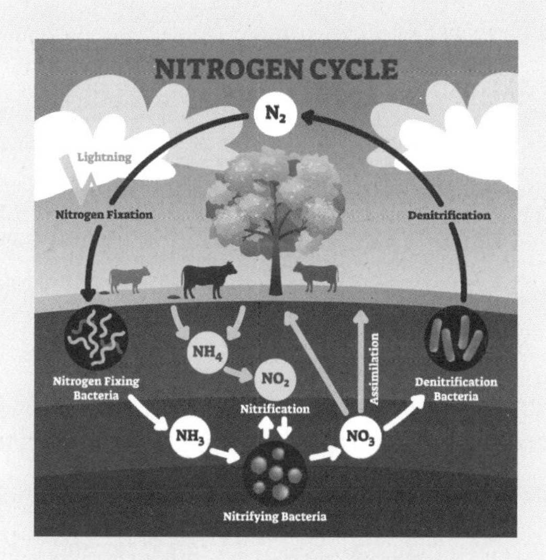

A diagram of the nitrogen cycle

Nitrogen is an essential component of all life on the Earth as it comprises parts of amino acids, proteins, and chlorophyll, which plants utilize for photosynthesis. Without nitrogen, life on the Earth would not be possible. It comprises around 78% of the Earth's atmosphere but, in its gaseous form, is unusable to plants and animals. Plants must obtain nitrogen in a fixed form that comes from the soil while animals obtain the nitrogen they need either directly from plants or indirectly by eating animals that have consumed plants. The process through which nitrogen moves from the atmosphere to the land and then back to the atmosphere again is the nitrogen cycle. There are four major steps in this process: nitrogen fixation, decay, nitrification, and denitrification.

Nitrogen fixation involves nitrogen moving from the atmosphere into the land and may occur in several ways. Lightning can cause the breakup of nitrogen molecules in the atmosphere so that they combine with oxygen to form nitrogen compounds. These fall to the ground when it rains. Some nitrogen compounds are introduced to the atmosphere by pollution created by vehicles and factories; these too may fall to the ground when it rains. Nitrogen may also be taken from the atmosphere and subjected to industrial procedures that convert it into fertilizers such as ammonia and ammonia nitrate, which farmers use in their fields. Another method of nitrogen fixation is a natural process that occurs thanks to bacteria in the soil. These bacteria have **symbiotic relationships** with some plants, which permit the bacteria to create the nitrogen compounds the plants need. Most of these plants are from the legume family, which includes soybeans and alfalfa.

The decay stage involves the absorption of nitrogen by plants and animals and its subsequent conversion to waste material, where it can be transformed into ammonia. Once nitrogen enters the soil, it is assimilated by plants through their roots. Animals eat these plants and absorb nitrogen into their bodies. At some point, the animals' metabolisms create organic nitrogen compounds which are expelled from the body as waste. This organic waste matter must then be broken down by bacteria, which convert it into ammonia. This process not only happens to waste material but also occurs when animals die. Their bodies decay, and the organic matter is eventually converted into ammonia.

The third stage of the nitrogen cycle—nitrification—involves specialized bacteria converting the ammonia into two nitrogen compounds. The ammonia is changed into two **nitrates**: NO_2, also known as nitrogen dioxide, and NO_3. In some instances, plant roots directly absorb ammonia from the soil, but most depend upon bacteria to create nitrates. Plants can then make use of them to grow. Some of these nitrates can cause problems in that they are easily soluble in water and thus often enter lakes, streams, and rivers. High nitrate levels in water may result in excessive algae growth, which can dramatically affect aquatic life.

The final stage of the nitrogen cycle is denitrification. In this state, nitrates are converted back into atmospheric nitrogen by specialized bacteria. These bacteria reside in environments where there is a limited supply of oxygen, including soil, wetlands, and certain parts of the ocean. Due to the lack of oxygen, the bacteria have evolved to breathe nitrogen instead. They take in nitrates and later expel them as N_2, the gaseous form of nitrogen, which then returns to the atmosphere to complete the nitrogen cycle.

There is some concern nowadays that too much nitrogen is entering the soil and water systems because of modern agricultural methods, so the denitrification process might not keep pace, which will result in there being too much nitrogen in the soil and water. In some parts of the oceans near heavily farmed land, large quantities of nitrates are entering the water, which has increased the amount of algae in the ocean waters. These algae create dead zones since they consume much of the oxygen in the water, which limits the survivability of most marine life forms. As a result, little or no life can be found in these dead zones. If this continues, large parts of the world's oceans will soon be uninhabitable too all but the tiniest life forms.

Glossary

symbiotic relationship: a relationship between two organisms that benefits at least one of the organisms

nitrate: any compound that contains NO_2 or NO_3

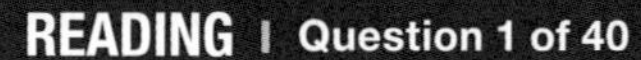

1 Which of the sentences below best expresses the essential information in the highlighted sentence in the passage? *Incorrect* answer choices change the meaning in important ways or leave out essential information.

(A) Animals obtain nitrogen when they eat plants or when they consume other animals.

(B) Nitrogen is found in the soil, where both plants and animals can get it for themselves.

(C) The only way that plants are able to obtain nitrogen is by absorbing it from the soil.

(D) Plants get nitrogen from the soil while animals get it by eating plants or other animals.

The Nitrogen Cycle

Nitrogen is an essential component of all life on the Earth as it comprises parts of amino acids, proteins, and chlorophyll, which plants utilize for photosynthesis. Without nitrogen, life on the Earth would not be possible. It comprises around 78% of the Earth's atmosphere but, in its gaseous form, is unusable to plants and animals. Plants must obtain nitrogen in a fixed form that comes from the soil while animals obtain the nitrogen they need either directly from plants or indirectly by eating animals that have consumed plants. The process through which nitrogen moves from the atmosphere to the land and then back to the atmosphere again is the nitrogen cycle. There are four major steps in this process: nitrogen fixation, decay, nitrification, and denitrification.

2 The word subjected in the passage is closest in meaning to

(A) applied

(B) exposed

(C) reduced

(D) condensed

3 According to paragraph 2, nitrogen fixation may occur when

(A) bacteria found in some plants help create fertilizer in the ground

(B) manmade pollution descends to the ground on account of rain

(C) lightning strikes the ground and creates nitrogen compounds in it

(D) nitrogen combines with hydrogen and oxygen to create compounds

2→ Nitrogen fixation involves nitrogen moving from the atmosphere into the land and may occur in several ways. Lightning can cause the breakup of nitrogen molecules in the atmosphere so that they combine with oxygen to form nitrogen compounds. These fall to the ground when it rains. Some nitrogen compounds are introduced to the atmosphere by pollution created by vehicles and factories; these too may fall to the ground when it rains. Nitrogen may also be taken from the atmosphere and subjected to industrial procedures that convert it into fertilizers such as ammonia and ammonia nitrate, which farmers use in their fields. Another method of nitrogen fixation is a natural process that occurs thanks to bacteria in the soil. These bacteria have **symbiotic relationships** with some plants, which permit the bacteria to create the nitrogen compounds the plants need. Most of these plants are from the legume family, which includes soybeans and alfalfa.

Glossary

symbiotic relationship: a relationship between two organisms that benefits at least one of the organisms

4 According to paragraph 3, which of the following is true of the decay stage of the nitrogen cycle?

Ⓐ It takes longer to occur than any of the other stages do.

Ⓑ The ammonia created during it comes from animals' metabolisms.

Ⓒ It involves the changing of waste material into ammonia.

Ⓓ The only time that it happens is when animals die.

5 The author's description of nitrification in paragraph 4 mentions all of the following EXCEPT:

Ⓐ the chemical composition of the nitrates that are formed during it

Ⓑ a negative effect that this stage may have on the environment

Ⓒ a medium through which nitrates are created from ammonia

Ⓓ the manner in which plants make use of the nitrates they absorb

6 According to paragraph 4, how can nitrates sometimes cause problems?

Ⓐ Plants absorb too many of them and grow very quickly.

Ⓑ They can kill certain plants that live in some bodies of water.

Ⓒ The soil that they are in can become too acidic at times.

Ⓓ It is possible for them to kill the bacteria that create them.

[3]→ The decay stage involves the absorption of nitrogen by plants and animals and its subsequent conversion to waste material, where it can be transformed into ammonia. Once nitrogen enters the soil, it is assimilated by plants through their roots. Animals eat these plants and absorb nitrogen into their bodies. At some point, the animals' metabolisms create organic nitrogen compounds which are expelled from the body as waste. This organic waste matter must then be broken down by bacteria, which convert it into ammonia. This process not only happens to waste material but also occurs when animals die. Their bodies decay, and the organic matter is eventually converted into ammonia.

[4]→ The third stage of the nitrogen cycle—nitrification—involves specialized bacteria converting the ammonia into two nitrogen compounds. The ammonia is changed into two **nitrates**: NO_2, also known as nitrogen dioxide, and NO_3. In some instances, plant roots directly absorb ammonia from the soil, but most depend upon bacteria to create nitrates. Plants can then make use of them to grow. Some of these nitrates can cause problems in that they are easily soluble in water and thus often enter lakes, streams, and rivers. High nitrate levels in water may result in excessive algae growth, which can dramatically affect aquatic life.

Glossary

nitrate: any compound that contains NO_2 or NO_3

7 According to paragraph 5, which of the following is true of denitrification?

Ⓐ N_2 combines with nitrates to form another compound of nitrogen.

Ⓑ The process cannot be completed without the presence of oxygen.

Ⓒ The only places where it can occur are in the soil and in the oceans.

Ⓓ It involves the turning of nitrates into nitrogen in its gaseous state.

8 In stating that the denitrification process might not keep pace, the author means that the denitrification process may

Ⓐ be less effective

Ⓑ cause more problems

Ⓒ become less obvious

Ⓓ occur too slowly

5→ The final stage of the nitrogen cycle is denitrification. In this state, nitrates are converted back into atmospheric nitrogen by specialized bacteria. These bacteria reside in environments where there is a limited supply of oxygen, including soil, wetlands, and certain parts of the ocean. Due to the lack of oxygen, the bacteria have evolved to breathe nitrogen instead. They take in nitrates and later expel them as N_2, the gaseous form of nitrogen, which then returns to the atmosphere to complete the nitrogen cycle.

There is some concern nowadays that too much nitrogen is entering the soil and water systems because of modern agricultural methods, so the denitrification process might not keep pace, which will result in there being too much nitrogen in the soil and water. In some parts of the oceans near heavily farmed land, large quantities of nitrates are entering the water, which has increased the amount of algae in the ocean waters. These algae create dead zones since they consume much of the oxygen in the water, which limits the survivability of most marine life forms. As a result, little or no life can be found in these dead zones. If this continues, large parts of the world's oceans will soon be uninhabitable too all but the tiniest life forms.

9 Look at the four squares [■] that indicate where the following sentence could be added to the passage.

Basically, fish are deprived of oxygen, causing many of them to die.

Where would the sentence best fit?

Click on a square [■] to add the sentence to the passage.

The third stage of the nitrogen cycle—nitrification—involves specialized bacteria converting the ammonia into two nitrogen compounds. The ammonia is changed into two **nitrates**: NO_2, also known as nitrogen dioxide, and NO_3. In some instances, plant roots directly absorb ammonia from the soil, but most depend upon bacteria to create nitrates. [1] Plants can then make use of them to grow. [2] Some of these nitrates can cause problems in that they are easily soluble in water and thus often enter lakes, streams, and rivers. [3] High nitrate levels in water may result in excessive algae growth, which can dramatically affect aquatic life. [4]

Glossary

nitrate: any compound that contains NO_2 or NO_3

10 **Directions:** An introductory sentence for a brief summary of the passage is provided below. Complete the summary by selecting the THREE answer choices that express the most important ideas of the passage. Some sentences do not belong because they express ideas that are not presented in the passage or are minor ideas in the passage. **This question is worth 2 points.**

Drag your answer choices to the spaces where they belong.
To remove an answer choice, click on it. To review the passage, click on **View Text**.

In the nitrogen cycle, nitrogen is removed from the atmosphere, utilized by plants and animals, and then returned to the atmosphere.

-
-
-

Answer Choices

1. NO_2 and NO_3 are two nitrates that are formed by various bacteria.
2. There are four distinct stages that make up the entire nitrogen cycle.
3. Some nitrates run off into the water and cause environmental problems.
4. During the denitrification stage, nitrogen in compounds returns to its gaseous state.
5. Ammonia is often created when organic material begins to break down and decompose.
6. Thanks to the nitrogen cycle, both plants and animals are able to survive.

The Textile Trade during the Industrial Revolution in England

The Industrial Revolution transformed much of the world from a rural agrarian society to an urban industrial-based one. It began in England during the middle of the 1700s. The first business that became industrialized was the textile industry. In fact, much of the machinery built early in the Industrial Revolution was designed specifically for the making of textiles. However, the transition from a cottage-based textile industry to one that employed workers in factories using machines was not smooth, and there was great resistance to change. Over time though, factories increased in number, those seeking work moved to live near them, and small towns grew to become enormous cities.

The textile industry produces cloth, which is used to make clothing, a basic necessity of life. In the early eighteenth century, all textiles were made from natural products. In England, the two most widespread of these were wool and flax with wool dominating the industry. Cotton, however, was becoming increasingly more common, so by the end of the eighteenth century, it had become the leading material used in the manufacturing of textiles. At that time, textiles were made in cottage-based businesses as people did work in individual homes. Oftentimes, entire families took part in preparing the raw material and making it into spools of yarn. This yarn was then weaved into large bolts of cloth on **looms** operated by hand. The preparation of the yarn and the weaving of the cloth both frequently took place in the same household. The bolts of cloth were then made into clothing—again in individual homes—by **seamstresses** and tailors who did all of the work by hand. Even after the textile industry became industrialized, most clothing continued to be made by hand until the sewing machine was invented in the nineteenth century.

England was uniquely prepared for the transition from the cottage-based textile industry to the factory-based one in the middle of the eighteenth century. A revolution in farming methods had resulted in increased food production and population yet simultaneously had reduced the need for human labor on farms. England therefore had a surplus labor pool that the factories could utilize. Additionally, ingenious people in England and elsewhere created machines that helped speed the process of preparing the natural materials and weaving the cloth. Some examples of these were improved looms that could be run by water or, later, steam power, the flying shuttle, which let weavers make wider cloth much faster than before, and the spinning jenny, which permitted more yarn to be produced by one person in a shorter period of time. Textile production steadily became more industrialized, and, in the process, businesses gathered their employees together in buildings, which were often located near sources of falling water that could provide power for their machines.

The ultimate invention that sent the entire textile industry propelling toward industrialization was the perfection of the steam engine in the late eighteenth century. Once steam-powered engines were coupled with textile machinery, the need to build factories near falling water ceased. Instead, they could be constructed anywhere, and they were. For the textile industry in England, countless factories sprung up around the northern city of Manchester. This was not the only place in England that became industrialized though. Numerous other cities saw factories erected in them as large parts of England became industrialized seemingly overnight.

Yet there was much resistance to the burgeoning textile industry. For centuries, certain families and towns in England had been the center of textile manufacturing in their cottage-based industries. As new machines that worked faster and that required less labor started to appear, large numbers of textile workers resisted using them, and some of them even rioted and smashed the machines at times. Sheep farmers, who depended on the textile industry by selling their wool to make cloth, opposed the change to cotton and got legislation passed by Parliament that restricted its importation from foreign lands. But the industrialization of the textile industry continued, and the methods used in textile factories became models for other types of industries. In the process, industrialization brought enormous profits to England and helped it become the world's wealthiest nation during the nineteenth century.

Glossary

loom: a piece of equipment that can weave cloth

seamstress: a woman who sews for a living

11 According to paragraph 1, which of the following is true of the textile industry during the Industrial Revolution?

Ⓐ The workers in the textile industry approved of the new machines.

Ⓑ It made use of machinery prior to any other industry at that time.

Ⓒ Thanks to several inventions, England's textile industry led the world.

Ⓓ More people were involved in making textiles than in any other industry.

The Textile Trade during the Industrial Revolution in England

1→ The Industrial Revolution transformed much of the world from a rural agrarian society to an urban industrial-based one. It began in England during the middle of the 1700s. The first business that became industrialized was the textile industry. In fact, much of the machinery built early in the Industrial Revolution was designed specifically for the making of textiles. However, the transition from a cottage-based textile industry to one that employed workers in factories using machines was not smooth, and there was great resistance to change. Over time though, factories increased in number, those seeking work moved to live near them, and small towns grew to become enormous cities.

12 The word it in the passage refers to

Ⓐ flax

Ⓑ wool

Ⓒ cotton

Ⓓ the end of the eighteenth century

13 According to paragraph 2, seamstresses and tailors made clothes by hand in the eighteenth century because

Ⓐ it guaranteed that the clothes they made were of good quality

Ⓑ their guilds insisted that they make all clothes by hand

Ⓒ there was not yet a way to make clothes by using machines

Ⓓ this enabled them to charge more for their services

Glossary

loom: a piece of equipment that can weave cloth

seamstress: a woman who sews for a living

2→ The textile industry produces cloth, which is used to make clothing, a basic necessity of life. In the early eighteenth century, all textiles were made from natural products. In England, the two most widespread of these were wool and flax with wool dominating the industry. Cotton, however, was becoming increasingly more common, so by the end of the eighteenth century, it had become the leading material used in the manufacturing of textiles. At that time, textiles were made in cottage-based businesses as people did work in individual homes. Oftentimes, entire families took part in preparing the raw material and making it into spools of yarn. This yarn was then weaved into large bolts of cloth on **looms** operated by hand. The preparation of the yarn and the weaving of the cloth both frequently took place in the same household. The bolts of cloth were then made into clothing—again in individual homes—by **seamstresses** and tailors who did all of the work by hand. Even after the textile industry became industrialized, most clothing continued to be made by hand until the sewing machine was invented in the nineteenth century.

14 The word ingenious in the passage is closest in meaning to

Ⓐ resourceful

Ⓑ notorious

Ⓒ affluent

Ⓓ profuse

15 In paragraph 3, the author uses the flying shuttle as an example of

Ⓐ a machine that worked much better than the spinning jenny

Ⓑ a piece of equipment that allowed one person to spin yarn

Ⓒ a loom that could be run by the power of falling water

Ⓓ an invention that made the process of creating cloth faster

16 In paragraph 4, the author implies that factories in England

Ⓐ were built at a rapid pace during the Industrial Revolution

Ⓑ were not well constructed so were dangerous workplaces

Ⓒ affected the health of many workers in a negative manner

Ⓓ were relatively inexpensive for a person to construct

[3] → England was uniquely prepared for the transition from the cottage-based textile industry to the factory-based one in the middle of the eighteenth century. A revolution in farming methods had resulted in increased food production and population yet simultaneously had reduced the need for human labor on farms. England therefore had a surplus labor pool that the factories could utilize. Additionally, ingenious people in England and elsewhere created machines that helped speed the process of preparing the natural materials and weaving the cloth. Some examples of these were improved looms that could be run by water or, later, steam power, the flying shuttle, which let weavers make wider cloth much faster than before, and the spinning jenny, which permitted more yarn to be produced by one person in a shorter period of time. Textile production steadily became more industrialized, and, in the process, businesses gathered their employees together in buildings, which were often located near sources of falling water that could provide power for their machines.

[4] → The ultimate invention that sent the entire textile industry propelling toward industrialization was the perfection of the steam engine in the late eighteenth century. Once steam-powered engines were coupled with textile machinery, the need to build factories near falling water ceased. Instead, they could be constructed anywhere, and they were. For the textile industry in England, countless factories sprung up around the northern city of Manchester. This was not the only place in England that became industrialized though. Numerous other cities saw factories erected in them as large parts of England became industrialized seemingly overnight.

17 Which of the sentences below best expresses the essential information in the highlighted sentence in the passage? *Incorrect* answer choices change the meaning in important ways or leave out essential information.

Ⓐ The efficient new machines were opposed, sometimes violently, by some textile workers.

Ⓑ There were occasionally riots by textile workers afraid they were going to lose their jobs.

Ⓒ A large number of new machines appeared, which changed the textile industry forever.

Ⓓ The textile workers became frustrated when their new machines often failed to work.

18 According to paragraph 5, Parliament restricted the amount of cotton that could be imported because

Ⓐ most people wanted their clothes to be made of wool or flax

Ⓑ it was encouraged to do so by the country's sheep farmers

Ⓒ English farmers wanted to sell all of the cotton that they grew

Ⓓ imported cotton could not be used on the new machines

5→ Yet there was much resistance to the burgeoning textile industry. For centuries, certain families and towns in England had been the center of textile manufacturing in their cottage-based industries. As new machines that worked faster and that required less labor started to appear, large numbers of textile workers resisted using them, and some of them even rioted and smashed the machines at times. Sheep farmers, who depended on the textile industry by selling their wool to make cloth, opposed the change to cotton and got legislation passed by Parliament that restricted its importation from foreign lands. But the industrialization of the textile industry continued, and the methods used in textile factories became models for other types of industries. In the process, industrialization brought enormous profits to England and helped it become the world's wealthiest nation during the nineteenth century.

19 Look at the four squares [■] that indicate where the following sentence could be added to the passage.

James Watt was the person who was the most responsible for this feat.

Where would the sentence best fit?

Click on a square [■] to add the sentence to the passage.

1 The ultimate invention that sent the entire textile industry propelling toward industrialization was the perfection of the steam engine in the late eighteenth century. **2** Once steam-powered engines were coupled with textile machinery, the need to build factories near falling water ceased. **3** Instead, they could be constructed anywhere, and they were. **4** For the textile industry in England, countless factories sprung up around the northern city of Manchester. This was not the only place in England that became industrialized though. Numerous other cities saw factories erected in them as large parts of England became industrialized seemingly overnight.

20 **Directions:** An introductory sentence for a brief summary of the passage is provided below. Complete the summary by selecting the THREE answer choices that express the most important ideas of the passage. Some sentences do not belong because they express ideas that are not presented in the passage or are minor ideas in the passage. **This question is worth 2 points.**

Drag your answer choices to the spaces where they belong.
To remove an answer choice, click on it. To review the passage, click on **View Text**.

The Industrial Revolution in England brought about many changes in the country's textile industry.

-
-
-

Answer Choices

1. Cottage-based industries were the primary manner in which people made cloth before the Industrial Revolution.
2. Some groups of people opposed the changes in the textile industry because their lives were affected negatively.
3. Factories that used machinery were built in many cities, so people went to urban centers to work in them.
4. England had to import a small amount of the cotton that its textile industry used to make cloth with.
5. The steam engine was an important invention that let people build factories anywhere they wanted.
6. Numerous new inventions made the creating of cloth a much faster and more efficient process.

Portraits

Girl with a Pearl Earring (1665) by Johannes Vermeer

Portrait art depicts a human subject or subjects and is one of the most common types of art produced. Paintings of people have been created since ancient times, but few examples from thousands of years ago have survived until the present day. In ancient Egypt, Greece, and Rome, portrait art was more public than private with portraits of rulers and religious figures placed on display in communal areas, often as stone sculptures rather than as paintings or frescoes. Centuries later during the Middle Ages and the Renaissance, portrait painting became more prominent and private. Wealthy **patrons** commissioned artists to paint their images, which frequently flattered the paying subject instead of displaying any unattractive details. During this time, three main styles of portrait painting based upon the size of the portrait were developed.

Full-length portraits showed the entire subject of the work along with a detailed background. This style came into vogue in Europe during the seventeenth century as individuals of means enjoyed displaying themselves in full-length portraits to flaunt their status. Of significance in full-length portraits is the harmony between the subject and the background, which tends to be fairly colorful with deep, rich backgrounds. One famous example of a full-length portrait is Thomas Gainsborough's *The Blue Boy* (1770), which was painted in oil. The portrait depicts the full figure of a youth dressed in blue silk clothing while standing with one hand on his hip and a determined look on his face. The background has rich browns and greens with a tree-covered mountain being the dominant feature. Art historians believe the figure depicts the son of a wealthy merchant; however, concrete evidence for this is lacking. In fact, the work was more of a costume study than a display of wealth since the subject is irrelevant with the focus being on the youth's extravagant clothing.

Half-length portraits depict the upper body from the waist to the head, show the subject either standing or sitting, and feature backgrounds with more muted color schemes than those that are displayed in full-length portraits. The pictures, most of which are painted with watercolors or oil paints on canvas, place more emphasis on their subjects' facial features. The subjects are typically painted with the face at an angle to the viewer, thereby giving one side of the face more prominence. This type of portrait painting became especially popular during the Renaissance, and while many artists pocketed commissions from the wealthy and powerful, they also painted everyday people by using the half-length portrait form. Arguably the most famous painting in this genre is the *Mona Lisa* (1503-1506) by Leonardo da Vinci, which emphasizes the woman depicted, particularly her enigmatic smile, while the background is of much less significance.

Bust-view portraits depict only the head and the shoulders of their subjects while stressing the subject's facial expressions, and the background is almost entirely insignificant. As a result, bust-view portraits show their subjects' faces with extremely detailed features. Such pictures are done with watercolors and oils as well as with pencils in sketches. One of the most famous bust-view portraits is *Girl with a Pearl Earring* (1665) by Dutch master Johannes Vermeer. Vermeer's masterpiece was done with oil paint on canvas and depicts a side view of a young girl wearing what appears to be an Oriental turban as well as a pearl earring. In the past, Dutch **grandmasters** did not consider works of that nature to be portrait art, but they instead called them tronies, a Dutch word meaning "faces," and these works were often paintings of common people featuring exaggerated expressions.

There are also some subordinate types included amongst the major categories of portrait art. One is called the kit-cat portrait, which is a half-length portrait that additionally includes the subject's hands in the work. The name is derived from the famous London gentleman's Kit Cat Club, where every single one of the club's members had their portrait done in this style. Art historians also categorize portrait art according to the direction the subject is facing with the angle of the subject's face toward the viewer serving as a means to categorize the work in question.

Glossary

patron: a person who supports an artist with money, gifts, or other items of value

grandmaster: a person who has achieved the highest level of ability in a field

21 In paragraph 1, the author implies that portraits

Ⓐ during the Renaissance sometimes failed to portray people as they really looked

Ⓑ made by the ancient Greeks are of higher quality than portraits from Roman times

Ⓒ were painted of both rich individuals as well as those with little or no money

Ⓓ became an art genre when artists in the Middle Ages started to paint them

Glossary

patron: a person who supports an artist with money, gifts, or other items of value

Portraits

1→ Portrait art depicts a human subject or subjects and is one of the most common types of art produced. Paintings of people have been created since ancient times, but few examples from thousands of years ago have survived until the present day. In ancient Egypt, Greece, and Rome, portrait art was more public than private with portraits of rulers and religious figures placed on display in communal areas, often as stone sculptures rather than as paintings or frescoes. Centuries later during the Middle Ages and the Renaissance, portrait painting became more prominent and private. Wealthy **patrons** commissioned artists to paint their images, which frequently flattered the paying subject instead of displaying any unattractive details. During this time, three main styles of portrait painting based upon the size of the portrait were developed.

22 The word flaunt in the passage is closest in meaning to

Ⓐ be aware of

Ⓑ approve of

Ⓒ show off

Ⓓ insist on

23 According to paragraph 2, which of the following is NOT true of *The Blue Boy*?

Ⓐ The painting focuses more on clothes than it does on the boy featured in it.

Ⓑ It was made by Thomas Gainsborough during the seventeenth century.

Ⓒ There is an outdoor scene that includes a mountain in the painting's background.

Ⓓ It is a full-length portrait that shows a boy posing in fine clothes.

2→ Full-length portraits showed the entire subject of the work along with a detailed background. This style came into vogue in Europe during the seventeenth century as individuals of means enjoyed displaying themselves in full-length portraits to flaunt their status. Of significance in full-length portraits is the harmony between the subject and the background, which tends to be fairly colorful with deep, rich backgrounds. One famous example of a full-length portrait is Thomas Gainsborough's *The Blue Boy* (1770), which was painted in oil. The portrait depicts the full figure of a youth dressed in blue silk clothing while standing with one hand on his hip and a determined look on his face. The background has rich browns and greens with a tree-covered mountain being the dominant feature. Art historians believe the figure depicts the son of a wealthy merchant; however, concrete evidence for this is lacking. In fact, the work was more of a costume study than a display of wealth since the subject is irrelevant with the focus being on the youth's extravagant clothing.

24 Which of the sentences below best expresses the essential information in the highlighted sentence in the passage? *Incorrect* answer choices change the meaning in important ways or leave out essential information.

Ⓐ Most of the subjects are painted while they are directly facing the viewer.

Ⓑ One side of each subject's face is featured since the subject is shown at an angle.

Ⓒ The face is featured very prominently since it is shown at an angle to the viewer.

Ⓓ These paintings show prominent faces and make use of angles to depict subjects.

25 The word enigmatic in the passage is closest in meaning to

Ⓐ revealing

Ⓑ genuine

Ⓒ reflective

Ⓓ mysterious

26 According to paragraph 3, which of the following is true of half-length portraits?

Ⓐ They always show the subject from the waist to the head in a standing position.

Ⓑ These paintings showed both rich people and regular ones during the Renaissance.

Ⓒ The genre is considered to have started when Leonardo da Vinci painted the *Mona Lisa*.

Ⓓ The majority of these paintings were done by artists who used watercolors.

3→ Half-length portraits depict the upper body from the waist to the head, show the subject either standing or sitting, and feature backgrounds with more muted color schemes than those that are displayed in full-length portraits. The pictures, most of which are painted with watercolors or oil paints on canvas, place more emphasis on their subjects' facial features. The subjects are typically painted with the face at an angle to the viewer, thereby giving one side of the face more prominence. This type of portrait painting became especially popular during the Renaissance, and while many artists pocketed commissions from the wealthy and powerful, they also painted everyday people by using the half-length portrait form. Arguably the most famous painting in this genre is the *Mona Lisa* (1503-1506) by Leonardo da Vinci, which emphasizes the woman depicted, particularly her enigmatic smile, while the background is of much less significance.

27 In paragraph 4, why does the author mention tronies?

Ⓐ To explain why they should not be considered to be real portrait art

Ⓑ To point out that they were first made by Dutch grandmasters

Ⓒ To provide an alternative name for some bust-view portraits

Ⓓ To claim that *Girl with a Pearl Earring* is the most famous of them

28 According to paragraph 5, kit-kat portraits acquired their name because

Ⓐ the members of a certain club were all painted in an identical manner

Ⓑ paintings which were in that genre featured a subject seated with a cat

Ⓒ the hands of the subjects who were in the paintings had to be included

Ⓓ the angle of a subject's face was supposed to be positioned in a certain way

29 Look at the four squares [■] that indicate where the following sentence could be added to the passage.

Dutchman Vincent van Gogh, who painted in the nineteenth century, also created a large number of self-portraits that used this style.

Where would the sentence best fit?

Click on a square [■] to add the sentence to the passage.

4→ Bust-view portraits depict only the head and the shoulders of their subjects while stressing the subject's facial expressions, and the background is almost entirely insignificant. As a result, bust-view portraits show their subjects' faces with extremely detailed features. **1** Such pictures are done with watercolors and oils as well as with pencils in sketches. **2** One of the most famous bust-view portraits is *Girl with a Pearl Earring* (1665) by Dutch master Johannes Vermeer. **3** Vermeer's masterpiece was done with oil paint on canvas and depicts a side view of a young girl wearing what appears to be an Oriental turban as well as a pearl earring. **4** In the past, Dutch grandmasters did not consider works of that nature to be portrait art, but they instead called them tronies, a Dutch word meaning "faces," and these works were often paintings of common people featuring exaggerated expressions.

5→ There are also some subordinate types included amongst the major categories of portrait art. One is called the kit-cat portrait, which is a half-length portrait that additionally includes the subject's hands in the work. The name is derived from the famous London gentleman's Kit Cat Club, where every single one of the club's members had their portrait done in this style. Art historians also categorize portrait art according to the direction the subject is facing with the angle of the subject's face toward the viewer serving as a means to categorize the work in question.

Glossary

grandmaster: a person who has achieved the highest level of ability in a field

30 Directions: Select the appropriate statements from the answer choices and match them to the type of portrait to which they relate. TWO of the answer choices will NOT be used. **This question is worth 4 points.**

Drag your answer choices to the spaces where they belong.
To remove an answer choice, click on it. To review the passage, click on **View Text**.

Answer Choices

1. Was the style of a famous painting by Leonardo da Vinci
2. Was made by Dutch artists and could feature regular people
3. Became popular in the 1600s because rich people wanted that style
4. Could be created with either various paints or even pencils
5. Always included the hands of the subjects in the paintings
6. Was the genre that *The Blue Boy* by Gainsborough was painted in
7. Was the main type of portrait created by the ancient Greeks and Romans
8. Featured a background with more subdued colors than other portraits
9. Had a colorful background that went well with the subject

TYPE OF PORTRAIT

Full-Length Portrait

-
-
-

Half-Length Portrait

-
-

Bust-View Portrait

-
-

Education in the Renaissance

During the fifteenth and sixteenth centuries, Europe went through the period known as the Renaissance. In Europe then, the education a child received typically depended upon the social status of the child's family. The vast majority of Europeans were poor peasants, so their children received no formal schooling, yet wealthier merchants and members of the nobility often ensured that their children were educated. Despite the facts that education was stressed in the Renaissance and that many universities were founded then, most children—regardless of their social status—were educated in their homes in some manner.

In the Renaissance, life was harsh for the majority of children born to peasants. If they survived infancy, boys farmed the land with their fathers or learned their fathers' trades. Some fortunate individuals were accepted as apprentices by craftsmen and learned specialized skills from them. As for girls, most learned how to become good wives and to raise children. The children of wealthier merchants frequently received some formal education from private tutors in their homes as they at least learned to read, write, and do mathematics since it was expected that they would take part in their family businesses.

Members of the nobility often went to great extents to educate their children in all facets of life. Aside from the basics of reading, writing, and some languages, young noble boys were taught horseback riding, practical skills with weapons, and dancing. Some also received military training or learned the basics of engineering. Noble girls were educated less than boys, yet they still learned to read and write and were also taught languages, art, music, and dancing. This was particularly true during the Renaissance, which was an age of art and music, so many young boys and girls were taught these subjects at specialized schools, particularly in Italy.

After childhood ended, there were few opportunities for peasant youths to receive any type of education. A few were occasionally trained to become members of the clergy at either churches or monasteries, but, for the most part, only upper-class youths received this type of education. During the Renaissance, merchants and noblemen with many sons usually sent their youngest to receive religious training. These children began their studies at young ages, were trained in Latin and sometimes Greek, and learned the Bible as well as the ceremonial aspects of church life. A few daughters of noblemen were sent to convents, where they were trained to become nuns. This normally happened when a family had many daughters because it spared the family the expense of providing a rich **dowry**, which they were obligated to do when their daughters married.

When the sons of merchants and nobles became teenagers, they joined their fathers' businesses, took part in court life, became soldiers, or attended universities. Universities had first appeared during the Middle Ages, yet during the Renaissance, which emphasized learning, more universities were established. Nevertheless, the universities students could attend then varied in quality from place to place. Additionally, some specialized in one field of study even though most offered classes in various subjects. Typical fields were astronomy, medicine, philosophy, rhetoric, history, mathematics, logic, and grammar. The rediscovery of ancient Greek and Latin texts during the Renaissance and the subsequent development of the philosophy of **humanism** had profound influences on university educations. University students were expected to study the works of the ancient Greeks and Romans, particularly those of Aristotle.

The methods of learning that happened in the Renaissance dominated Europe for years. However, Renaissance ideas on education were gradually modified and eventually replaced during the eighteenth and nineteenth centuries. The emergence of nation-states and the onset of democracy during these two centuries led reformers to push for mass education for all children regardless of their social status. Still, despite receiving a basic education paid for by the state, most boys continued to follow in their fathers' footsteps while most girls learned to become wives and mothers. Universities remained like they had been during the Renaissance: places for the rich and privileged that were dominated by male students. It was not until the second half of the twentieth century that the Renaissance model disappeared in Europe and university educations became possible to all people no matter what their status or gender.

Glossary

dowry: money that a bride's family pays to her new family when she gets married

humanism: a philosophy that emphasizes the place of man in the world and puts less emphasis on religion

31 The word ensured in the passage is closest in meaning to

Ⓐ guaranteed

Ⓑ considered

Ⓒ requested

Ⓓ remembered

32 According to paragraph 1, which of the following is NOT true of the Renaissance?

Ⓐ The educations that people received then depended upon their positions in society.

Ⓑ More people were educated at universities then than they were at their homes.

Ⓒ The children of rich parents were educated better than those of poor ones at that time.

Ⓓ A lot of universities were established during this particular period of history.

Education in the Renaissance

[1]→ During the fifteenth and sixteenth centuries, Europe went through the period known as the Renaissance. In Europe then, the education a child received typically depended upon the social status of the child's family. The vast majority of Europeans were poor peasants, so their children received no formal schooling, yet wealthier merchants and members of the nobility often ensured that their children were educated. Despite the facts that education was stressed in the Renaissance and that many universities were founded then, most children—regardless of their social status—were educated in their homes in some manner.

33 The author discusses private tutors in paragraph 2 in order to

Ⓐ list the subjects that they often taught their students

Ⓑ explain how some children were taught during the Renaissance

Ⓒ claim that many of them had been educated at universities

Ⓓ note their importance to families that had their own businesses

34 In paragraph 2, the author implies that the children of peasants

Ⓐ frequently died when they were still young

Ⓑ were taught to read and write if they seemed intelligent

Ⓒ expected to get paid for the work that they did

Ⓓ seldom interacted with the children of merchants

35 The word facets in the passage is closest in meaning to

Ⓐ aspects

Ⓑ regimes

Ⓒ ideas

Ⓓ philosophies

2→ In the Renaissance, life was harsh for the majority of children born to peasants. If they survived infancy, boys farmed the land with their fathers or learned their fathers' trades. Some fortunate individuals were accepted as apprentices by craftsmen and learned specialized skills from them. As for girls, most learned how to become good wives and to raise children. The children of wealthier merchants frequently received some formal education from private tutors in their homes as they at least learned to read, write, and do mathematics since it was expected that they would take part in their family businesses.

Members of the nobility often went to great extents to educate their children in all facets of life. Aside from the basics of reading, writing, and some languages, young noble boys were taught horseback riding, practical skills with weapons, and dancing. Some also received military training or learned the basics of engineering. Noble girls were educated less than boys, yet they still learned to read and write and were also taught languages, art, music, and dancing. This was particularly true during the Renaissance, which was an age of art and music, so many young boys and girls were taught these subjects at specialized schools, particularly in Italy.

36 According to paragraph 4, which of the following is true of the religious educations some youths received in the Renaissance?

Ⓐ A family with many children was expected to have at least one become a priest.

Ⓑ Latin and Greek were core courses that all students learned at monasteries.

Ⓒ Families paid large sums of money to monasteries to instruct their children.

Ⓓ The people who received these religious educations came from all social groups.

37 In paragraph 5, the author implies that Aristotle

Ⓐ was highly respected by people during the Renaissance

Ⓑ was one of the greatest of all scholars who wrote in Latin

Ⓒ established the philosophy of humanism during ancient times

Ⓓ was knowledgeable in a number of different academic fields

Glossary

dowry: money that a bride's family pays to her new family when she gets married

humanism: a philosophy that emphasizes the place of man in the world and puts less emphasis on religion

4→ After childhood ended, there were few opportunities for peasant youths to receive any type of education. A few were occasionally trained to become members of the clergy at either churches or monasteries, but, for the most part, only upper-class youths received this type of education. During the Renaissance, merchants and noblemen with many sons usually sent their youngest to receive religious training. These children began their studies at young ages, were trained in Latin and sometimes Greek, and learned the Bible as well as the ceremonial aspects of church life. A few daughters of noblemen were sent to convents, where they were trained to become nuns. This normally happened when a family had many daughters because it spared the family the expense of providing a rich **dowry**, which they were obligated to do when their daughters married.

5→ When the sons of merchants and nobles became teenagers, they joined their fathers' businesses, took part in court life, became soldiers, or attended universities. Universities had first appeared during the Middle Ages, yet during the Renaissance, which emphasized learning, more universities were established. Nevertheless, the universities students could attend then varied in quality from place to place. Additionally, some specialized in one field of study even though most offered classes in various subjects. Typical fields were astronomy, medicine, philosophy, rhetoric, history, mathematics, logic, and grammar. The rediscovery of ancient Greek and Latin texts during the Renaissance and the subsequent development of the philosophy of **humanism** had profound influences on university educations. University students were expected to study the works of the ancient Greeks and Romans, particularly those of Aristotle.

38 According to paragraph 6, people began to promote mass education when

Ⓐ they realized that the Renaissance model of education had failed Europe

Ⓑ countries changed their political systems to ones that followed democracy

Ⓒ reformers realized what the economic benefits of doing so would be

Ⓓ the onset of the Industrial Revolution required workers to be well educated

[6]→ The methods of learning that happened in the Renaissance dominated Europe for years. However, Renaissance ideas on education were gradually modified and eventually replaced during the eighteenth and nineteenth centuries. The emergence of nation-states and the onset of democracy during these two centuries led reformers to push for mass education for all children regardless of their social status. Still, despite receiving a basic education paid for by the state, most boys continued to follow in their fathers' footsteps while most girls learned to become wives and mothers. Universities remained like they had been during the Renaissance: places for the rich and privileged that were dominated by male students. It was not until the second half of the twentieth century that the Renaissance model disappeared in Europe and university educations became possible to all people no matter what their status or gender.

39 Look at the four squares [■] that indicate where the following sentence could be added to the passage.

Consequently, they became priests when they grew up.

Where would the sentence best fit?

Click on a square [■] to add the sentence to the passage.

After childhood ended, there were few opportunities for peasant youths to receive any type of education. A few were occasionally trained to become members of the clergy at either churches or monasteries, but, for the most part, only upper-class youths received this type of education. During the Renaissance, merchants and noblemen with many sons usually sent their youngest to receive religious training. **1** These children began their studies at young ages, were trained in Latin and sometimes Greek, and learned the Bible as well as the ceremonial aspects of church life. **2** A few daughters of noblemen were sent to convents, where they were trained to become nuns. **3** This normally happened when a family had many daughters because it spared the family the expense of providing a rich **dowry**, which they were obligated to do when their daughters married. **4**

Glossary

dowry: money that a bride's family pays to her new family when she gets married

40 **Directions:** An introductory sentence for a brief summary of the passage is provided below. Complete the summary by selecting the THREE answer choices that express the most important ideas of the passage. Some sentences do not belong because they express ideas that are not presented in the passage or are minor ideas in the passage. **This question is worth 2 points.**

Drag your answer choices to the spaces where they belong.
To remove an answer choice, click on it. To review the passage, click on **View Text**.

The methods of education during the European Renaissance affected all classes of society for several centuries.

-
-
-

Answer Choices

1. Sons of noblemen were trained in military matters so that they would be effective officers in the army.
2. The Renaissance style of education did not start to disappear from Europe until the eighteenth century.
3. The philosophy of humanism played an important role in the stressing of education during the Renaissance.
4. A lot of wealthy families sent their daughters to convents to avoid having to pay dowries when they married.
5. During the Renaissance, the children of poor people received the least amount of education.
6. Universities began to play a more prominent role in the education of youths during the Renaissance.

TOEFL® MAP

ACTUAL TEST

Reading 2

CONTINUE

Reading Section Directions

This section measures your ability to understand academic passages in English. You will have **54 minutes** to read and answer questions about **3 passages**. A clock at the top of the screen will show you how much time is remaining.

Most questions are worth 1 point but the last question for each passage is worth more than 1 point. The directions for the last question indicate how many points you may receive.

Some passages include a word or phrase that is **underlined** in blue. Click on the word or phrase to see a definition or an explanation.

When you want to move to the next question, click on **Next**. You may skip questions and go back to them later. If you want to return to previous questions, click on **Back**. You can click on **Reivew** at any time, and the review screen will show you which questions you have answered and which you have not answered. From this review screen, you may go directly to any question you have already seen in the Reading section.

Click on **Continue** to go on.

Primitive South American Cultures

The South American continent is presently home to numerous modern cities, and many of its people enjoy relatively high standards of living. But much of the continent, particularly the inner basin of the Amazon River and its countless **tributaries**, is still an untamed region. Consequently, large numbers of the people who live in these areas lead a virtual Stone Age existence, and some South American tribes have not yet even made contact with the outside world. The people living in these primitive communities have lifestyles that parallel those of early humans: They live off the land as slash-and-burn farmers, hunter-gatherers, or a combination of the two. While their simple lives may seem ideal to some, there remains an undercurrent of violence between some tribes, and many practiced **headhunting** well into the twentieth century. Today, the tribe members struggle to maintain their cultures while also trying to enjoy some benefits of modern society.

Currently, there are more than 200 distinct tribes of Native Americans who live in South America. It is estimated that there were more than 2,000 when the Europeans arrived, but most were wiped out for various reasons. The tribes that have survived to the present vary in size, location, and lifestyle. One tribe, the Waroa, lives around the delta of the Orinoco River in Venezuela and has around 20,000 members. The Waroa were a viable community prior to the Spanish arrival in the 1500s and have been able to maintain much of their cultural identity up to the present day. On the other hand, the Assurini people of the Amazon Rainforest were unknown to the outside world until 1971. They occupy one small region that lies between tributaries of the Amazon River and survive by growing crops, fishing, and hunting. The tribe has never been large and today has only slightly more than one hundred members. The Assurini have avoided disappearing by intermarrying with people from other tribes.

Unfortunately, the stories of many of these tribes are lost. The coming of the Spanish and the Portuguese in the early 1500s upset the balance of life in South America forever. Some tribes were eradicated by European diseases while some were defeated in wars. Others fled from conquered lands and headed into the remote interior of the continent. Some anthropologists conjecture that a few tribes were much more sophisticated in the past and perhaps lived in large towns, engaged in trade, made pottery, and employed relatively advanced farming techniques. But, intent on conquering the land, enslaving the people, and forcing them to abandon their traditional shamanistic religions in favor of Catholicism, the Europeans drove lots of tribes away from their homelands and into the jungles. There, the people learned to survive and how to make do with whatever resources they could find. Thus they became more primitive not by choice but by necessity. When they were rediscovered by outsiders centuries later, the histories of these tribes had been long forgotten.

Today, most tribesmen have adjusted to living with the rest of the people in South America. Tribal warfare is mostly a relic of the past, and intertribal relations and unity are on the rise. There is even a tribal Olympic Games, during which members of various tribes gather to display their prowess at traditional activities such as running, spear-throwing, and archery. Furthermore, many tribes engage in external economic activities, especially tourism, by marketing their traditional clothing, pottery, baskets, and other handcrafted items to the numerous tourists curious about the tribes' primitive lifestyles. In the past, most of the money they earned was used by the tribes to ward off developers intent on encroaching on their territories since they were eager to exploit the resources of the tribes' lands.

However, in recent decades, the lands and the rights of these tribes have gradually come to be protected by the law. Most South American countries have made efforts to protect their native tribes. In Brazil, for instance, there are many tribal reservations—mostly in the Amazon Rainforest—where the lands of the tribes are protected. Except for violence against others, the tribesmen's traditional lifestyles are protected by Brazilian law. Consequently, tribes such as the Assurini can continue to live as they have for centuries.

Glossary

tributary: a river or stream that flows into a larger river or stream

headhunting: the practice of killing people and keeping their heads as trophies

1 The word untamed in the passage is closest in meaning to

Ⓐ uncharted

Ⓑ dangerous

Ⓒ deserted

Ⓓ wild

2 According to paragraph 1, which of the following is true of the primitive tribes living in South America?

Ⓐ Almost all of them live somewhere close to the Amazon River.

Ⓑ They have been living the same lifestyles since the Stone Age.

Ⓒ Some of these tribes know nothing about modern civilization.

Ⓓ The majority of them are eager to integrate with the modern world.

3 In paragraph 1, the author implies that the primitive tribes

Ⓐ are being exploited by various governments

Ⓑ are trying to learn modern agricultural methods

Ⓒ sometimes go to war against one another

Ⓓ are known to engage in cannibalism nowadays

Glossary

tributary: a river or stream that flows into a larger river or stream

headhunting: the practice of killing people and keeping their heads as trophies

Primitive South American Cultures

[1] → The South American continent is presently home to numerous modern cities, and many of its people enjoy relatively high standards of living. But much of the continent, particularly the inner basin of the Amazon River and its countless **tributaries**, is still an untamed region. Consequently, large numbers of the people who live in these areas lead a virtual Stone Age existence, and some South American tribes have not yet even made contact with the outside world. The people living in these primitive communities have lifestyles that parallel those of early humans: They live off the land as slash-and-burn farmers, hunter-gatherers, or a combination of the two. While their simple lives may seem ideal to some, there remains an undercurrent of violence between some tribes, and many practiced **headhunting** well into the twentieth century. Today, the tribe members struggle to maintain their cultures while also trying to enjoy some benefits of modern society.

4 The author discusses the Waroa in paragraph 2 in order to

Ⓐ describe one tribe that has survived for hundreds of years

Ⓑ explain how they managed to resist the Spanish invaders

Ⓒ compare the number of people they have with the Assurini tribe

Ⓓ emphasize some aspects of their cultural heritage

5 The author's description of the Assurini people in paragraph 2 mentions all of the following EXCEPT:

Ⓐ the manner in which they have avoided vanishing completely

Ⓑ the relative size of the territory in which they reside

Ⓒ the types of crops that their farmers usually raise

Ⓓ the year in which they made contact with the modern world

2→ Currently, there are more than 200 distinct tribes of Native Americans who live in South America. It is estimated that there were more than 2,000 when the Europeans arrived, but most were wiped out for various reasons. The tribes that have survived to the present vary in size, location, and lifestyle. One tribe, the Waroa, lives around the delta of the Orinoco River in Venezuela and has around 20,000 members. The Waroa were a viable community prior to the Spanish arrival in the 1500s and have been able to maintain much of their cultural identity up to the present day. On the other hand, the Assurini people of the Amazon Rainforest were unknown to the outside world until 1971. They occupy one small region that lies between tributaries of the Amazon River and survive by growing crops, fishing, and hunting. The tribe has never been large and today has only slightly more than one hundred members. The Assurini have avoided disappearing by intermarrying with people from other tribes.

6 According to paragraph 3, which of the following is NOT true of the Europeans that went to South America?

Ⓐ They were interested in converting the natives to their own religion.

Ⓑ They were responsible for forcing people off the land that they lived on.

Ⓒ They made slaves of many of the people whom they defeated in battle.

Ⓓ They taught many South American tribes how to survive in the jungle.

3→ Unfortunately, the stories of many of these tribes are lost. The coming of the Spanish and the Portuguese in the early 1500s upset the balance of life in South America forever. Some tribes were eradicated by European diseases while some were defeated in wars. Others fled from conquered lands and headed into the remote interior of the continent. Some anthropologists conjecture that a few tribes were much more sophisticated in the past and perhaps lived in large towns, engaged in trade, made pottery, and employed relatively advanced farming techniques. But, intent on conquering the land, enslaving the people, and forcing them to abandon their traditional shamanistic religions in favor of Catholicism, the Europeans drove lots of tribes away from their homelands and into the jungles. There, the people learned to survive and how to make do with whatever resources they could find. Thus they became more primitive not by choice but by necessity. When they were rediscovered by outsiders centuries later, the histories of these tribes had been long forgotten.

7 The phrase ward off in the passage is closest in meaning to

Ⓐ fight off

Ⓑ refuse

Ⓒ negotiate with

Ⓓ plead with

8 According to paragraph 5, Brazil has created tribal reservations because

Ⓐ the government is eager to force tribesmen to live there

Ⓑ the country is trying to protect the lands of its native tribes

Ⓒ too many developers have been stealing land that belongs to tribes

Ⓓ tribes take much better care of the land than do other people

Today, most tribesmen have adjusted to living with the rest of the people in South America. Tribal warfare is mostly a relic of the past, and intertribal relations and unity are on the rise. There is even a tribal Olympic Games, during which members of various tribes gather to display their prowess at traditional activities such as running, spear-throwing, and archery. Furthermore, many tribes engage in external economic activities, especially tourism, by marketing their traditional clothing, pottery, baskets, and other handcrafted items to the numerous tourists curious about the tribes' primitive lifestyles. In the past, most of the money they earned was used by the tribes to ward off developers intent on encroaching on their territories since they were eager to exploit the resources of the tribes' lands.

5→ However, in recent decades, the lands and the rights of these tribes have gradually come to be protected by the law. Most South American countries have made efforts to protect their native tribes. In Brazil, for instance, there are many tribal reservations—mostly in the Amazon Rainforest—where the lands of the tribes are protected. Except for violence against others, the tribesmen's traditional lifestyles are protected by Brazilian law. Consequently, tribes such as the Assurini can continue to live as they have for centuries.

9 Look at the four squares [■] that indicate where the following sentence could be added to the passage.

This is a common activity for many of the smallest tribes living in South America.

Where would the sentence best fit?

Click on a square [■] to add the sentence to the passage.

Currently, there are more than 200 distinct tribes of Native Americans who live in South America. It is estimated that there were more than 2,000 when the Europeans arrived, but most were wiped out for various reasons. The tribes that have survived to the present vary in size, location, and lifestyle. One tribe, the Waroa, lives around the delta of the Orinoco River in Venezuela and has around 20,000 members. The Waroa were a viable community prior to the Spanish arrival in the 1500s and have been able to maintain much of their cultural identity up to the present day. On the other hand, the Assurini people of the Amazon Rainforest were unknown to the outside world until 1971. [1] They occupy one small region that lies between tributaries of the Amazon River and survive by growing crops, fishing, and hunting. [2] The tribe has never been large and today has only slightly more than one hundred members. [3] The Assurini have avoided disappearing by intermarrying with people from other tribes. [4]

10 **Directions:** An introductory sentence for a brief summary of the passage is provided below. Complete the summary by selecting the THREE answer choices that express the most important ideas of the passage. Some sentences do not belong because they express ideas that are not presented in the passage or are minor ideas in the passage. **This question is worth 2 points.**

Drag your answer choices to the spaces where they belong.
To remove an answer choice, click on it. To review the passage, click on **View Text**.

There are many primitive tribes that live in areas all throughout South America.

-
-
-

Answer Choices

1. The Spanish killed few tribesmen when they visited South America in the 1500s.
2. Some of the tribes have lived in the same locations for hundreds of years.
3. There are currently efforts in many countries to protect the lands of these tribes.
4. The world only became aware of the Assurini people around four decades ago.
5. Many tribes are making efforts to integrate into modern society and to earn money.
6. There were once more than 2,000 native tribes that lived in South America.

Jupiter's Moon Io

An image of Io

Jupiter has more moons than every planet in the solar system except Saturn. Of its seventy-nine moons, most are small, but four are rather sizable as they are nearly as large as some of the solar system's smaller planets. These four moons orbit close to Jupiter and are named the Galilean moons because they were discovered by Italian scientist Galileo Galilei in 1610. Of these four moons, Io is perhaps the most unusual. It is the most geologically active moon in the entire solar system as it receives an extensive amount of volcanic activity, which has produced a terrain featuring mountains and plains comprised of various hues of sulfur. In addition, the volcanic activity on Io accounts for its large number of craters and partly for its unique orbit around Jupiter.

Io is the fifth closest moon to Jupiter and the nearest to the planet of the Galilean moons. It is the third largest of Jupiter's moons and is similar in size to Earth's moon. Io orbits Jupiter once approximately every forty-two hours, giving it a very swift rotational period around the massive planet. Io's own rotational period is such that one side of it continually faces Jupiter. This is similar to the manner in which the moon orbits Earth. Io's orbital track is eccentric, so it is not a perfect circle. Its orbital eccentricity is a result of powerful gravitational forces from Jupiter as well as from the two nearest Galilean moons, Europa and Ganymede. Io is caught in between the gravitational effects of these heavenly bodies, so its orbital path is affected, and there are a large number of tidal effects on its interior as well.

Io's interior consists of silicate-based rocks, iron, and large amounts of sulfur. Its composition is based on external space observations, so there is some disagreement as to whether or not Io has a mantle-core system similar to what Earth has. What astronomers agree on is that Io's interior is extremely active. This is due to a process called tidal heating, which is the result of the effects of the gravitational pull of Jupiter and some nearby moons. Because of tidal heating, Io is highly volcanically active with a surface that has numerous active and extinct volcanoes. During one satellite flyby, at least nine active volcanoes were observed. These volcanoes frequently spew vast amounts of sulfur and other materials several hundred kilometers into Io's thin atmosphere. One consequence is that the moon's surface has numerous large flat plains comprised of sulfur. These plains are mostly yellow and white in color, but some also appear to be red, orange, and green since they are composed of various **allotropes** of sulfur.

To the surprise of many astronomers, when the first satellites reached Io in the late twentieth century, the images they returned to Earth showed that Io was devoid of impact craters. Unlike Earth's moon and various other bodies in the solar system, Io has a relatively smooth surface. The explanation for its lack of impact craters soon became evident. The incessant volcanic activity has resulted in Io's surface being constantly reshaped since the volcanic eruptions either fill in or cover up any impact craters on the moon.

When a volcano on Io erupts, most of the material that is ejected from the moon's interior first rises high above the moon prior to falling back to the surface. However, some of it stays high above the surface, which produces a thin atmosphere around Io. A significant amount of this material also escapes into space, where it forms a cloud that surrounds Io at a distance of up to six times the moon's radius. Even more of this material—at a rate of about one ton a second—gets sucked up by Jupiter's magnetic field. This material is mainly comprised of **ionized** elements such as sulfur, oxygen, and chlorine. The particles form a wide magnetic belt around Jupiter that astronomers have dubbed the torus. These particles from Io remain in Jupiter's torus for an average of forty days, whereupon they are then ejected into Jupiter's magnetosphere, which helps account for its unusually large size.

Glossary

allotrope: one of the two or more forms that an element can take

ionized: having been changed into an ion, which is a charged particle

11 The word hues in the passage is closest in meaning to

Ⓐ elements

Ⓑ divisions

Ⓒ shades

Ⓓ styles

12 In paragraph 1, the author's description of the Galilean moons mentions all of the following EXCEPT:

Ⓐ the year during which they were first observed

Ⓑ their sizes in comparison with Jupiter's other moons

Ⓒ the person who was responsible for finding them

Ⓓ the names that people have given to all of them

13 The word eccentric in the passage is closest in meaning to

Ⓐ peculiar

Ⓑ individual

Ⓒ perpendicular

Ⓓ triangular

Jupiter's Moon Io

[1]➔ Jupiter has more moons than every planet in the solar system except Saturn. Of its seventy-nine moons, most are small, but four are rather sizable as they are nearly as large as some of the solar system's smaller planets. These four moons orbit close to Jupiter and are named the Galilean moons because they were discovered by Italian scientist Galileo Galilei in 1610. Of these four moons, Io is perhaps the most unusual. It is the most geologically active moon in the entire solar system as it receives an extensive amount of volcanic activity, which has produced a terrain featuring mountains and plains comprised of various hues of sulfur. In addition, the volcanic activity on Io accounts for its large number of craters and partly for its unique orbit around Jupiter.

Io is the fifth closest moon to Jupiter and the nearest to the planet of the Galilean moons. It is the third largest of Jupiter's moons and is similar in size to Earth's moon. Io orbits Jupiter once approximately every forty-two hours, giving it a very swift rotational period around the massive planet. Io's own rotational period is such that one side of it continually faces Jupiter. This is similar to the manner in which the moon orbits Earth. Io's orbital track is eccentric, so it is not a perfect circle. Its orbital eccentricity is a result of powerful gravitational forces from Jupiter as well as from the two nearest Galilean moons, Europa and Ganymede. Io is caught in between the gravitational effects of these heavenly bodies, so its orbital path is affected, and there are a large number of tidal effects on its interior as well.

14 According to paragraph 2, Io is similar to Earth's moon because

Ⓐ it affects the tides on Jupiter much like the moon does to Earth

Ⓑ it completes a rotation of Jupiter in the same amount of time

Ⓒ it has an orbital track almost identical to the moon's

Ⓓ it rotates so that only one of its sides ever faces Jupiter

15 Which of the following can be inferred from paragraph 2 about Io?

Ⓐ It orbits Jupiter faster than any of the planet's moons.

Ⓑ It is the smallest of all four of the Galilean moons.

Ⓒ Its orbit is similar to no other heavenly body in the solar system.

Ⓓ It orbits Jupiter more closely than Europa or Ganymede do.

16 The author discusses tidal heating in paragraph 3 in order to

Ⓐ explain why Io is comprised of iron and silicate-based rocks

Ⓑ compare its volcanoes with some of those that are on the Earth

Ⓒ explain why Io has a large amount of volcanic activity

Ⓓ account for the presence of many sulfur plains on Io

Glossary

allotrope: one of the two or more forms that an element can take

2→ Io is the fifth closest moon to Jupiter and the nearest to the planet of the Galilean moons. It is the third largest of Jupiter's moons and is similar in size to Earth's moon. Io orbits Jupiter once approximately every forty-two hours, giving it a very swift rotational period around the massive planet. Io's own rotational period is such that one side of it continually faces Jupiter. This is similar to the manner in which the moon orbits Earth. Io's orbital track is eccentric, so it is not a perfect circle. Its orbital eccentricity is a result of powerful gravitational forces from Jupiter as well as from the two nearest Galilean moons, Europa and Ganymede. Io is caught in between the gravitational effects of these heavenly bodies, so its orbital path is affected, and there are a large number of tidal effects on its interior as well.

3→ Io's interior consists of silicate-based rocks, iron, and large amounts of sulfur. Its composition is based on external space observations, so there is some disagreement as to whether or not Io has a mantle-core system similar to what Earth has. What astronomers agree on is that Io's interior is extremely active. This is due to a process called tidal heating, which is the result of the effects of the gravitational pull of Jupiter and some nearby moons. Because of tidal heating, Io is highly volcanically active with a surface that has numerous active and extinct volcanoes. During one satellite flyby, at least nine active volcanoes were observed. These volcanoes frequently spew vast amounts of sulfur and other materials several hundred kilometers into Io's thin atmosphere. One consequence is that the moon's surface has numerous large flat plains comprised of sulfur. These plains are mostly yellow and white in color, but some also appear to be red, orange, and green since they are composed of various allotropes of sulfur.

17 According to paragraph 4, the surface of Io is relatively smooth because

Ⓐ no asteroids or meteors have ever hit the moon's surface

Ⓑ earthquakes on the moon prevent mountains from being too high

Ⓒ lava that volcanoes spew covers any irregular spots on the surface

Ⓓ the volcanic activity quickly removes all impact craters

18 According to paragraph 5, which of the following is NOT true of the material ejected by Io's volcanoes?

Ⓐ Most of the material that falls back is formed of ionized elements.

Ⓑ It contributes to the creation of a thin atmosphere on Io.

Ⓒ Some of it enters outer space and then forms the torus of Jupiter.

Ⓓ A certain amount of it does not fall back to the moon's surface.

Glossary

ionized: having been changed into an ion, which is a charged particle

4→ To the surprise of many astronomers, when the first satellites reached Io in the late twentieth century, the images they returned to Earth showed that Io was devoid of impact craters. Unlike Earth's moon and various other bodies in the solar system, Io has a relatively smooth surface. The explanation for its lack of impact craters soon became evident. The incessant volcanic activity has resulted in Io's surface being constantly reshaped since the volcanic eruptions either fill in or cover up any impact craters on the moon.

5→ When a volcano on Io erupts, most of the material that is ejected from the moon's interior first rises high above the moon prior to falling back to the surface. However, some of it stays high above the surface, which produces a thin atmosphere around Io. A significant amount of this material also escapes into space, where it forms a cloud that surrounds Io at a distance of up to six times the moon's radius. Even more of this material—at a rate of about one ton a second—gets sucked up by Jupiter's magnetic field. This material is mainly comprised of **ionized** elements such as sulfur, oxygen, and chlorine. The particles form a wide magnetic belt around Jupiter that astronomers have dubbed the torus. These particles from Io remain in Jupiter's torus for an average of forty days, whereupon they are then ejected into Jupiter's magnetosphere, which helps account for its unusually large size.

19 Look at the four squares [■] that indicate where the following sentence could be added to the passage.

In fact, the largest, Ganymede, is bigger than Mercury and almost the same size as Mars.

Where would the sentence best fit?

Click on a square [■] to add the sentence to the passage.

Jupiter has more moons than every planet in the solar system except Saturn. **1** Of its seventy-nine moons, most are small, but four are rather sizable as they are nearly as large as some of the solar system's smaller planets. **2** These four moons orbit close to Jupiter and are named the Galilean moons because they were discovered by Italian scientist Galileo Galilei in 1610. **3** Of these four moons, Io is perhaps the most unusual. **4** It is the most geologically active moon in the entire solar system as it receives an extensive amount of volcanic activity, which has produced a terrain featuring mountains and plains comprised of various hues of sulfur. In addition, the volcanic activity on Io accounts for its large number of craters and partly for its unique orbit around Jupiter.

20 Directions: An introductory sentence for a brief summary of the passage is provided below. Complete the summary by selecting the THREE answer choices that express the most important ideas of the passage. Some sentences do not belong because they express ideas that are not presented in the passage or are minor ideas in the passage. **This question is worth 2 points.**

Drag your answer choices to the spaces where they belong.
To remove an answer choice, click on it. To review the passage, click on **View Text**.

Jupiter's moon Io has an exceptional amount of volcanic activity, which contributes to its unique features.

-
-
-

Answer Choices

1. Several satellites have flown by Io, but none of them has ever entered its atmosphere.
2. Because of its volcanic eruptions, the surface of Io is almost entirely smooth.
3. Io is known as one of the four Galilean moons that were discovered by Galileo.
4. There are a number of colorful sulfur plains that are found all over Io.
5. Io has an atmosphere thanks to material that is spewed high above its surface.
6. Io's orbit of Jupiter is eccentric because Jupiter and some other moons affect it.

The Economic Development of London

The London Stock Exchange

London today is the political and financial capital of Great Britain. It began, however, as a Roman **stronghold**, and following the Romans departure, the Anglo-Saxons and then the Normans controlled it. London grew considerably during the medieval period and, by the sixteenth century, was primed to be the center of unprecedented growth. Most of this can be attributed to the city's economic development. Located on the Thames River with easy access to the North Sea, London became a shipping and commerce center. Large corporations were based there, bringing further wealth. Finally, when the Industrial Revolution began, London was transformed even more and became the world's financial center by the nineteenth century.

The Romans conquered Britain in 43 A.D. and founded London—called Londinium by them—as a garrison town, and it became a center of seaborne trade soon afterward. London's location was ideal: It was centrally situated on the Thames River far from the coast but not so far inland that ships could not navigate upriver to it. As such, it became a center of trade in Roman Britain and may have had as many as 60,000 people at its height. But the fall of the Roman Empire in the fifth century resulted in the Roman abandonment of Britain, so, for some time, London was virtually empty. Anglo-Saxon incursions led to the reoccupation of the area, but Viking invasions and decades of instability resulted in the region seeing little economic growth. When the Normans invaded from France in 1066, they chose London as their center of government, which began the city's revival.

During the mid and late Middle Ages, London expanded as both a town and economic center when the European world became more connected due to increased shipbuilding and maritime trade. London was poised to take advantage of this thanks to its geographical location and political power. The city continued to grow in size and wealth throughout the medieval period as well as during the Renaissance. When Britain began to gain colonies in the Americas and elsewhere in the sixteenth century, fabulous amounts of money started finding their way to London.

At that time, mercantilism was the reigning economic philosophy in Britain. It called for the protecting of British trade between the home island and its colonies. The government accordingly enacted laws imposing taxes on imports and protecting British trade. The main objectives were to attain a trade surplus and to amass gold and silver. One result of this mercantilist philosophy was that extraordinary wealth poured into London. At the center of British economic activity, London grew rapidly and expanded in size and population.

At the same time, the founding of several great companies and institutions paved the way for London to become the center of world trade and finance. The British East India Company, for instance, was granted a **monopoly** on trade in India. It was based in London, so treasures from India made their way there. The company had to raise money for its initial ventures, so it sold shares of stock that gave investors pieces of the wealth it was amassing. This helped establish the London Stock Exchange, which had its humble beginnings in London's coffee shops, where merchants gathered to trade stocks and to learn global financial news. Other important institutions, such as the Bank of England and the insurance firm Lloyd's of London, were started then as well.

During the eighteenth century, the Industrial Revolution caused the British economic philosophy to change from mercantilism to capitalism. Trade with overseas colonies became less important when investors in factories started becoming rich. Britain initiated a policy of free trade, sought to establish a worldwide market, and traded products from its manufacturing industry with anyone who would purchase them. London was at the center of this economic action. The development of fast steamships, the telegraph, and the telephone in the nineteenth century connected London with the entire world, so it became the world's financial center. Its banks were used to transfer funds worldwide, its financial institutions provided capital for investors, and its docks and warehouses were filled with raw materials and goods from around the world. Unfortunately, the onset of World War I in 1914 brought this entire system to a halt.

Glossary

stronghold: a fortified area

monopoly: the complete domination of one economic sector by an individual, company, or government

PREVIEW

HELP

BACK

NEXT

21 The word primed in the passage is closest in meaning to

Ⓐ positioned

Ⓑ inspired

Ⓒ appointed

Ⓓ expected

22 According to paragraph 2, the Romans left London because

Ⓐ the Anglo-Saxons invaded Britain and defeated the Romans in battle

Ⓑ the entire Roman empire fell, so the Romans in London departed

Ⓒ there were few economic benefits to gain by living there

Ⓓ the Romans had no need for a seaport so far north of Rome

Glossary

stronghold: a fortified area

The Economic Development of London

London today is the political and financial capital of Great Britain. It began, however, as a Roman **stronghold**, and following the Romans departure, the Anglo-Saxons and then the Normans controlled it. London grew considerably during the medieval period and, by the sixteenth century, was primed to be the center of unprecedented growth. Most of this can be attributed to the city's economic development. Located on the Thames River with easy access to the North Sea, London became a shipping and commerce center. Large corporations were based there, bringing further wealth. Finally, when the Industrial Revolution began, London was transformed even more and became the world's financial center by the nineteenth century.

2→ The Romans conquered Britain in 43 A.D. and founded London—called Londinium by them—as a garrison town, and it became a center of seaborne trade soon afterward. London's location was ideal: It was centrally situated on the Thames River far from the coast but not so far inland that ships could not navigate upriver to it. As such, it became a center of trade in Roman Britain and may have had as many as 60,000 people at its height. But the fall of the Roman Empire in the fifth century resulted in the Roman abandonment of Britain, so, for some time, London was virtually empty. Anglo-Saxon incursions led to the reoccupation of the area, but Viking invasions and decades of instability resulted in the region seeing little economic growth. When the Normans invaded from France in 1066, they chose London as their center of government, which began the city's revival.

23 In paragraph 3, the author uses shipbuilding and maritime trade as examples of

Ⓐ two aspects of the medieval economy in which London was a European leader

Ⓑ the reasons that Britain made an effort to acquire colonies in the Americas

Ⓒ the primary factors why Britain became wealthy during the Renaissance

Ⓓ reasons that London started to become more prominent in the Middle Ages

24 According to paragraph 4, which of the following is true of mercantilism?

Ⓐ It focused on selling goods to others rather than purchasing them.

Ⓑ It was an economic philosophy that had its origins in Great Britain.

Ⓒ It enabled London to grow rich at the expense of other British cities.

Ⓓ It contributed to the British colonies being less wealthy than the home island.

25 In paragraph 4, the author implies that mercantilism

Ⓐ was practiced by almost every country in Europe

Ⓑ led to the outbreak of several wars in Europe

Ⓒ was financially beneficial to much of Great Britain

Ⓓ began because of the colonization of the Americas

[3]→ During the mid and late Middle Ages, London expanded as both a town and economic center when the European world became more connected due to increased shipbuilding and maritime trade. London was poised to take advantage of this thanks to its geographical location and political power. The city continued to grow in size and wealth throughout the medieval period as well as during the Renaissance. When Britain began to gain colonies in the Americas and elsewhere in the sixteenth century, fabulous amounts of money started finding their way to London.

[4]→ At that time, mercantilism was the reigning economic philosophy in Britain. It called for the protecting of British trade between the home island and its colonies. The government accordingly enacted laws imposing taxes on imports and protecting British trade. The main objectives were to attain a trade surplus and to amass gold and silver. One result of this mercantilist philosophy was that extraordinary wealth poured into London. At the center of British economic activity, London grew rapidly and expanded in size and population.

26 The word It in the passage refers to

Ⓐ The British East India Company

Ⓑ A monopoly

Ⓒ Trade

Ⓓ India

27 The word capital in the passage is closest in meaning to

Ⓐ government

Ⓑ funds

Ⓒ advice

Ⓓ regulations

28 According to paragraph 6, which of the following is NOT true of London in the nineteenth century?

Ⓐ Both raw materials and finished products were imported there.

Ⓑ The city benefitted greatly from a number of new inventions that were made.

Ⓒ It was dramatically affected by the breaking out of hostilities in some wars.

Ⓓ No other city in the world was more powerful in the financial sector.

Glossary

monopoly: the complete domination of one economic sector by an individual, company, or government

At the same time, the founding of several great companies and institutions paved the way for London to become the center of world trade and finance. The British East India Company, for instance, was granted a **monopoly** on trade in India. It was based in London, so treasures from India made their way there. The company had to raise money for its initial ventures, so it sold shares of stock that gave investors pieces of the wealth it was amassing. This helped establish the London Stock Exchange, which had its humble beginnings in London's coffee shops, where merchants gathered to trade stocks and to learn global financial news. Other important institutions, such as the Bank of England and the insurance firm Lloyd's of London, were started then as well.

6→ During the eighteenth century, the Industrial Revolution caused the British economic philosophy to change from mercantilism to capitalism. Trade with overseas colonies became less important when investors in factories started becoming rich. Britain initiated a policy of free trade, sought to establish a worldwide market, and traded products from its manufacturing industry with anyone who would purchase them. London was at the center of this economic action. The development of fast steamships, the telegraph, and the telephone in the nineteenth century connected London with the entire world, so it became the world's financial center. Its banks were used to transfer funds worldwide, its financial institutions provided capital for investors, and its docks and warehouses were filled with raw materials and goods from around the world. Unfortunately, the onset of World War I in 1914 brought this entire system to a halt.

29 Look at the four squares [■] that indicate where the following sentence could be added to the passage.

It also conducted business in many other British colonies.

Where would the sentence best fit?

Click on a square [■] to add the sentence to the passage.

At the same time, the founding of several great companies and institutions paved the way for London to become the center of world trade and finance. The British East India Company, for instance, was granted a **monopoly** on trade in India. It was based in London, so treasures from India made their way there. [1] The company had to raise money for its initial ventures, so it sold shares of stock that gave investors pieces of the wealth it was amassing. [2] This helped establish the London Stock Exchange, which had its humble beginnings in London's coffee shops, where merchants gathered to trade stocks and to learn global financial news. [3] Other important institutions, such as the Bank of England and the insurance firm Lloyd's of London, were started then as well. [4]

Glossary

monopoly: the complete domination of one economic sector by an individual, company, or government

30 **Directions:** Select the appropriate statements from the answer choices and match them to the cause and effect of the economic development of London to which they relate. TWO of the answer choices will NOT be used. **This question is worth 3 points.**

Drag your answer choices to the spaces where they belong.
To remove an answer choice, click on it. To review the passage, click on **View Text**.

Answer Choices

1. The Romans founded London in 43 A.D. and called the town Londinium.
2. London was the financial center of the world in the nineteenth century.
3. The British East India Company helped establish the London Stock Exchange.
4. Great Britain practiced the political philosophy of mercantilism.
5. The city had an ideal location on the Thames River near the North Sea.
6. Capitalism and mercantilism were two competing economic philosophies.
7. The population and wealth of London rose during the mid and late Middle Ages.

THE ECONOMIC DEVELOPMENT OF LONDON

Cause

-
-
-

Effect

-
-

TOEFL® MAP

ACTUAL TEST

Reading 2

04

CONTINUE

Reading Section Directions

This section measures your ability to understand academic passages in English. You will have **72 minutes** to read and answer questions about **4 passages**. A clock at the top of the screen will show you how much time is remaining.

Most questions are worth 1 point but the last question for each passage is worth more than 1 point. The directions for the last question indicate how many points you may receive.

Some passages include a word or phrase that is **underlined** in blue. Click on the word or phrase to see a definition or an explanation.

When you want to move to the next question, click on **Next**. You may skip questions and go back to them later. If you want to return to previous questions, click on **Back**. You can click on **Reivew** at any time, and the review screen will show you which questions you have answered and which you have not answered. From this review screen, you may go directly to any question you have already seen in the Reading section.

Click on **Continue** to go on.

The Longleaf Pine Tree

The crowns of a longleaf pine tree

Of the numerous species of pine trees in the United States, one of the most noticeable, on account of its long needles, is the longleaf pine tree. It grows in a unique manner that encompasses several individual stages. The longleaf pine has long been valued for the quality of its wood, which has led to vast areas in the Southeast United States being deforested. Currently, steps are being taken to reintroduce the tree in several states though.

The longleaf pine is native to the Southeastern United States, and its territory ranges from eastern Texas in the west to the Atlantic coast of Virginia in the east. The forests in which longleaf pines are found contain a rich diversity of life, mainly because of the largeness and nutritional value of the trees' seeds, which many animals are partial to eating. Yet unlike most other pine trees, the longleaf pine grows extremely slowly as a typical tree does not attain its full height until it is between 100 and 150 years old.

The seeds of most longleaf pines fall to the ground in mid-autumn and subsequently germinate a few weeks later. Then, the trees enter the grass stage, a period when they resemble clumps of grass and look nothing like trees. One benefit is that trees in the grass stage are protected from the forest fires that sometimes affect their regions. Some needles may get singed, but the tree itself remains safe from the flames. Additionally, although trees in the grass stage do not grow high above the ground, they develop **taproots** that eventually become approximately two to three meters long. The grass stage normally lasts between one and seven years, yet some trees have remained in it for around two decades.

When the grass stage concludes, the trees enter the **bottlebrush** stage, whereupon they begin growing taller above the ground. The trees experience a growth spurt and often become a meter or two higher in merely a few months' time. During this time, the trees do not develop outward-growing branches, which makes them resemble bottlebrush trees, hence the name of this particular stage. The trees' rapid growth enables them to get positioned to collect as much sunlight as possible, yet they become somewhat vulnerable to forest fires because their bark develops at a slower pace than the rest of the trees' parts.

It is during the sapling stage, when longleaf pines are about two to three meters high, that their branches finally start to grow horizontally. The trees' trunks and bark begin to thicken, and the trees themselves grow at a rate of approximately one meter each year. During the sapling stage, as the bark toughens, the trees once again become practically impervious to fire, so most longleaf pines that are more than 2.5 meters high virtually never get killed by forest fires.

Longleaf pines do not fully mature until they have been alive for around three decades. At that point, the mature stage begins, and they produce cones with fertile seeds. The trees remain in this stage for around 100 years, after which they enter the old-growth stage. Most longleaf pines live to be around 300 years old, yet there are documented cases of some living for nearly 500 years. It is during these final two stages that longleaf pines become incredibly valuable for their timber. Ever since they were discovered during America's colonial period, the trees, which grow tall and straight, have been utilized to make the masts of ships. Presently, their wood is employed to make paper, rayon, turpentine, and even plastics.

On account of their value to humans, longleaf pines were chopped down so quickly that they could not reproduce fast enough to replenish their numbers. It is estimated that 97% of longleaf pine forests no longer exist as a result of this overharvesting. Fortunately, in modern times, the value of the longleaf pine has been recognized. In many states, including Florida, Georgia, and Alabama, where it has been named the state tree, there are longleaf pine nurseries in which trees are raised and then reintroduced to forests whenever they are healthy enough to survive in the wild. With luck, the number of longleaf pines in the Southeastern United States will increase in the future.

Glossary

taproot: a main root that descends straight down from a plant and from which other smaller roots may extend

bottlebrush: a group of trees and bushes that belong to the myrtle family

1 The word encompasses in the passage is closest in meaning to

(A) appoints

(B) entitles

(C) includes

(D) appeals to

2 The phrase partial to in the passage is closest in meaning to

(A) fond of

(B) considerate of

(C) aware of

(D) resolve to

3 The author's description of the longleaf pine tree in paragraph 2 mentions all of the following EXCEPT:

(A) the number of years it requires to grow to its maximum height

(B) the places in the United States where it most normally grows

(C) the greatest height that most of the trees are able to attain

(D) the reason that many animals live in forests with these trees

The Longleaf Pine Tree

Of the numerous species of pine trees in the United States, one of the most noticeable, on account of its long needles, is the longleaf pine tree. It grows in a unique manner that encompasses several individual stages. The longleaf pine has long been valued for the quality of its wood, which has led to vast areas in the Southeast United States being deforested. Currently, steps are being taken to reintroduce the tree in several states though.

2→ The longleaf pine is native to the Southeastern United States, and its territory ranges from eastern Texas in the west to the Atlantic coast of Virginia in the east. The forests in which longleaf pines are found contain a rich diversity of life, mainly because of the largeness and nutritional value of the trees' seeds, which many animals are partial to eating. Yet unlike most other pine trees, the longleaf pine grows extremely slowly as a typical tree does not attain its full height until it is between 100 and 150 years old.

4 The author describes the grass stage in paragraph 3 in order to

Ⓐ focus on the fact that the longleaf pine tree's taproot becomes so long

Ⓑ explain the reason that longleaf pine tree seeds germinate in winter

Ⓒ emphasize that many longleaf pine trees are affected by forest fires in this stage

Ⓓ go into detail about the initial stage of growth of longleaf pine trees

5 According to paragraph 4, what happens when the longleaf pine tree enters the bottlebrush stage?

Ⓐ The trunk of the tree becomes much thicker than before.

Ⓑ The tree starts to grow at a rate that is faster than usual.

Ⓒ The needles begin to resemble those of other trees.

Ⓓ The taproot ceases growing as smaller roots expand in size.

Glossary

taproot: a main root that descends straight down from a plant and from which other smaller roots may extend

bottlebrush: a group of trees and bushes that belong to the myrtle family

[3]→ The seeds of most longleaf pines fall to the ground in mid-autumn and subsequently germinate a few weeks later. Then, the trees enter the grass stage, a period when they resemble clumps of grass and look nothing like trees. One benefit is that trees in the grass stage are protected from the forest fires that sometimes affect their regions. Some needles may get singed, but the tree itself remains safe from the flames. Additionally, although trees in the grass stage do not grow high above the ground, they develop **taproots** that eventually become approximately two to three meters long. The grass stage normally lasts between one and seven years, yet some trees have remained in it for around two decades.

[4]→ When the grass stage concludes, the trees enter the **bottlebrush** stage, whereupon they begin growing taller above the ground. The trees experience a growth spurt and often become a meter or two higher in merely a few months' time. During this time, the trees do not develop outward-growing branches, which makes them resemble bottlebrush trees, hence the name of this particular stage. The trees' rapid growth enables them to get positioned to collect as much sunlight as possible, yet they become somewhat vulnerable to forest fires because their bark develops at a slower pace than the rest of the trees' parts.

6 Which of the sentences below best expresses the essential information in the highlighted sentence in the passage? *Incorrect* answer choices change the meaning in important ways or leave out essential information.

Ⓐ While most longleaf pine trees in their sapling stage cannot get killed by forest fires, it is possible for some of the bigger ones to get burned and die.

Ⓑ It is virtually impossible for a forest fire to kill a longleaf pine tree that is 2.5 meters high and is in any of its numerous stages of life.

Ⓒ Longleaf pine trees at least 2.5 meters high that are in their sapling stage almost never succumb to forest fires because their bark becomes too tough.

Ⓓ When forest fires start in an area that has longleaf pine trees in it, the trees that are 2.5 meters high or higher live while all of the other trees die.

7 Which of the following can be inferred from paragraph 6 about longleaf pine trees in the mature stage?

Ⓐ They can suffer from a variety of diseases during this period.

Ⓑ They grow at their most rapid pace when in the mature stage.

Ⓒ They can be consumed by forest fires due to their great height.

Ⓓ They develop the ability to reproduce during that stage.

It is during the sapling stage, when longleaf pines are about two to three meters high, that their branches finally start to grow horizontally. The trees' trunks and bark begin to thicken, and the trees themselves grow at a rate of approximately one meter each year. During the sapling stage, as the bark toughens, the trees once again become practically impervious to fire, so most longleaf pines that are more than 2.5 meters high virtually never get killed by forest fires.

6→ Longleaf pines do not fully mature until they have been alive for around three decades. At that point, the mature stage begins, and they produce cones with fertile seeds. The trees remain in this stage for around 100 years, after which they enter the old-growth stage. Most longleaf pines live to be around 300 years old, yet there are documented cases of some living for nearly 500 years. It is during these final two stages that longleaf pines become incredibly valuable for their timber. Ever since they were discovered during America's colonial period, the trees, which grow tall and straight, have been utilized to make the masts of ships. Presently, their wood is employed to make paper, rayon, turpentine, and even plastics.

8 According to paragraph 7, one way in which people are trying to help the longleaf pine tree is by

Ⓐ growing the trees in nurseries and then transplanting them in forests

Ⓑ eliminating some of the diseases that commonly afflict the trees

Ⓒ asking loggers to chop down fewer trees to keep them from being depleted

Ⓓ setting aside large areas of land where the trees cannot be harvested

[7] ➜ On account of their value to humans, longleaf pines were chopped down so quickly that they could not reproduce fast enough to replenish their numbers. It is estimated that 97% of longleaf pine forests no longer exist as a result of this overharvesting. Fortunately, in modern times, the value of the longleaf pine has been recognized. In many states, including Florida, Georgia, and Alabama, where it has been named the state tree, there are longleaf pine nurseries in which trees are raised and then reintroduced to forests whenever they are healthy enough to survive in the wild. With luck, the number of longleaf pines in the Southeastern United States will increase in the future.

9 Look at the four squares [■] that indicate where the following sentence could be added to the passage.

Of course, many trees succumb to natural disasters or diseases before reaching this age.

Where would the sentence best fit?

Click on a square [■] to add the sentence to the passage.

Longleaf pines do not fully mature until they have been alive for around three decades. At that point, the mature stage begins, and they produce cones with fertile seeds. The trees remain in this stage for around 100 years, after which they enter the old-growth stage. Most longleaf pines live to be around 300 years old, yet there are documented cases of some living for nearly 500 years. **1** It is during these final two stages that longleaf pines become incredibly valuable for their timber. **2** Ever since they were discovered during America's colonial period, the trees, which grow tall and straight, have been utilized to make the masts of ships. **3** Presently, their wood is employed to make paper, rayon, turpentine, and even plastics. **4**

10 Directions: An introductory sentence for a brief summary of the passage is provided below. Complete the summary by selecting the THREE answer choices that express the most important ideas of the passage. Some sentences do not belong because they express ideas that are not presented in the passage or are minor ideas in the passage. **This question is worth 2 points.**

Drag your answer choices to the spaces where they belong.
To remove an answer choice, click on it. To review the passage, click on **View Text**.

The longleaf pine tree goes through several unique stages of growth during its lifetime.

-
-
-

Answer Choices

1. Longleaf pine tree seeds germinate soon after falling to the ground and then begin to grow into adult trees.
2. People in some parts of the Southeastern United States have established nurseries to grow longleaf pine trees in.
3. There are some instances of longleaf pine trees living for nearly 500 years even though most only live around 350 years.
4. Over the course of many years in the mature stage, the longleaf pine tree reaches its greatest height.
5. The grass stage enables the longleaf pine tree to grow a deep taproot while its needles keep it safe from fires.
6. When a longleaf pine tree becomes a sapling, it grows quickly for a few months and regains its resistance to fire.

The Onset of the Greek Dark Ages

A Mycenaean ruins complex in Mycenae, Greece

Prior to the Classical Period of Greek history, which began around 800 B.C., there was a long period that historians call the Greek Dark Ages. Sometime around 1200 B.C., the Bronze Age civilization in the region by the eastern Mediterranean Sea collapsed entirely. The dominant people there—the Mycenaeans—occupied mainland Greece, Crete, and other islands, but their civilization was overwhelmed, so Greece and the nearby area entered a 400-year-period which saw little progress. The exact cause of this downfall is unknown to historians, but there are some theories that provide plausible explanations.

Despite its influence, little is actually known about Mycenaean civilization. It appeared around 1600 B.C., and some of its pottery, weapons, clothing, and other artifacts have been unearthed from burial sites in mainland Greece, thereby providing historians with some knowledge of the Mycenaeans and their culture. Additionally, the remains of some Mycenaean buildings with **frescoes** have been excavated, so this has provided historians with further glances into the ancient culture. It has been determined that the Mycenaeans lived in small city-states and worshiped a large number of deities. It is commonly believed that many of the later Greek gods, including Athena and Poseidon, and a large number of Greek myths were adopted from the Mycenaeans by the Greeks. Among these stories was that of the Trojan War, which was detailed in Homer's *Iliad* and other epic poems. While it is unknown if the Mycenaeans were really the people who destroyed ancient Troy, they were highly aggressive, had a strong military, and invaded Crete, where they conquered the Minoan people living there.

However, around 1200 B.C., something happened to the Mycenaeans that resulted in their civilization coming to an end. The traditional story is that a group called the Dorians invaded the Mycenaeans' land. The Dorians are thought to have hailed from the Balkans, an area north of Greece. Another theory proposes that a seaborne invasion was responsible for the Mycenaeans' downfall. There is historical evidence that a marauding group of seafarers disrupted life in Egypt and other Mediterranean lands around this time, but their origin and motives have been lost over time. Whatever the case, there is proof of the widespread collapse of Mycenaean civilization, and the numerous ruins, the lack of art and writing, and the decline in the quality of **metallurgy** and pottery from this time suggests they were overwhelmed by an outside invader.

Some historians suggest that both events happened. They claim the Dorians, who remained in Greece after invading, attacked the Mycenaeans as did the group from the sea. Yet historians face a conundrum in that they wonder why civilization in Greece declined so much since the Dorians were powerful enough to have defeated the Mycenaeans. Some believe the invaders from the sea attacked first, which left the Greek mainland ripe for invasion from the Dorians, who were less advanced. Others theorize that after the seafarers departed, the Dorians migrated to Mycenaean territory and assimilated with the remaining people.

A third possibility that has been raised in recent decades is that a natural disaster occurred. A few people deem it possible that a powerful earthquake, of which the region gets many, could have destroyed a significant amount of Mycenaean civilization, which would have sent the survivors into a period of decline. Some have also proposed that a change in the climate, possibly caused by a drought, could have disrupted agriculture so much that the Mycenaeans could not recover and were accordingly defeated by others while in a weakened state. Although there is little evidence to support the natural disaster theory, it could explain how the militarily strong Mycenaeans could not successfully defend their land.

While the cause of the Greek Dark Ages is disputed, the fact that they were a bleak period in that region's history is not. Starting around 1200 B.C., for the next four centuries, there was little in the way of progress, and much of the history of that region remains unknown since there are no written records from then. It was not until around 800 B.C. that the people on the Greek mainland emerged from the Dark Ages, founded city-states, and began creating a civilization that would influence the world up to the present day.

Glossary

fresco: a painting that is done on a plaster surface

metallurgy: the science of working with metals to give them particular shapes and characteristics

11 According to paragraph 1, which of the following is true of the Mycenaeans?

Ⓐ They were living in Greece at the time when the Greek Dark Ages began.

Ⓑ They resided in the area around Greece for fewer than four centuries.

Ⓒ They invaded the Greek mainland and helped start the Greek Dark Ages.

Ⓓ They created a long-lasting Bronze Age civilization in the Mediterranean area.

The Onset of the Greek Dark Ages

[1]→ Prior to the Classical Period of Greek history, which began around 800 B.C., there was a long period that historians call the Greek Dark Ages. Sometime around 1200 B.C., the Bronze Age civilization in the region by the eastern Mediterranean Sea collapsed entirely. The dominant people there—the Mycenaeans—occupied mainland Greece, Crete, and other islands, but their civilization was overwhelmed, so Greece and the nearby area entered a 400-year-period which saw little progress. The exact cause of this downfall is unknown to historians, but there are some theories that provide plausible explanations.

12 Which of the sentences below best expresses the essential information in the highlighted sentence in the passage? *Incorrect* answer choices change the meaning in important ways or leave out essential information.

(A) Historians are trying to learn more about the Mycenaeans by studying some of the artifacts that they have found in ancient tombs.

(B) Since the Mycenaeans lived thousands of years ago, they left many artifacts, some of which have been found in modern times.

(C) Little is known about Mycenaean civilization despite the fact that large numbers of relics from their civilization have been unearthed.

(D) Historians have learned when the Mycenaeans appeared and have also discovered many of their relics in places throughout Greece.

13 Which of the following can be inferred from paragraph 2 about the Mycenaeans?

(A) It is possible they were the conquerors written about in the *Iliad*.

(B) Their culture was superior to that of the Greeks in many regards.

(C) The fact that they conquered Crete proved they were great warriors.

(D) They got the idea for city-states from the ancient Greeks themselves.

Glossary

fresco: a painting that is done on a plaster surface

2→ Despite its influence, little is actually known about Mycenaean civilization. It appeared around 1600 B.C., and some of its pottery, weapons, clothing, and other artifacts have been unearthed from burial sites in mainland Greece, thereby providing historians with some knowledge of the Mycenaeans and their culture. Additionally, the remains of some Mycenaean buildings with **frescoes** have been excavated, so this has provided historians with further glances into the ancient culture. It has been determined that the Mycenaeans lived in small city-states and worshiped a large number of deities. It is commonly believed that many of the later Greek gods, including Athena and Poseidon, and a large number of Greek myths were adopted from the Mycenaeans by the Greeks. Among these stories was that of the Trojan War, which was detailed in Homer's *Iliad* and other epic poems. While it is unknown if the Mycenaeans were really the people who destroyed ancient Troy, they were highly aggressive, had a strong military, and invaded Crete, where they conquered the Minoan people living there.

14 The phrase hailed from in the passage is closest in meaning to

(A) summoned with

(B) traveled through

(C) originated from

(D) appeared in

15 According to paragraph 3, which of the following is NOT true of the downfall of the Mycenaeans?

(A) A group of Egyptian seafarers is thought to have caused it.

(B) The exact circumstances that caused it have not been proven.

(C) Mycenaean society promptly declined after it was invaded.

(D) It might have been caused by a northern group called the Dorians.

16 The word conundrum in the passage is closest in meaning to

(A) mystery

(B) connection

(C) decision

(D) interpretation

Glossary

metallurgy: the science of working with metals to give them particular shapes and characteristics

3→ However, around 1200 B.C., something happened to the Mycenaeans that resulted in their civilization coming to an end. The traditional story is that a group called the Dorians invaded the Mycenaeans' land. The Dorians are thought to have hailed from the Balkans, an area north of Greece. Another theory proposes that a seaborne invasion was responsible for the Mycenaeans' downfall. There is historical evidence that a marauding group of seafarers disrupted life in Egypt and other Mediterranean lands around this time, but their origin and motives have been lost over time. Whatever the case, there is proof of the widespread collapse of Mycenaean civilization, and the numerous ruins, the lack of art and writing, and the decline in the quality of **metallurgy** and pottery from this time suggests they were overwhelmed by an outside invader.

Some historians suggest that both events happened. They claim the Dorians, who remained in Greece after invading, attacked the Mycenaeans as did the group from the sea. Yet historians face a conundrum in that they wonder why civilization in Greece declined so much since the Dorians were powerful enough to have defeated the Mycenaeans. Some believe the invaders from the sea attacked first, which left the Greek mainland ripe for invasion from the Dorians, who were less advanced. Others theorize that after the seafarers departed, the Dorians migrated to Mycenaean territory and assimilated with the remaining people.

17 According to paragraph 5, the natural disaster theory is likely incorrect because

Ⓐ the written records from that period mention no such event

Ⓑ no proof of a natural disaster has ever been found

Ⓒ there is no history of droughts ever happening in Greece

Ⓓ earthquakes rarely ever occurred in that part of the world

18 The word bleak in the passage is closest in meaning to

Ⓐ pessimistic

Ⓑ unforgettable

Ⓒ regrettable

Ⓓ miserable

5➜ A third possibility that has been raised in recent decades is that a natural disaster occurred. A few people deem it possible that a powerful earthquake, of which the region gets many, could have destroyed a significant amount of Mycenaean civilization, which would have sent the survivors into a period of decline. Some have also proposed that a change in the climate, possibly caused by a drought, could have disrupted agriculture so much that the Mycenaeans could not recover and were accordingly defeated by others while in a weakened state. Although there is little evidence to support the natural disaster theory, it could explain how the militarily strong Mycenaeans could not successfully defend their land.

While the cause of the Greek Dark Ages is disputed, the fact that they were a bleak period in that region's history is not. Starting around 1200 B.C., for the next four centuries, there was little in the way of progress, and much of the history of that region remains unknown since there are no written records from then. It was not until around 800 B.C. that the people on the Greek mainland emerged from the Dark Ages, founded city-states, and began creating a civilization that would influence the world up to the present day.

19 Look at the four squares [■] that indicate where the following sentence could be added to the passage.

They would have therefore had an easy time reaching Greece from their homeland.

Where would the sentence best fit?

Click on a square [■] to add the sentence to the passage.

However, around 1200 B.C., something happened to the Mycenaeans that resulted in their civilization coming to an end. **1** The traditional story is that a group called the Dorians invaded the Mycenaeans' land. **2** The Dorians are thought to have hailed from the Balkans, an area north of Greece. **3** Another theory proposes that a seaborne invasion was responsible for the Mycenaeans' downfall. **4** There is historical evidence that a marauding group of seafarers disrupted life in Egypt and other Mediterranean lands around this time, but their origin and motives have been lost over time. Whatever the case, there is proof of the widespread collapse of Mycenaean civilization, and the numerous ruins, the lack of art and writing, and the decline in the quality of **metallurgy** and pottery from this time suggests they were overwhelmed by an outside invader.

Glossary

metallurgy: the science of working with metals to give them particular shapes and characteristics

20 Directions: An introductory sentence for a brief summary of the passage is provided below. Complete the summary by selecting the THREE answer choices that express the most important ideas of the passage. Some sentences do not belong because they express ideas that are not presented in the passage or are minor ideas in the passage. **This question is worth 2 points.**

Drag your answer choices to the spaces where they belong.
To remove an answer choice, click on it. To review the passage, click on **View Text**.

Historians have proposed several theories concerning why the downfall of Mycenaean civilization, which initiated the Greek Dark Ages, happened.

-
-
-

Answer Choices

1. Some academics have proposed a theory that an earthquake or other natural disaster caused the Greek Dark Ages to begin.
2. It is possible that a group known as the Dorians invaded and subsequently conquered the Mycenaean people.
3. The Mycenaeans had a tremendous influence on the Greeks, particularly with regard to their mythology.
4. There are some who believe that the Mycenaeans were invaded by people who sailed from the Mediterranean Sea.
5. The Greek Dark Ages lasted for about four centuries, but there is virtually nothing known about this period.
6. Historians try to piece together information about ancient history by exploring the ruins and artifacts of past civilizations.

Advanced Telescopes

The Hubble Space Telescope

Modern optical telescopes are vast improvements over those utilized in the past. All optical telescopes gather light in order to produce an image that the eye can see. They can accomplish this in two ways: by passing light through a lens or by reflecting it off a mirror. As lenses and mirrors increase in size, they become able to gather more light and thus can enable a person to see farther into space while simultaneously providing fairly clear images. Prior to the twentieth century, making relatively large lenses and mirrors was a virtual impossibility. However, nowadays, thanks to advanced techniques in lens and mirror construction, modern telescopes can see farther than ever before. Yet these telescopes still face the problem of distorted images caused by the Earth's atmosphere. This issue has been solved by the inventing of even better types of telescopes, all of which have greatly improved mankind's knowledge of the universe.

To gather information about the universe, telescopes obtain it from the electromagnetic spectrum, which includes visible light, radio waves, gamma rays, and X-rays. From the Earth's surface, only a limited part of the electromagnetic spectrum can be observed. Radio waves and visible light can be observed, yet X-rays and gamma rays cannot since they are mostly absorbed by the atmosphere. However, every part of the electromagnetic spectrum can be picked up from space without any distortion at all. Prior to the **Space Age**, which began in the 1950s, the only types of telescopes were optical and radio in nature. Optical telescopes were typically built on mountaintops far from the bright lights of cities. Still, even high in the atmosphere, there was some distortion of visible light. But once the Space Age began, telescopes could be mounted on satellites in near-Earth orbit.

One of the largest and most advanced space-based optical telescopes is the Hubble Space Telescope (HST). It was built during the 1980s and was carried into orbit aboard the space shuttle in 1990. It promptly suffered some technical problems with its mirror, so NASA had to train a space shuttle crew how to conduct repairs on it, which were ultimately successful. Since then, the HST has transmitted an enormous quantity of data about the universe back to Earth. One of its most impressive achievements is the Hubble Ultra-Deep Field photograph, which shows a section of the universe where many galaxies and other objects are clearly visible. It is the farthest that any human has ever looked into deep space. The HST is still operational and should be in use until around 2040, and some other space telescopes are also in orbit while others are in the planning stages.

As for radio telescopes, they are utilized for radio astronomy. This branch of astronomy detects radio wave emissions from objects in space, including galaxies, quasars, and pulsars. Radio astronomy and radio telescopes were first conceived in the United States in the 1930s, and the first radio telescope became operational in 1937. Radio telescopes differ from optical telescopes in that they require no lens or mirror. Instead, they have large parabolic antennae which pick up radio signals from space. Some operate as individual telescopes while others are grouped together to improve their capabilities. Radio telescopes have been responsible for several discoveries, including quasars, pulsars, and the presence of cosmic microwave background radiation, which has helped scientists determine the age of the universe.

Optical and radio telescopes are the two most common types, but they are not the only ones. There are also gamma ray and X-ray telescopes, both of which must be mounted on satellites in space. They employ sophisticated mirrors, lenses, and **apertures** to capture gamma rays and X-rays. Scientists use images of gamma rays and X-rays coming from celestial bodies to help them better understand stellar phenomena, especially those which are extremely distant. For instance, gamma ray telescopes provide detailed images and data of gamma ray bursts in faraway galaxies. These are high-energy explosions that last for a short time and are the most intense outbursts of energy ever observed in the universe. Scientists hope that all of the various types of advanced telescopes will combine to provide information about the universe's mysteries, among them black holes, dark energy, and dark matter.

Glossary

Space Age: the period that began when humans began sending rockets into space

aperture: a device on an optical instrument that limits the amount of radiation entering or leaving

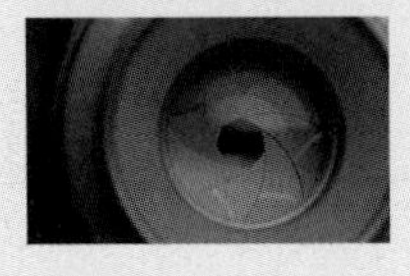

21 The word distorted in the passage is closest in meaning to

Ⓐ inaccurate

Ⓑ fuzzy

Ⓒ pristine

Ⓓ blank

22 According to paragraph 1, optical telescopes can let people see more distant objects when

Ⓐ people use them in darkened areas

Ⓑ they are placed at higher elevations

Ⓒ the eyepieces that people utilize are cleaned

Ⓓ their mirrors or lenses become larger

Advanced Telescopes

[1]→ Modern optical telescopes are vast improvements over those utilized in the past. All optical telescopes gather light in order to produce an image that the eye can see. They can accomplish this in two ways: by passing light through a lens or by reflecting it off a mirror. As lenses and mirrors increase in size, they become able to gather more light and thus can enable a person to see farther into space while simultaneously providing fairly clear images. Prior to the twentieth century, making relatively large lenses and mirrors was a virtual impossibility. However, nowadays, thanks to advanced techniques in lens and mirror construction, modern telescopes can see farther than ever before. Yet these telescopes still face the problem of distorted images caused by the Earth's atmosphere. This issue has been solved by the inventing of even better types of telescopes, all of which have greatly improved mankind's knowledge of the universe.

23 According to paragraph 2, there are no gamma ray telescopes on the Earth because

Ⓐ the atmosphere distorts any gamma ray images that are received

Ⓑ gamma rays from space cannot be detected from the ground

Ⓒ the cost of building one of them on the Earth's surface is too great

Ⓓ lights from cities cause the images they return to be distorted

24 The word it in the passage refers to

Ⓐ the space shuttle

Ⓑ its mirror

Ⓒ NASA

Ⓓ a space shuttle crew

25 The author discusses the Hubble Ultra-Deep Field photograph in paragraph 3 in order to

Ⓐ prove that the repairs on the Hubble Space Telescope were necessary

Ⓑ detail a notable accomplishment of the Hubble Space Telescope

Ⓒ mention that it is a picture of the very edge of the universe

Ⓓ argue in favor of sending more telescopes into orbit around the Earth

Glossary

Space Age: the period that began when humans began sending rockets into space

2→ To gather information about the universe, telescopes obtain it from the electromagnetic spectrum, which includes visible light, radio waves, gamma rays, and X-rays. From the Earth's surface, only a limited part of the electromagnetic spectrum can be observed. Radio waves and visible light can be observed, yet X-rays and gamma rays cannot since they are mostly absorbed by the atmosphere. However, every part of the electromagnetic spectrum can be picked up from space without any distortion at all. Prior to the **Space Age**, which began in the 1950s, the only types of telescopes were optical and radio in nature. Optical telescopes were typically built on mountaintops far from the bright lights of cities. Still, even high in the atmosphere, there was some distortion of visible light. But once the Space Age began, telescopes could be mounted on satellites in near-Earth orbit.

3→ One of the largest and most advanced space-based optical telescopes is the Hubble Space Telescope (HST). It was built during the 1980s and was carried into orbit aboard the space shuttle in 1990. It promptly suffered some technical problems with its mirror, so NASA had to train a space shuttle crew how to conduct repairs on it, which were ultimately successful. Since then, the HST has transmitted an enormous quantity of data about the universe back to Earth. One of its most impressive achievements is the Hubble Ultra-Deep Field photograph, which shows a section of the universe where many galaxies and other objects are clearly visible. It is the farthest that any human has ever looked into deep space. The HST is still operational and should be in use until around 2040, and some other space telescopes are also in orbit while others are in the planning stages.

26 In paragraph 4, the author of the passage implies that the first radio telescope

(A) was later grouped with another to increase its power

(B) was constructed somewhere in the United States

(C) was erected at a location high in the mountains

(D) had many faults as little was known about radio astronomy then

27 The word sophisticated in the passage is closest in meaning to

(A) debonair

(B) advanced

(C) costly

(D) fabricated

28 In paragraph 5, the author uses black holes, dark energy, and dark matter as examples of

(A) phenomena that can be created by high-energy explosions

(B) aspects of the universe that astronomers know little about

(C) three things that astronomers theorize may possibly exist

(D) unique phenomena that must be understood more fully

Glossary

aperture: a device on an optical instrument that limits the amount of radiation entering or leaving

[4]→ As for radio telescopes, they are utilized for radio astronomy. This branch of astronomy detects radio wave emissions from objects in space, including galaxies, quasars, and pulsars. Radio astronomy and radio telescopes were first conceived in the United States in the 1930s, and the first radio telescope became operational in 1937. Radio telescopes differ from optical telescopes in that they require no lens or mirror. Instead, they have large parabolic antennae which pick up radio signals from space. Some operate as individual telescopes while others are grouped together to improve their capabilities. Radio telescopes have been responsible for several discoveries, including quasars, pulsars, and the presence of cosmic microwave background radiation, which has helped scientists determine the age of the universe.

[5]→ Optical and radio telescopes are the two most common types, but they are not the only ones. There are also gamma ray and X-ray telescopes, both of which must be mounted on satellites in space. They employ sophisticated mirrors, lenses, and **apertures** to capture gamma rays and X-rays. Scientists use images of gamma rays and X-rays coming from celestial bodies to help them better understand stellar phenomena, especially those which are extremely distant. For instance, gamma ray telescopes provide detailed images and data of gamma ray bursts in faraway galaxies. These are high-energy explosions that last for a short time and are the most intense outbursts of energy ever observed in the universe. Scientists hope that all of the various types of advanced telescopes will combine to provide information about the universe's mysteries, among them black holes, dark energy, and dark matter.

29 Look at the four squares [■] that indicate where the following sentence could be added to the passage.

In contrast, radio telescopes can be built anywhere, even at or below sea level.

Where would the sentence best fit?

Click on a square [■] to add the sentence to the passage.

To gather information about the universe, telescopes obtain it from the electromagnetic spectrum, which includes visible light, radio waves, gamma rays, and X-rays. From the Earth's surface, only a limited part of the electromagnetic spectrum can be observed. Radio waves and visible light can be observed, yet X-rays and gamma rays cannot since they are mostly absorbed by the atmosphere. However, every part of the electromagnetic spectrum can be picked up from space without any distortion at all. [1] Prior to the **Space Age**, which began in the 1950s, the only types of telescopes were optical and radio in nature. [2] Optical telescopes were typically built on mountaintops far from the bright lights of cities. [3] Still, even high in the atmosphere, there was some distortion of visible light. [4] But once the Space Age began, telescopes could be mounted on satellites in near-Earth orbit.

Glossary

Space Age: the period that began when humans began sending rockets into space

30 Directions: Select the appropriate statements from the answer choices and match them to the type of telescope to which they relate. TWO of the answer choices will NOT be used. **This question is worth 3 points.**

Drag your answer choices to the spaces where they belong.
To remove an answer choice, click on it. To review the passage, click on **View Text**.

Answer Choices

1. Can be combined with others of its kind to increase its output
2. Must be located in outer space to be effective
3. Is what the Hubble Space Telescope is equipped with
4. Was first constructed during the mid-1900s
5. Employs either a mirror or a lens to create images
6. Can produce imperfect images when disturbed by light
7. Has been used to observe gamma ray bursts in other galaxies

TYPE OF TELESCOPE

Optical Telescope

-
-
-

Radio Telescope

-
-

The Development of Photography

A Kodak Box Brownie film camera

Modern digital cameras can take clear, sharp pictures that can be viewed instantly; however, in photography's early days, cameras were not nearly so advanced. Photography started in France in the mid-1800s, but at that time, producing pictures was time consuming and difficult, and the cameras themselves were heavy and bulky, which meant that most pictures were taken in studios. Over time though, cameras and the photographic process were refined. Cameras became lighter and smaller, and **celluloid** film replaced the heavy plates that had previously been used. By the early 1900s, companies were manufacturing cameras and film that made photography accessible to almost anyone.

Two Frenchmen, Joseph Niepce and Louis Daguerre, are credited with inventing photography during the 1830s. They conducted experiments with chemicals which proved that a polished metal plate covered in **silver nitrate** would, when exposed to light, leave a latent image on the plate. Once the image was exposed to some other chemicals, it could be fixed to the plate. In this manner, they created the first photographs. This process and the resulting photographs were called daguerreotype after one of the inventors. As time passed, others improved the daguerreotype, but the major concern with it was the length of time required to take a picture. In some instances, the plate had to be exposed to bright light for fifteen to thirty minutes in order to produce a viable photograph.

As a result, human subjects had to remain absolutely still, or photographs of them would be blurry. Thus the majority of photographs were taken in studios, where the subjects were either seated in chairs or were positioned so that they were leaning against stands that supported their bodies during the long period of time required to remain motionless. Despite this limitation, early photography was extremely popular, and many people made use of it to have portrait pictures taken. Prior to the advent of photography, all portraits were painted by artists, but most people lacked the money to do this. Photography, however, was much cheaper, which made it a more affordable option than portrait painting.

Another problem with the daguerreotype and later imitations was that copies of the resulting photographs could not easily be made. This was an issue for decades until, in 1884, American George Eastman developed a process using chemically treated paper which could take photographs and from which duplicates could be made. After a while, Eastman's paper film was replaced by celluloid, which was a more flexible and durable material. Eastman also invented a camera in 1888 that could utilize a roll of film to take many pictures before it needed to be developed. The film was inserted into the camera, and the photographer merely pressed a button that would open the lens and expose the film to light.

Eastman's camera was revolutionary for a couple of reasons. First, the heavy plates used by daguerreotypes and other similar cameras were no longer required, nor were long exposure times necessary anymore. Additionally, the photographer did not have to become an expert at utilizing the chemical processes necessary to develop the photographs, as was the case at that time. Instead, photographers simply ejected the film and sent it to the Kodak Company, which processed the film and then returned it to the photographer.

Eastman's system became the standard and was imitated around the world. Then, in 1901, he introduced yet another new camera, the Kodak Brownie, which was cheap and simple to use. This camera was mass produced and marketed to the general public, thereby enabling anyone to take pictures. This set the stage for photography for practically the entire century as people took pictures and then sent the film away to be processed. The later inventing of 35mm film, colored film, and highly sophisticated cameras throughout the 1900s allowed photography to become an art form.

The development of photography had several important results. First, portrait paintings declined greatly by the end of the 1800s. Second, photography influenced several schools of art, such as Realism in France, as artists attempted to duplicate photographic images on their canvases. Third, mass-produced cameras such as Eastman's removed photography from the hands of experts and gave photographers the freedom to go anywhere and to photograph anything.

Glossary

celluloid: a tough material used in the manufacture of film

silver nitrate: a substance that is a combination of silver and nitric acid

31 According to paragraph 1, which of the following is NOT true of photography's early days?

Ⓐ The process of developing a picture took a lot of time.

Ⓑ Cameras utilized celluloid into order to produce photographs.

Ⓒ The first cameras weighed a lot and were difficult to carry.

Ⓓ Most photographers took pictures in indoor locations.

32 In paragraph 2, why does the author mention Joseph Niepce and Louis Daguerre?

Ⓐ To point out the faults that the daguerreotype they made possessed

Ⓑ To note the importance of their using silver nitrate to develop photographs

Ⓒ To admit that they were pioneers in the field in which they worked

Ⓓ To name them as the two men responsible for inventing photography

Glossary 

celluloid: a tough material used in the manufacture of film

silver nitrate: a substance that is a combination of silver and nitric acid

The Development of Photography

[1]→ Modern digital cameras can take clear, sharp pictures that can be viewed instantly; however, in photography's early days, cameras were not nearly so advanced. Photography started in France in the mid-1800s, but at that time, producing pictures was time consuming and difficult, and the cameras themselves were heavy and bulky, which meant that most pictures were taken in studios. Over time though, cameras and the photographic process were refined. Cameras became lighter and smaller, and **celluloid** film replaced the heavy plates that had previously been used. By the early 1900s, companies were manufacturing cameras and film that made photography accessible to almost anyone.

[2]→ Two Frenchmen, Joseph Niepce and Louis Daguerre, are credited with inventing photography during the 1830s. They conducted experiments with chemicals which proved that a polished metal plate covered in **silver nitrate** would, when exposed to light, leave a latent image on the plate. Once the image was exposed to some other chemicals, it could be fixed to the plate. In this manner, they created the first photographs. This process and the resulting photographs were called daguerreotype after one of the inventors. As time passed, others improved the daguerreotype, but the major concern with it was the length of time required to take a picture. In some instances, the plate had to be exposed to bright light for fifteen to thirty minutes in order to produce a viable photograph.

33 According to paragraph 2, how did the daguerreotype take pictures?

Ⓐ By reflecting light off a mirror coated with silver nitrate

Ⓑ By applying chemicals to celluloid film to produce an image

Ⓒ By letting bright light shine onto a plate for some time

Ⓓ By briefly opening a lens to capture an image onto film

34 Which of the sentences below best expresses the essential information in the highlighted sentence in the passage? *Incorrect* answer choices change the meaning in important ways or leave out essential information.

Ⓐ Early pictures typically show people either in seated positions or leaning against something while standing.

Ⓑ Most pictures were taken indoors with people posing in ways that would allow them not to move for several minutes.

Ⓒ It was difficult for most people to remain still for a long time while they were posing for pictures.

Ⓓ When people went to studios, the photographers put them in poses that did not require them to move.

Glossary

silver nitrate: a substance that is a combination of silver and nitric acid

[2]→ Two Frenchmen, Joseph Niepce and Louis Daguerre, are credited with inventing photography during the 1830s. They conducted experiments with chemicals which proved that a polished metal plate covered in **silver nitrate** would, when exposed to light, leave a latent image on the plate. Once the image was exposed to some other chemicals, it could be fixed to the plate. In this manner, they created the first photographs. This process and the resulting photographs were called daguerreotype after one of the inventors. As time passed, others improved the daguerreotype, but the major concern with it was the length of time required to take a picture. In some instances, the plate had to be exposed to bright light for fifteen to thirty minutes in order to produce a viable photograph.

As a result, human subjects had to remain absolutely still, or photographs of them would be blurry. Thus the majority of photographs were taken in studios, where the subjects were either seated in chairs or were positioned so that they were leaning against stands that supported their bodies during the long period of time required to remain motionless. Despite this limitation, early photography was extremely popular, and many people made use of it to have portrait pictures taken. Prior to the advent of photography, all portraits were painted by artists, but most people lacked the money to do this. Photography, however, was much cheaper, which made it a more affordable option than portrait painting.

35 The word durable in the passage is closest in meaning to

- (A) profuse
- (B) sturdy
- (C) abundant
- (D) inexpensive

36 According to paragraph 5, which of the following is true of Eastman's camera?

- (A) The time necessary to expose the film in it to light was decreased.
- (B) It utilized plates much in the same manner as the daguerreotype.
- (C) People sent their cameras to the Kodak Company to develop their film.
- (D) The film that was inserted in it was developed by the photographer.

Another problem with the daguerreotype and later imitations was that copies of the resulting photographs could not easily be made. This was an issue for decades until, in 1884, American George Eastman developed a process using chemically treated paper which could take photographs and from which duplicates could be made. After a while, Eastman's paper film was replaced by celluloid, which was a more flexible and durable material. Eastman also invented a camera in 1888 that could utilize a roll of film to take many pictures before it needed to be developed. The film was inserted into the camera, and the photographer merely pressed a button that would open the lens and expose the film to light.

[5]→ Eastman's camera was revolutionary for a couple of reasons. First, the heavy plates used by daguerreotypes and other similar cameras were no longer required, nor were long exposure times necessary anymore. Additionally, the photographer did not have to become an expert at utilizing the chemical processes necessary to develop the photographs, as was the case at that time. Instead, photographers simply ejected the film and sent it to the Kodak Company, which processed the film and then returned it to the photographer.

37 The author discusses the Kodak Brownie in paragraph 6 in order to

- (A) proclaim it as the forerunner of 35mm film and colored film
- (B) mention the number of cameras that were sold to the public
- (C) describe the manner in which it revolutionized photography
- (D) stress that it was the first camera to be sold to the general populace

38 The author's description of the effects of photography in paragraph 7 mentions all of the following EXCEPT:

- (A) a school of art that was affected by the invention of the camera
- (B) how cameras that were mass produced changed photography
- (C) the decline in the number of people who used portrait painting
- (D) how photography came to be considered a unique form of art

39 Look at the four squares [■] that indicate where the following sentence could be added to the passage.

These enabled photographers such as Ansel Adams to become recognized for being great artists.

Where would the sentence best fit?

Click on a square [■] to add the sentence to the passage.

[6]→ Eastman's system became the standard and was imitated around the world. Then, in 1901, he introduced yet another new camera, the Kodak Brownie, which was cheap and simple to use. [1] This camera was mass produced and marketed to the general public, thereby enabling anyone to take pictures. [2] This set the stage for photography for practically the entire century as people took pictures and then sent the film away to be processed. [3] The later inventing of 35mm film, colored film, and highly sophisticated cameras throughout the 1900s allowed photography to become an art form. [4]

[7]→ The development of photography had several important results. First, portrait paintings declined greatly by the end of the 1800s. Second, photography influenced several schools of art, such as Realism in France, as artists attempted to duplicate photographic images on their canvases. Third, mass-produced cameras such as Eastman's removed photography from the hands of experts and gave photographers the freedom to go anywhere and to photograph anything.

40 **Directions:** An introductory sentence for a brief summary of the passage is provided below. Complete the summary by selecting the THREE answer choices that express the most important ideas of the passage. Some sentences do not belong because they express ideas that are not presented in the passage or are minor ideas in the passage. **This question is worth 2 points.**

Drag your answer choices to the spaces where they belong.
To remove an answer choice, click on it. To review the passage, click on **View Text**.

In the first few decades of photography, there were many changes that made taking pictures both easy and accessible to people in general.

-
-
-

Answer Choices

1. Most early pictures were taken of people assuming poses in which they were either seated or leaning against something.
2. George Eastman was responsible for a number of inventions that made cameras smaller, lighter, and easier to use.
3. Photography affected the world of art in that some schools, such as Realism, sought to imitate the looks of photographs.
4. One advance in camera technology involved the use of celluloid, which resulted in duplicate photographs being easy to produce.
5. In the 1900s, there were many inventions in camera technology, including motion pictures and digital cameras.
6. The daguerreotype, which exposed light to a metal plate, was the first form of photography to be developed.

TOEFL® MAP

ACTUAL TEST

Reading 2

05

CONTINUE

Reading Section Directions

This section measures your ability to understand academic passages in English. You will have **54 minutes** to read and answer questions about **3 passages**. A clock at the top of the screen will show you how much time is remaining.

Most questions are worth 1 point but the last question for each passage is worth more than 1 point. The directions for the last question indicate how many points you may receive.

Some passages include a word or phrase that is **underlined** in blue. Click on the word or phrase to see a definition or an explanation.

When you want to move to the next question, click on **Next**. You may skip questions and go back to them later. If you want to return to previous questions, click on **Back**. You can click on **Reivew** at any time, and the review screen will show you which questions you have answered and which you have not answered. From this review screen, you may go directly to any question you have already seen in the Reading section.

Click on **Continue** to go on.

Population Decline in Ancient Rome

The most populous city in the ancient world was Rome. During both the Roman Republic and the Roman Empire, the once-sleepy town on the banks of the Tiber River eventually grew to have a population of approximately one million people by around the year 200. But it was sometime then that Rome's population began a precipitous decline, one leaving it with a population of about 60,000 individuals by the year 500. A multitude of factors led to this occurring. Among them were numerous barbarian invasions, civil wars, **epidemics**, and the transfer of imperial power from Rome to Constantinople in the Eastern Roman Empire. For centuries, Rome remained but a shell of its former self, and it was not until the nineteenth century, when Italy was unified and Rome named its capital, that its population would once again be the same as it once was during the height of the Roman Empire.

Modern historians have based their calculations on Rome's population by examining the surviving records of grain shipments to the city. While not infallible, this method has provided scholars with a rough estimate of the number of people who resided there. The best guess is that one million people—and perhaps even more—lived in Rome when the city was at its height. The number of individuals who were free citizens and who were slaves has not been easy to determine though. But it is known that Rome's population peaked by the end of the second century and then started to decline. One cause of this decline was a plague of some sort that swept through the city and killed more than a thousand people a day in the late second century.

Years later in the early third century, a series of disasters further cut Rome's population. Roman soldiers, dissatisfied with the rule of Emperor Alexander Severus, assassinated him in 235. This triggered a long period of civil war and instability which, coupled with new plagues that killed more people, further reduced Rome's population. Additionally, during that period, there was an economic crisis that limited internal trade within the empire and made the provinces more independent from Rome's rule. Because of that, smaller amounts of tax revenues and fewer agricultural products were sent to the capital, so Rome could not afford to feed so many mouths. By the end of the third century, it is likely that Rome's population had been reduced to half a million people.

During the late third century, the civil wars ceased when Emperor Diocletian assumed power. Yet Rome's decline continued when Diocletian divided the empire into two and created an eastern and western empire. He ruled the eastern empire and appointed an emperor for the western empire, which was secondary in power and importance. Following Diocletian, Emperor Constantine I built his capital city of Constantinople in the east. While Diocletian had begun the process of transferring power to the east, Constantine continued doing so, focusing on making sure that both the bureaucracy and military were concentrated there. As Constantinople accordingly grew in size and importance, Rome declined.

During the fifth century, the Western Roman Empire finally collapsed. Germanic tribes from the north invaded the Italian peninsula, and they **sacked** Rome three times during that century. This resulted in tremendous damage to the city, great loss of life, and a dramatic decrease in Rome's population. The aqueduct system that brought fresh water to the city was seriously disrupted, and food shipments virtually ceased, so in order to survive, most of the city's population fled. By the end of the century, perhaps 60,000 people remained there.

For the next 1,000 years, Rome was practically a ghost town, especially when compared to its previous glory years. The northern provinces and city-states such as Venice and Genoa became the new centers of Italian life during the Middle Ages and Renaissance. Then, during the Industrial Revolution in the eighteenth century, Rome's population slowly began edging upward. Finally, in the nineteenth century, the independent Italian states united to establish the modern nation state of Italy. Rome was chosen to be its capital, and it reclaimed its position as the first city of Italy, so its population eventually rose to its present-day number of approximately 2.8 million people.

Glossary

epidemic: a disease that affects many people in one area at the same time

sack: to loot; to plunder

1 According to paragraph 1, which of the following is NOT true of the decline in Rome's population?

Ⓐ Over a period lasting three centuries, Rome's population declined more than 90%.

Ⓑ Invasions originating from Constantinople in the east killed many of Rome's citizens.

Ⓒ There were many reasons that the number of people living in the city decreased.

Ⓓ Rome's population was less than one million for a period lasting longer than a millennium.

Glossary 

epidemic: a disease that affects many people in one area at the same time

Population Decline in Ancient Rome

[1]➜ The most populous city in the ancient world was Rome. During both the Roman Republic and the Roman Empire, the once-sleepy town on the banks of the Tiber River eventually grew to have a population of approximately one million people by around the year 200. But it was sometime then that Rome's population began a precipitous decline, one leaving it with a population of about 60,000 individuals by the year 500. A multitude of factors led to this occurring. Among them were numerous barbarian invasions, civil wars, **epidemics**, and the transfer of imperial power from Rome to Constantinople in the Eastern Roman Empire. For centuries, Rome remained but a shell of its former self, and it was not until the nineteenth century, when Italy was unified and Rome named its capital, that its population would once again be the same as it once was during the height of the Roman Empire.

[2]→ Modern historians have based their calculations on Rome's population by examining the surviving records of grain shipments to the city. While not infallible, this method has provided scholars with a rough estimate of the number of people who resided there. The best guess is that one million people—and perhaps even more—lived in Rome when the city was at its height. The number of individuals who were free citizens and who were slaves has not been easy to determine though. But it is known that Rome's population peaked by the end of the second century and then started to decline. One cause of this decline was a plague of some sort that swept through the city and killed more than a thousand people a day in the late second century.

[3]→ Years later in the early third century, a series of disasters further cut Rome's population. Roman soldiers, dissatisfied with the rule of Emperor Alexander Severus, assassinated him in 235. This triggered a long period of civil war and instability which, coupled with new plagues that killed more people, further reduced Rome's population. Additionally, during that period, there was an economic crisis that limited internal trade within the empire and made the provinces more independent from Rome's rule. Because of that, smaller amounts of tax revenues and fewer agricultural products were sent to the capital, so Rome could not afford to feed so many mouths. By the end of the third century, it is likely that Rome's population had been reduced to half a million people.

2 The word infallible in the passage is closest in meaning to

Ⓐ perfect

Ⓑ exquisite

Ⓒ original

Ⓓ appreciated

3 Which of the following can be inferred from paragraph 2 about the plague that affected Rome?

Ⓐ It killed nearly one quarter of Rome's population.

Ⓑ The plague was the first that ever affected Rome.

Ⓒ It killed people living all throughout the Roman Empire.

Ⓓ The disease that was spread during it is unknown.

4 According to paragraph 3, one result of the economic crisis in the Roman Empire was that

Ⓐ the Roman provinces came to rely on Rome much less

Ⓑ Rome raised taxes on people in all of the empire's provinces

Ⓒ the empire was not able to finance large standing armies

Ⓓ Rome began to trade more with empires abroad

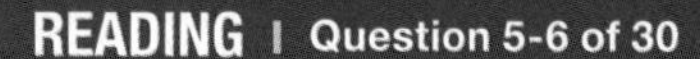

5 According to paragraph 4, which of the following is true of Emperor Diocletian?

Ⓐ The split of the Roman Empire into two parts happened during his reign.

Ⓑ He appointed Constantine I to rule over the empire prior to his death.

Ⓒ He was assassinated by soldiers that were displeased with his rule.

Ⓓ A new round of civil wars broke out as soon as he became emperor.

6 The author's description of the Germanic tribes that invaded the Italian peninsula in paragraph 5 mentions which of the following?

Ⓐ The reasons they focused on destroying Rome's aqueducts

Ⓑ The number of times that they managed to loot Rome

Ⓒ The military methods they used to fight against the Romans

Ⓓ The number of Romans they killed when they sacked the city

Glossary

sack: to loot; to plunder

[4]→ During the late third century, the civil wars ceased when Emperor Diocletian assumed power. Yet Rome's decline continued when Diocletian divided the empire into two and created an eastern and western empire. He ruled the eastern empire and appointed an emperor for the western empire, which was secondary in power and importance. Following Diocletian, Emperor Constantine I built his capital city of Constantinople in the east. While Diocletian had begun the process of transferring power to the east, Constantine continued doing so, focusing on making sure that both the bureaucracy and military were concentrated there. As Constantinople accordingly grew in size and importance, Rome declined.

[5]→ During the fifth century, the Western Roman Empire finally collapsed. Germanic tribes from the north invaded the Italian peninsula, and they **sacked** Rome three times during that century. This resulted in tremendous damage to the city, great loss of life, and a dramatic decrease in Rome's population. The aqueduct system that brought fresh water to the city was seriously disrupted, and food shipments virtually ceased, so in order to survive, most of the city's population fled. By the end of the century, perhaps 60,000 people remained there.

7 In paragraph 6, the author uses Venice and Genoa as examples of

Ⓐ the two largest city-states situated on the Italian peninsula

Ⓑ two city-states that were located in the northern provinces

Ⓒ Italian city-states that became more prominent than Rome

Ⓓ city-states that modeled themselves upon the city of Rome

8 According to paragraph 6, Rome's population started to increase once again when

Ⓐ the Industrial Revolution took place in Italy

Ⓑ the Italy city-states began contemplating unification

Ⓒ Rome was named the capital of a united Italy

Ⓓ the Renaissance finally came to an end

6➜ For the next 1,000 years, Rome was practically a ghost town, especially when compared to its previous glory years. The northern provinces and city-states such as Venice and Genoa became the new centers of Italian life during the Middle Ages and Renaissance. Then, during the Industrial Revolution in the eighteenth century, Rome's population slowly began edging upward. Finally, in the nineteenth century, the independent Italian states united to establish the modern nation state of Italy. Rome was chosen to be its capital, and it reclaimed its position as the first city of Italy, so its population eventually rose to its present-day number of approximately 2.8 million people.

9 Look at the four squares [■] that indicate where the following sentence could be added to the passage.

The massive construction project took six years and was completed in 330.

Where would the sentence best fit?

Click on a square [■] to add the sentence to the passage.

During the late third century, the civil wars ceased when Emperor Diocletian assumed power. Yet Rome's decline continued when Diocletian divided the empire into two and created an eastern and western empire. He ruled the eastern empire and appointed an emperor for the western empire, which was secondary in power and importance. **1** Following Diocletian, Emperor Constantine I built his capital city of Constantinople in the east. **2** While Diocletian had begun the process of transferring power to the east, Constantine continued doing so, focusing on making sure that both the bureaucracy and military were concentrated there. **3** As Constantinople accordingly grew in size and importance, Rome declined. **4**

10 **Directions:** An introductory sentence for a brief summary of the passage is provided below. Complete the summary by selecting the THREE answer choices that express the most important ideas of the passage. Some sentences do not belong because they express ideas that are not presented in the passage or are minor ideas in the passage. **This question is worth 2 points.**

Drag your answer choices to the spaces where they belong.
To remove an answer choice, click on it. To review the passage, click on **View Text**.

Rome underwent a tremendous decrease in its population on account of a number of different reasons.

-
-
-

Answer Choices

1 There were several plagues that killed thousands of people who were living in Rome.

2 Emperor Alexander Severus was extremely popular with the Roman army.

3 Much of the empire's bureaucracy was moved out of Rome and went to Constantinople.

4 At its greatest point in the past, the population of Rome was somewhere around one million people.

5 Armies from Germanic regions captured Rome and forced many people to leave the city.

6 Rome's population was fewer than 100,000 people during the entire Middle Ages.

How Animals Adapt to Extreme Temperatures

Living creatures are affected by temperature to some extent, and many must adapt to temperature changes to survive. As a result, countless animals have evolved so that they can live in either cold or hot environments, in wet and humid tropical regions, and in the extreme dry heat of deserts. They can survive on account of certain mechanisms in their bodies and by making use of various external means. Altogether, these prevent animals from either overheating or getting too cold.

All animals are either warm or cold blooded. Warm-blooded animals include virtually all mammals and birds while the vast majority of reptiles, amphibians, and fish are cold blooded. Warm-blooded animals produce heat through an internal process which allows them to control their body temperatures even in extremely cold conditions. They accomplish this by consuming food, which their bodies then utilize as fuel to produce heat. Cold-blooded animals, however, cannot control their body temperatures. Instead, their body temperatures are directly affected by the weather conditions surrounding them. When the temperature is cold, cold-blooded creatures are too, and when the weather becomes hot, so do they. As a result of these differences, in some environments, either warm-blooded or cold-blooded animals constitute the majority of species. In the Arctic, for instance, most creatures are warm blooded as cold-blooded animals would die easily in the frigid conditions.

Evolution has also bestowed upon animals some body conditions that allow them to adapt to extreme weather. Mammals in very cold places have **squat**, rounded bodies with short external limbs. This enables them to concentrate their body heat in the areas where their organs are rather than sending valuable body heat to their extremities. Additionally, many animals in the Polar Regions have thick fur or feathers to help them preserve their body heat and to keep their bodies dry in snowy or icy conditions. Some, such as polar bears and walruses, have thick layers of fat that stop their bodies from getting too cold. Mammals can also shiver, which lets them generate heat in their limbs when the weather is too cold.

In exceptionally hot conditions, mammals sweat or pant to cool their bodies, but when the weather is too hot, they could wind up losing so much water that they die. As a result, animals such as the camel have adapted to survive in desert conditions. Camels have either one or two humps on their backs. They store fat in these humps, which they can convert to energy or water should the need arise. Camels can also drink enormous amounts of water at a single time, and when they urinate or defecate, they lose little water in either process. Camels do not sweat except in very high temperatures, and in those conditions, their bodies manage to retain much of the moisture.

As for reptiles and amphibians, they lack fur and feathers, which would be unsuitable for the desert and tropical regions in which most of them reside. Instead, they have tough outer hides that are **scaly**. For some reptiles, such as crocodiles, their hides are rather thick, so they protect the animals' insides from overheating. Reptiles also have slow metabolisms since they have no need to burn food to generate heat. Consequently, they can survive without eating anything far longer than mammals can. This lets them live in environments such as the desert, where food is not particularly abundant. Due to their slow metabolisms, most reptiles that live in hot climates remain inactive for most of the day so frequently appear sluggish.

Even with these adaptations, reptiles and other animals are still subject to extreme heat, so they must find external means to cool their bodies when the outside temperature rises too much. In the desert, animals seek shade during the hottest parts of the day or move underground. At night, when desert temperatures may plunge, snakes, lizards, and other reptiles often lie on rocks that were exposed to the sun's rays during the day to absorb their heat. In the tropics, many animals find places with water or mud to lie in during the hottest parts of the day. Finally, reptiles and many mammals, including squirrels and bears, hibernate, so they sleep through the winter months to avoid cold weather conditions.

Glossary

squat: short and broad

scaly: having many scales, as in a fish or a reptile

11 According to paragraph 1, animals can live in places with extreme temperatures because

Ⓐ they understand when the weather is going to get worse

Ⓑ their bodies have changed to permit them to survive

Ⓒ they migrate to areas to avoid cold or hot temperatures

Ⓓ humans ensure that their environments are comfortable

12 According to paragraph 2, which of the following is NOT true of warm-blooded animals?

Ⓐ They can survive in cold climates since they can regulate their bodies.

Ⓑ They can keep their bodies warm by eating food to create energy.

Ⓒ The majority of birds and mammals are warm-blooded animals.

Ⓓ Their body temperatures may be affected by the local temperatures.

How Animals Adapt to Extreme Temperatures

1→ Living creatures are affected by temperature to some extent, and many must adapt to temperature changes to survive. As a result, countless animals have evolved so that they can live in either cold or hot environments, in wet and humid tropical regions, and in the extreme dry heat of deserts. They can survive on account of certain mechanisms in their bodies and by making use of various external means. Altogether, these prevent animals from either overheating or getting too cold.

2→ All animals are either warm or cold blooded. Warm-blooded animals include virtually all mammals and birds while the vast majority of reptiles, amphibians, and fish are cold blooded. Warm-blooded animals produce heat through an internal process which allows them to control their body temperatures even in extremely cold conditions. They accomplish this by consuming food, which their bodies then utilize as fuel to produce heat. Cold-blooded animals, however, cannot control their body temperatures. Instead, their body temperatures are directly affected by the weather conditions surrounding them. When the temperature is cold, cold-blooded creatures are too, and when the weather becomes hot, so do they. As a result of these differences, in some environments, either warm-blooded or cold-blooded animals constitute the majority of species. In the Arctic, for instance, most creatures are warm blooded as cold-blooded animals would die easily in the frigid conditions.

13 In paragraph 3, the author uses polar bears and walruses as examples of

(A) animals with an adaptation that lets them live in frigid weather

(B) two species of mammals that are able to keep warm by shivering

(C) the two largest mammals that reside at the Earth's Polar Regions

(D) mammals that have short, squat bodies with tiny extremities

14 The word shiver in the passage is closest in meaning to

(A) tremble

(B) flee

(C) ambulate

(D) disperse

15 The author's description of the camel in paragraph 4 mentions all of the following EXCEPT:

(A) a way in which their bodies can store extra water

(B) one region where they have adapted to be able to live

(C) the temperature at which their bodies begin to sweat

(D) their capability to consume large amounts of water

Glossary

squat: short and broad

[3]→ Evolution has also bestowed upon animals some body conditions that allow them to adapt to extreme weather. Mammals in very cold places have **squat**, rounded bodies with short external limbs. This enables them to concentrate their body heat in the areas where their organs are rather than sending valuable body heat to their extremities. Additionally, many animals in the Polar Regions have thick fur or feathers to help them preserve their body heat and to keep their bodies dry in snowy or icy conditions. Some, such as polar bears and walruses, have thick layers of fat that stop their bodies from getting too cold. Mammals can also shiver, which lets them generate heat in their limbs when the weather is too cold.

[4]→ In exceptionally hot conditions, mammals sweat or pant to cool their bodies, but when the weather is too hot, they could wind up losing so much water that they die. As a result, animals such as the camel have adapted to survive in desert conditions. Camels have either one or two humps on their backs. They store fat in these humps, which they can convert to energy or water should the need arise. Camels can also drink enormous amounts of water at a single time, and when they urinate or defecate, they lose little water in either process. Camels do not sweat except in very high temperatures, and in those conditions, their bodies manage to retain much of the moisture.

16 The word sluggish in the passage is closest in meaning to

Ⓐ asleep

Ⓑ lethargic

Ⓒ uninterested

Ⓓ unconscious

17 Which of the sentences below best expresses the essential information in the highlighted sentence in the passage? *Incorrect* answer choices change the meaning in important ways or leave out essential information.

Ⓐ Animals, including reptiles, must often utilize outside methods to keep cool in very hot weather.

Ⓑ Reptiles have still not adapted to live in extremely hot weather since it can affect them negatively.

Ⓒ Some reptiles rely upon external methods to keep themselves cool during particularly hot times.

Ⓓ If an animal has no bodily adaptations, it will have a hard time getting used to living in hot weather.

18 According to paragraph 6, some animals heat themselves at night by

Ⓐ staying underground in dens and lairs that keep the cold out

Ⓑ hibernating in their lairs so that they can preserve their body heat

Ⓒ resting upon rocks that absorbed heat from the sun during the day

Ⓓ lying in waterholes or mud in order to keep cold air off them

As for reptiles and amphibians, they lack fur and feathers, which would be unsuitable for the desert and tropical regions in which most of them reside. Instead, they have tough outer hides that are **scaly**. For some reptiles, such as crocodiles, their hides are rather thick, so they protect the animals' insides from overheating. Reptiles also have slow metabolisms since they have no need to burn food to generate heat. Consequently, they can survive without eating anything far longer than mammals can. This lets them live in environments such as the desert, where food is not particularly abundant. Due to their slow metabolisms, most reptiles that live in hot climates remain inactive for most of the day so frequently appear sluggish.

6→ Even with these adaptations, reptiles and other animals are still subject to extreme heat, so they must find external means to cool their bodies when the outside temperature rises too much. In the desert, animals seek shade during the hottest parts of the day or move underground. At night, when desert temperatures may plunge, snakes, lizards, and other reptiles often lie on rocks that were exposed to the sun's rays during the day to absorb their heat. In the tropics, many animals find places with water or mud to lie in during the hottest parts of the day. Finally, reptiles and many mammals, including squirrels and bears, hibernate, so they sleep through the winter months to avoid cold weather conditions.

Glossary

scaly: having many scales, as in a fish or a reptile

19 Look at the four squares [■] that indicate where the following sentence could be added to the passage.

For instance, the anaconda, a snake from South America, can go weeks or even months without consuming anything.

Where would the sentence best fit?

Click on a square [■] to add the sentence to the passage.

As for reptiles and amphibians, they lack fur and feathers, which would be unsuitable for the desert and tropical regions in which most of them reside. Instead, they have tough outer hides that are **scaly**. For some reptiles, such as crocodiles, their hides are rather thick, so they protect the animals' insides from overheating. Reptiles also have slow metabolisms since they have no need to burn food to generate heat. [1] Consequently, they can survive without eating anything far longer than mammals can. [2] This lets them live in environments such as the desert, where food is not particularly abundant. [3] Due to their slow metabolisms, most reptiles that live in hot climates remain inactive for most of the day so frequently appear sluggish. [4]

Glossary

scaly: having many scales, as in a fish or a reptile

20 Directions: An introductory sentence for a brief summary of the passage is provided below. Complete the summary by selecting the THREE answer choices that express the most important ideas of the passage. Some sentences do not belong because they express ideas that are not presented in the passage or are minor ideas in the passage. **This question is worth 2 points.**

Drag your answer choices to the spaces where they belong.
To remove an answer choice, click on it. To review the passage, click on **View Text**.

Animals use both internal and external means to enable themselves to live in places with very hot or cold temperatures.

-
-
-

Answer Choices

1. A large number of animals hibernate for several weeks or months of the year.
2. Camels are animals with one or two humps that are often found living in deserts.
3. All animals can be categorized as either warm blooded or cold blooded.
4. Mammals in cold environments may have fur or feathers to help keep them warm.
5. By eating food, warm-blooded animals can transform the energy created into heat.
6. Reptiles often hide in the shade or rest underground to keep from getting too hot.

How Plants Spread to New Regions

Like all living organisms, plants have a driving need to propagate. The main way flowering plants do this is by having their seeds spread to new areas. For a seed to become a plant, it must be buried in the soil and then **germinate**. There are numerous ways in which seeds can spread to different regions, including being transported by gravity, wind, water, and humans as well as other animals. Seeds may travel just a meter or move thousands of kilometers. They may also disperse into areas where others of their species are well established, colonize new lands if the growing conditions are sufficient, and even assist ecosystems in recovering from natural disasters.

Plants' seeds come in a variety of forms and sizes. Many are hidden by the outer husks of nuts or inside the soft flesh of fruits while others are so miniscule that they are scarcely visible. Seeds are the end result of plant reproduction. Once they start becoming plants, the reproduction process of the original plant is complete. Seeds need to move away from their parent plants to be able to grow into new plants, but many merely fall to the ground because of gravity when their connections to their parent plants are terminated.

The ground in the immediate vicinity of a parent plant is not always ideal for seeds since other plants—including the parent—are typically already utilizing the soil, the water, and the sunlight that is available. For instance, the seeds of apple, orange, and peach trees that get buried beside their parent trees are likely never to grow into adult trees because they will have to compete with their parent tree for vital resources. Resultantly, the best way for seeds to become mature plants is to disperse far from their parent plants.

Wind is one most common way that seeds disperse. Some plants have seeds so tiny and lightweight that they are easily picked up by the wind and transported great distances. In many cases, evolution has made seeds more aerodynamic, which lets even light breezes lift and move them. For example, the dandelion has hair-like growths on its seeds that give them the appearance of helicopter blades. Other seeds are **buoyant**, so they may be washed down streams and rivers until they float ashore in new locations. Some, like coconuts, may float vast distances on the oceans until they reach remote islands.

Seeds wrapped inside fleshy fruits and nuts are commonly dispersed by animals, which eat the fruits and the nuts and thereby simultaneously ingest the seeds. Later, the animals defecate, so the seeds, which are not digested inside their bodies, are deposited somewhere else. Many of these seeds, which have a good source of fertilizer in the animal feces, germinate and develop into new plants. Other seeds, including walnuts and acorns, are stored by animals such as squirrels and birds. These animals frequently store seeds underground, but, at times, they forget about their caches of nuts, so some germinate and become plants. Humans also play a role in the scattering of seeds by cultivating fruits and nuts and transporting them great distances, where some fall into the soil and then grow.

Ideally, seeds disperse in areas with good soil, abundant water resources, and plenty of sunlight. Seeds usually only germinate when the conditions for their survival are optimal, and many remain dormant to avoid dangers such as frost, which can kill them. Yet when seeds germinate, they must compete with plants that are already growing. Crowded forests, places with poor soil, and regions that receive little rainfall may not be the best locations for seeds to germinate.

Instead, one ideal place for seeds to colonize is an area beginning to recover from a natural disaster. A place that has recently experienced a forest fire, for example, is perfect for plant colonization. The organic matter from the burned dead plants improves the nutrient levels of the soil. Additionally, due to the lack of other plants—especially tall trees—growing, young plants are practically guaranteed access to abundant sunlight. This enables them to grow quickly and to become strong and healthy plants, which is one reason why areas destroyed by forest fires and floods typically recover so swiftly.

Glossary

germinate: to begin to grow, as in the seed of a plant

buoyant: able to float on water

21 The word propagate in the passage is closest in meaning to

Ⓐ evolve

Ⓑ mutate

Ⓒ reproduce

Ⓓ scatter

22 According to paragraph 2, how does gravity affect seeds?

Ⓐ It causes them to get buried beneath the surface of the ground.

Ⓑ It makes many of them fall to the ground beneath their parent plants.

Ⓒ It assists in the germination process that seeds go through to become plants.

Ⓓ It enables seeds to be hidden inside the fruits of some plants.

Glossary

germinate: to begin to grow, as in the seed of a plant

How Plants Spread to New Regions

Like all living organisms, plants have a driving need to propagate. The main way flowering plants do this is by having their seeds spread to new areas. For a seed to become a plant, it must be buried in the soil and then **germinate**. There are numerous ways in which seeds can spread to different regions, including being transported by gravity, wind, water, and humans as well as other animals. Seeds may travel just a meter or move thousands of kilometers. They may also disperse into areas where others of their species are well established, colonize new lands if the growing conditions are sufficient, and even assist ecosystems in recovering from natural disasters.

2→ Plants' seeds come in a variety of forms and sizes. Many are hidden by the outer husks of nuts or inside the soft flesh of fruits while others are so miniscule that they are scarcely visible. Seeds are the end result of plant reproduction. Once they start becoming plants, the reproduction process of the original plant is complete. Seeds need to move away from their parent plants to be able to grow into new plants, but many merely fall to the ground because of gravity when their connections to their parent plants are terminated.

23 Which of the sentences below best expresses the essential information in the highlighted sentence in the passage? *Incorrect* answer choices change the meaning in important ways or leave out essential information.

Ⓐ The area near a parent plant is not good for seeds since they must compete against other plants for resources.

Ⓑ The majority of the seeds that fall near their parent plants fail to get enough soil, water, and sunlight.

Ⓒ When a seed falls near its parent plant, it must compete with the parent for valuable natural resources.

Ⓓ Soil, water, and sunlight are hard for many seeds to attain when they fall to the ground in some places.

24 According to paragraph 3, which of the following is true of the seeds of apple, orange, and peach trees?

Ⓐ Very few of these seeds ever germinate and become mature plants.

Ⓑ It can take them many years before they germinate and start to grow.

Ⓒ They are among the largest seeds in the entire plant kingdom.

Ⓓ Those that get buried beside their parent trees rarely become adult trees.

3→ The ground in the immediate vicinity of a parent plant is not always ideal for seeds since other plants—including the parent—are typically already utilizing the soil, the water, and the sunlight that is available. For instance, the seeds of apple, orange, and peach trees that get buried beside their parent trees are likely never to grow into adult trees because they will have to compete with their parent tree for vital resources. Resultantly, the best way for seeds to become mature plants is to disperse far from their parent plants.

25 In paragraph 4, the author uses the dandelion as an example of

(A) a type of plant that can float on rivers and streams

(B) a plant whose seeds can be moved by the wind

(C) a flower that has tiny and lightweight seeds

(D) a kind of plant that is able to reproduce rapidly

26 The word ingest in the passage is closest in meaning to

(A) chew

(B) swallow

(C) avoid

(D) digest

Glossary

buoyant: able to float on water

4→ Wind is one most common way that seeds disperse. Some plants have seeds so tiny and lightweight that they are easily picked up by the wind and transported great distances. In many cases, evolution has made seeds more aerodynamic, which lets even light breezes lift and move them. For example, the dandelion has hair-like growths on its seeds that give them the appearance of helicopter blades. Other seeds are **buoyant**, so they may be washed down streams and rivers until they float ashore in new locations. Some, like coconuts, may float vast distances on the oceans until they reach remote islands.

Seeds wrapped inside fleshy fruits and nuts are commonly dispersed by animals, which eat the fruits and the nuts and thereby simultaneously ingest the seeds. Later, the animals defecate, so the seeds, which are not digested inside their bodies, are deposited somewhere else. Many of these seeds, which have a good source of fertilizer in the animal feces, germinate and develop into new plants. Other seeds, including walnuts and acorns, are stored by animals such as squirrels and birds. These animals frequently store seeds underground, but, at times, they forget about their caches of nuts, so some germinate and become plants. Humans also play a role in the scattering of seeds by cultivating fruits and nuts and transporting them great distances, where some fall into the soil and then grow.

27 In paragraph 6, the author implies that seeds

Ⓐ many not grow well in a place that already has many trees

Ⓑ can remain beneath the ground for years before germinating

Ⓒ only germinate in either the spring or summer months

Ⓓ require water every day in order to become healthy plants

28 According to paragraph 7, seeds can grow well in places that have recently experienced forest fires because

Ⓐ the regions have no obstructions that block sunlight

Ⓑ there are no animals living there that will eat the seeds

Ⓒ people spread fertilizers in the areas to make the soil better

Ⓓ water supplies in these regions are typically ample

29 Look at the four squares [■] that indicate where the following sentence could be added to the passage.

It is particularly dangerous for seeds in early spring, when the weather can suddenly drop below freezing in some places.

Where would the sentence best fit?

Click on a square [■] to add the sentence to the passage.

6→ Ideally, seeds disperse in areas with good soil, abundant water resources, and plenty of sunlight. **1** Seeds usually only germinate when the conditions for their survival are optimal, and many remain dormant to avoid dangers such as frost, which can kill them. **2** Yet when seeds germinate, they must compete with plants that are already growing. **3** Crowded forests, places with poor soil, and regions that receive little rainfall may not be the best locations for seeds to germinate. **4**

7→ Instead, one ideal place for seeds to colonize is an area beginning to recover from a natural disaster. A place that has recently experienced a forest fire, for example, is perfect for plant colonization. The organic matter from the burned dead plants improves the nutrient levels of the soil. Additionally, due to the lack of other plants—especially tall trees—growing, young plants are practically guaranteed access to abundant sunlight. This enables them to grow quickly and to become strong and healthy plants, which is one reason why areas destroyed by forest fires and floods typically recover so swiftly.

30 Directions: Select the appropriate statements from the answer choices and match them to the cause and effect of seed dispersal to which they relate. TWO of the answer choices will NOT be used. **This question is worth 3 points.**

Drag your answer choices to the spaces where they belong.
To remove an answer choice, click on it. To review the passage, click on **View Text**.

Answer Choices

1. Places that have been flooded may have new plants grow quickly.
2. Animals drop seeds in new places when they defecate.
3. Growing plants compete against one another for sunlight, soil, and water.
4. Plants start to grow in areas where they are not common.
5. Seeds do not usually germinate when weather conditions are poor.
6. Humans transport some fruits and nuts to faraway places.
7. The wind lifts light seeds and moves them to other areas.

SEED DISPERSAL

Cause

-
-
-

Effect

-
-

TOEFL® MAP

ACTUAL TEST

Reading 2

CONTINUE

Reading Section Directions

This section measures your ability to understand academic passages in English. You will have **72 minutes** to read and answer questions about **4 passages**. A clock at the top of the screen will show you how much time is remaining.

Most questions are worth 1 point but the last question for each passage is worth more than 1 point. The directions for the last question indicate how many points you may receive.

Some passages include a word or phrase that is **underlined** in blue. Click on the word or phrase to see a definition or an explanation.

When you want to move to the next question, click on **Next**. You may skip questions and go back to them later. If you want to return to previous questions, click on **Back**. You can click on **Reivew** at any time, and the review screen will show you which questions you have answered and which you have not answered. From this review screen, you may go directly to any question you have already seen in the Reading section.

Click on **Continue** to go on.

News in Colonial America

PLAIN TRUTH;
ADDRESSED TO THE
INHABITANTS
OF
AMERICA,
Containing, Remarks
ON A LATE PAMPHLET,
entitled
COMMON SENSE:
Wherein are ſhewn, that the Scheme of INDEPENDENCE is Ruinous, Deluſive, and Impracticable: That were the Author's Aſſeverations, Reſpecting the Power of AMERICA, as Real as Nugatory; Reconciliation on liberal Principles with GREAT BRITAIN, would be exalted Policy: And that circumſtanced as we are, Permanent Liberty, and True Happineſs, can only be

Common Sense, published in 1776

The American Revolution took place from 1775 to 1783 as the American colonies fought for their independence from Great Britain. At that time, newspapers, **pamphlets**, and mail were the main ways American colonists received the news. These sources of information, which the British levied taxes on and which resulted in increasing tensions between them and the colonists, were vital to the revolution. They helped unite people spread out over a large area and conveyed news on the progress of the revolution itself.

Prior to the twentieth century, virtually all news was passed on by word of mouth or through letters, newspapers, **broadsheets**, and pamphlets. When the British started establishing colonies in North America during the 1600s, they printed broadsheets containing news from home and the rest of Europe and distributed them around the colonies. Due to the nature of transportation then, news was usually at least six months old when it reached the most isolated places in the colonies. Additionally, people in the colonies seldom received much printed news about events in other American colonies.

This started changing during the early eighteenth century. In 1721, the first truly American newspaper, *The New-England Courant*, was published by James Franklin, Benjamin Franklin's older brother, in Boston, Massachusetts. While the paper only lasted for five years, it served as a model for later newspapers, which began to emerge all over the colonies. Roughly fifty years later when the American Revolution began, newspapers were common in all thirteen American colonies.

On the eve of the American Revolution, these newspapers served as places for American colonists to voice their opinions concerning British actions, which were gradually leading the two sides toward an armed confrontation. Many newspapers printed opinion pieces and published letters from their readers. A large number of Americans voiced their opinions of British actions in decidedly anti-British tones, so through the print media, feelings of ill will toward British rule spread throughout the colonies. How much influence these newspapers had on the outbreak of hostilities is difficult to measure, but their constant anti-British attitudes surely played a role in shaping people's opinions.

Other colonists resorted to publishing pamphlets as a further way to use the written word to influence others. No pamphlet played a greater role than *Common Sense*, which was written by Thomas Paine and printed in 1776 after the first shots of the revolution had already been fired. In his work, Paine presented a strong argument for American independence. *Common Sense* was widely printed and read throughout the colonies and played an integral role in increasing the people's support for the revolution in its early days.

Nonetheless, at the start of the revolution, many colonists were unprepared for the outbreak of violence. Fighting between the British and American colonists started in Massachusetts in spring of 1775. Slowly, news of the fighting spread, and, combined with the printing of *Common Sense* and the signing of the Declaration of Independence on July 4, 1776, the momentum for an armed rebellion became unstoppable. Even so, news of these events as well as later battles spread slowly throughout the colonies.

The reason was that both mail and news traveled in three main ways: by ship, by horse and carriage, and on foot. Ships were the fastest way to spread news, so people in ports usually received news from elsewhere long before those living inland did. In addition, during the war, news services were frequently interrupted, and many newspapers suffered delays in printing due to a lack of paper and worn-out printing presses. The British made a point of suppressing newspapers in areas they controlled. Consequently, many colonists only received news by word of mouth, so some information could not be trusted in its entirety.

Despite these problems, during the American Revolution, news in various forms still arrived, no matter how sporadically, so people were informed of the most crucial events. While measuring the importance of newspapers, pamphlets, and other means of conveying information to the success of the revolution is not easy, it is safe to state that without them, the revolution itself likely would never have occurred. It was, after all, the newspapers and the pamphlets which printed the material that helped unite the American colonists against the British.

Glossary

pamphlet: a short essay, often on a controversial matter of current interest

broadsheet: a newspaper that is printed on large paper

PREVIEW

HELP

BACK

NEXT

1 The word levied in the passage is closest in meaning to

(A) received

(B) considered

(C) charged

(D) proposed

2 According to paragraph 2, which of the following is true about news in the American colonies in the 1600s?

(A) It was printed in newspapers in Great Britain and then shipped to America.

(B) The people living in America were updated on news in other colonies.

(C) The colonists printed broadsheets that covered news about the colonies.

(D) People in some of the colonies received news that was at least half a year old.

Glossary

pamphlet: a short essay, often on a controversial matter of current interest

broadsheet: a newspaper that is printed on large paper

News in Colonial America

The American Revolution took place from 1775 to 1783 as the American colonies fought for their independence from Great Britain. At that time, newspapers, **pamphlets**, and mail were the main ways American colonists received the news. These sources of information, which the British levied taxes on and which resulted in increasing tensions between them and the colonists, were vital to the revolution. They helped unite people spread out over a large area and conveyed news on the progress of the revolution itself.

2→ Prior to the twentieth century, virtually all news was passed on by word of mouth or through letters, newspapers, **broadsheets**, and pamphlets. When the British started establishing colonies in North America during the 1600s, they printed broadsheets containing news from home and the rest of Europe and distributed them around the colonies. Due to the nature of transportation then, news was usually at least six months old when it reached the most isolated places in the colonies. Additionally, people in the colonies seldom received much printed news about events in other American colonies.

3 In paragraph 3, the author uses *The New-England Courant* as an example of

Ⓐ a newspaper that influenced the Americans to revolt against Great Britain

Ⓑ one of the least successful ventures attempted by the Franklin family

Ⓒ an American newspaper that was published in the colonies

Ⓓ the oldest newspaper that is still being printed in the United States

4 Which of the sentences below best expresses the essential information in the highlighted sentence in the passage? *Incorrect* answer choices change the meaning in important ways or leave out essential information.

Ⓐ American newspapers printed letters that were anti-British, so these helped people in the colonies turn against the British.

Ⓑ When the British realized that American newspapers were anti-British, they understood how much the Americans disliked them.

Ⓒ Because there were so many newspapers in America, it was hard to keep track of which ones were anti-British in nature.

Ⓓ American newspapers made a point of publishing as many anti-British letters to the editor as they could.

[3]→ This started changing during the early eighteenth century. In 1721, the first truly American newspaper, *The New-England Courant*, was published by James Franklin, Benjamin Franklin's older brother, in Boston, Massachusetts. While the paper only lasted for five years, it served as a model for later newspapers, which began to emerge all over the colonies. Roughly fifty years later when the American Revolution began, newspapers were common in all thirteen American colonies.

On the eve of the American Revolution, these newspapers served as places for American colonists to voice their opinions concerning British actions, which were gradually leading the two sides toward an armed confrontation. Many newspapers printed opinion pieces and published letters from their readers. A large number of Americans voiced their opinions of British actions in decidedly anti-British tones, so through the print media, feelings of ill will toward British rule spread throughout the colonies. How much influence these newspapers had on the outbreak of hostilities is difficult to measure, but their constant anti-British attitudes surely played a role in shaping people's opinions.

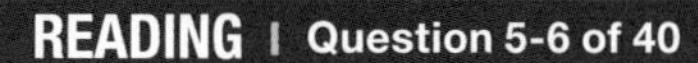

5 The author's description of *Common Sense* in paragraph 5 mentions which of the following?

Ⓐ It served as the inspiration for the writing of the Declaration of Independence.

Ⓑ It was the most influential pamphlet published during the American Revolution.

Ⓒ It is still read by people today who want to understand that period of history.

Ⓓ Paine decided to write it prior to the outbreak of hostilities in the revolution.

6 The word momentum in the passage is closest in meaning to

Ⓐ quest

Ⓑ desire

Ⓒ possibility

Ⓓ impetus

5→ Other colonists resorted to publishing pamphlets as a further way to use the written word to influence others. No pamphlet played a greater role than *Common Sense*, which was written by Thomas Paine and printed in 1776 after the first shots of the revolution had already been fired. In his work, Paine presented a strong argument for American independence. *Common Sense* was widely printed and read throughout the colonies and played an integral role in increasing the people's support for the revolution in its early days.

Nonetheless, at the start of the revolution, many colonists were unprepared for the outbreak of violence. Fighting between the British and American colonists started in Massachusetts in spring of 1775. Slowly, news of the fighting spread, and, combined with the printing of *Common Sense* and the signing of the Declaration of Independence on July 4, 1776, the momentum for an armed rebellion became unstoppable. Even so, news of these events as well as later battles spread slowly throughout the colonies.

7 In paragraph 7, the author implies that the American colonists

(A) imported printing presses from several other countries

(B) became more interested in news after the American Revolution

(C) were better informed of the news than the British

(D) often mistrusted some of the news that they received

8 According to paragraph 8, which of the following is true of newspapers and pamphlets?

(A) They accurately described the battles of the American Revolution.

(B) They were one of the main reasons the American Revolution occurred.

(C) Some of them supported the Americans while others supported the British.

(D) They were mostly written by people who were very well educated.

7→ The reason was that both mail and news traveled in three main ways: by ship, by horse and carriage, and on foot. Ships were the fastest way to spread news, so people in ports usually received news from elsewhere long before those living inland did. In addition, during the war, news services were frequently interrupted, and many newspapers suffered delays in printing due to a lack of paper and worn-out printing presses. The British made a point of suppressing newspapers in areas they controlled. Consequently, many colonists only received news by word of mouth, so some information could not be trusted in its entirety.

8→ Despite these problems, during the American Revolution, news in various forms still arrived, no matter how sporadically, so people were informed of the most crucial events. While measuring the importance of newspapers, pamphlets, and other means of conveying information to the success of the revolution is not easy, it is safe to state that without them, the revolution itself likely would never have occurred. It was, after all, the newspapers and the pamphlets which printed the material that helped unite the American colonists against the British.

9 Look at the four squares [■] that indicate where the following sentence could be added to the passage.

The first shots were fired on April 19 at the Battles of Lexington and Concord.

Where would the sentence best fit?

Click on a square [■] to add the sentence to the passage.

Nonetheless, at the start of the revolution, many colonists were unprepared for the outbreak of violence. [1] Fighting between the British and American colonists started in Massachusetts in spring of 1775. [2] Slowly, news of the fighting spread, and, combined with the printing of *Common Sense* and the signing of the Declaration of Independence on July 4, 1776, the momentum for an armed rebellion became unstoppable. [3] Even so, news of these events as well as later battles spread slowly throughout the colonies. [4]

10 **Directions:** An introductory sentence for a brief summary of the passage is provided below. Complete the summary by selecting the THREE answer choices that express the most important ideas of the passage. Some sentences do not belong because they express ideas that are not presented in the passage or are minor ideas in the passage. **This question is worth 2 points.**

Drag your answer choices to the spaces where they belong.
To remove an answer choice, click on it. To review the passage, click on **View Text**.

Newspapers and pamphlets helped unite the American colonists and led them to start the American Revolution against Great Britain.

-
-
-

Answer Choices

1 Newspapers spread news of events such as the fighting in 1775 and the signing of the Declaration of Independence.

2 *Common Sense* by Thomas Paine was a pivotal pamphlet in that it described why the American colonies should be free.

3 Benjamin Franklin's older brother was the first person to print a newspaper that could be considered American.

4 Many American newspapers were anti-British in attitude, which helped turn the colonists against the British.

5 It was often impossible for people in distant colonies to keep updated on events that were occurring in other colonies.

6 The British made a point of destroying printing presses in American cities during the American Revolution.

The Effects of Ice Ages

Over the course of the Earth's history, there have been countless ice ages, with the most recent major one happening around 15,000 to 20,000 years ago. During these ice ages, massive sheets of ice formed at the Polar Regions and in mountainous regions elsewhere. These grew to be several kilometers thick and moved slowly while gradually transforming the land by their actions. Not only did ice ages alter the land, but they also changed the oceans as they are given credit by scientists for establishing present-day currents such as the Gulf Stream.

During an ice age, the Earth's average temperatures plummet. This leads to the gradual freezing of both fresh water on land and salt water in the oceans. As ocean water freezes and gets trapped inside sheets of ice, ocean levels fall worldwide. It is estimated that in most places, the ocean level fell approximately 100 to 200 meters during the last ice age. This exposed the ocean floor in many places and created land bridges between regions which had been separated by vast expanses of water. This had a profound impact on both the shape of the land and the distribution of human life on the Earth.

During one ice age around 40,000 years ago, a land bridge appeared between Indonesia and New Guinea, so people subsequently moved south to New Guinea. Of even greater impact was the appearance of a land bridge connecting Siberia in Asia and Alaska in North America. Before the manifestation of this land bridge, both North and South America were devoid of human life. However, by the last major ice age, people had learned how to survive in frigid temperatures, so there were human tribes living in Siberia. When the land bridge appeared in the Bering Sea around 15,000 years ago, many tribespeople in Siberia followed wandering herds of animals across to Alaska.

Eventually, humans in North America made their way south, departed the glacial zone, and found warmer lands filled with animals that had never seen humans before. They promptly began slaughtering many of these animals. This happened primarily because humans were hunter-gatherers who had not learned about agriculture, so they relied upon animals as a major food source. However, many animal species became extinct because of overhunting. Nevertheless, within a thousand years, people had spread down to the southern tip of South America.

Past ice ages are also believed to have had a tremendous impact on modern-day ocean currents, which have important roles in determining the weather. During ice ages, there were sometimes short periods when temperatures rose, which caused some ice sheets to melt. For instance, during these warming periods, huge **icebergs** around Europe and North America broke off from gigantic sheets of ice and flowed into the Atlantic Ocean. As they moved southward, the icebergs began to melt, releasing large amounts of fresh water into the saltwater ocean. This altered the **salinity levels** of the Atlantic Ocean and may have played a role in determining the course and strength of the Gulf Stream, the most important current in the Atlantic. The Gulf Stream carries warm water from the south to the north and passes close to Europe, where it helps the continent maintain a climate more temperate than its northern latitude would otherwise permit.

Evidence for this comes from two main sources. First, ice cores drilled in the Greenland ice cap proved there were periods when the layers of ice were not as thick as during other times, which indicates there were warming periods when less ice and snow accumulated. Some warming periods are known to have lasted for decades. The second piece of evidence comes from rock samples taken from the floor of the Atlantic Ocean. These rocks are consistent with others found only in certain land masses in Northern Europe. The presence of these rocks in the middle of the ocean led scientists to conclude they had been carried there on icebergs. As the ice sheets advanced, they carved up the land and gathered rocks that were then buried in the ice. When icebergs broke off from these ice sheets and later melted in the ocean, the rocks fell to the bottom. Simultaneously, the icebergs released fresh water, which helped form the Gulf Stream.

Glossary

iceberg: a large floating mass of ice on the ocean

salinity level: the amount of salt in a liquid

11 In paragraph 1, the author's description of ice ages mentions all of the following EXCEPT:

Ⓐ how large it is possible for some of them to become

Ⓑ how frequently major ones tend to happen on the Earth

Ⓒ the manner in which they can have an effect on the Earth's oceans

Ⓓ which parts of the Earth they tend to create ice sheets on

12 The word plummet in the passage is closest in meaning to

Ⓐ subtract

Ⓑ stabilize

Ⓒ alternate

Ⓓ plunge

The Effects of Ice Ages

[1]→ Over the course of the Earth's history, there have been countless ice ages, with the most recent major one happening around 15,000 to 20,000 years ago. During these ice ages, massive sheets of ice formed at the Polar Regions and in mountainous regions elsewhere. These grew to be several kilometers thick and moved slowly while gradually transforming the land by their actions. Not only did ice ages alter the land, but they also changed the oceans as they are given credit by scientists for establishing present-day currents such as the Gulf Stream.

During an ice age, the Earth's average temperatures plummet. This leads to the gradual freezing of both fresh water on land and salt water in the oceans. As ocean water freezes and gets trapped inside sheets of ice, ocean levels fall worldwide. It is estimated that in most places, the ocean level fell approximately 100 to 200 meters during the last ice age. This exposed the ocean floor in many places and created land bridges between regions which had been separated by vast expanses of water. This had a profound impact on both the shape of the land and the distribution of human life on the Earth.

13 In paragraph 3, why does the author mention Indonesia and New Guinea?

- (A) To state that it was once possible for people to walk to North America
- (B) To compare the size of the land bridge there to the one in the Bering Sea
- (C) To claim that New Guinea was first populated around 40,000 years ago
- (D) To name one place where a land bridge appeared during an ice age

14 Which of the following can be inferred from paragraph 3 about the tribespeople living in Siberia?

- (A) The animals that they followed were crucial to their food supply.
- (B) They led many animals across the Bering Sea to go to North America.
- (C) Some went to North America while others went to New Guinea.
- (D) It took them hundreds of years to move from Siberia to Alaska.

15 According to paragraph 4, many animals in the Americas went extinct because

- (A) they were unable to adapt to cold temperatures during the ice age
- (B) humans hunted them too much and killed all of them
- (C) they were outcompeted for their food supplies by humans
- (D) animals that migrated from Asia succeeded at killing them

[3]→ During one ice age around 40,000 years ago, a land bridge appeared between Indonesia and New Guinea, so people subsequently moved south to New Guinea. Of even greater impact was the appearance of a land bridge connecting Siberia in Asia and Alaska in North America. Before the manifestation of this land bridge, both North and South America were devoid of human life. However, by the last major ice age, people had learned how to survive in frigid temperatures, so there were human tribes living in Siberia. When the land bridge appeared in the Bering Sea around 15,000 years ago, many tribespeople in Siberia followed wandering herds of animals across to Alaska.

[4]→ Eventually, humans in North America made their way south, departed the glacial zone, and found warmer lands filled with animals that had never seen humans before. They promptly began slaughtering many of these animals. This happened primarily because humans were hunter-gatherers who had not learned about agriculture, so they relied upon animals as a major food source. However, many animal species became extinct because of overhunting. Nevertheless, within a thousand years, people had spread down to the southern tip of South America.

16 According to paragraph 5, which of the following is true of the Gulf Stream?

Ⓐ It is the largest of all of the currents that flow through the Atlantic Ocean.

Ⓑ It carries icebergs that have broken off thousands of kilometers southward.

Ⓒ It was altered during some warming periods that happened in the last ice age.

Ⓓ It helps keep both North America and Europe warmer than they should be.

[5]→ Past ice ages are also believed to have had a tremendous impact on modern-day ocean currents, which have important roles in determining the weather. During ice ages, there were sometimes short periods when temperatures rose, which caused some ice sheets to melt. For instance, during these warming periods, huge **icebergs** around Europe and North America broke off from gigantic sheets of ice and flowed into the Atlantic Ocean. As they moved southward, the icebergs began to melt, releasing large amounts of fresh water into the saltwater ocean. This altered the **salinity levels** of the Atlantic Ocean and may have played a role in determining the course and strength of the Gulf Stream, the most important current in the Atlantic. The Gulf Stream carries warm water from the south to the north and passes close to Europe, where it helps the continent maintain a climate more temperate than its northern latitude would otherwise permit.

Glossary

iceberg: a large floating mass of ice on the ocean

salinity level: the amount of salt in a liquid

17 Which of the sentences below best expresses the essential information in the highlighted sentence in the passage? *Incorrect* answer choices change the meaning in important ways or leave out essential information.

Ⓐ According to research conducted in Greenland, there were times when the weather warmed, so there were less snow and ice.

Ⓑ During the last ice age, Greenland often received much less ice and snow than other places on the Earth did.

Ⓒ During warming periods, less ice and snow fell, so the layers of ice were not as thick as they were during other times.

Ⓓ Because Greenland did not get very much snow or ice, scientists decided to conduct their research on the last ice age there.

18 According to paragraph 6, how did rocks from Northern Europe get to the bottom of the Atlantic Ocean?

Ⓐ They were carried there by icebergs that then melted.

Ⓑ The Gulf Stream carried some of the rocks there.

Ⓒ Continental drift resulted in the rocks being brought there.

Ⓓ Scientists conducting experiments took the rocks there.

6→ Evidence for this comes from two main sources. First, ice cores drilled in the Greenland ice cap proved there were periods when the layers of ice were not as thick as during other times, which indicates there were warming periods when less ice and snow accumulated. Some warming periods are known to have lasted for decades. The second piece of evidence comes from rock samples taken from the floor of the Atlantic Ocean. These rocks are consistent with others found only in certain land masses in Northern Europe. The presence of these rocks in the middle of the ocean led scientists to conclude they had been carried there on icebergs. As the ice sheets advanced, they carved up the land and gathered rocks that were then buried in the ice. When icebergs broke off from these ice sheets and later melted in the ocean, the rocks fell to the bottom. Simultaneously, the icebergs released fresh water, which helped form the Gulf Stream.

19 Look at the four squares [■] that indicate where the following sentence could be added to the passage.

Among them were mammoths, saber-toothed tigers, dire wolves, and ground sloths.

Where would the sentence best fit?

Click on a square [■] to add the sentence to the passage.

[1] Eventually, humans in North America made their way south, departed the glacial zone, and found warmer lands filled with animals that had never seen humans before. [2] They promptly began slaughtering many of these animals. [3] This happened primarily because humans were hunter-gatherers who had not learned about agriculture, so they relied upon animals as a major food source. [4] However, many animal species became extinct because of overhunting. Nevertheless, within a thousand years, people had spread down to the southern tip of South America.

20 Directions: An introductory sentence for a brief summary of the passage is provided below. Complete the summary by selecting the THREE answer choices that express the most important ideas of the passage. Some sentences do not belong because they express ideas that are not presented in the passage or are minor ideas in the passage. **This question is worth 2 points.**

Drag your answer choices to the spaces where they belong.
To remove an answer choice, click on it. To review the passage, click on **View Text**.

Ice ages have affected both where on the Earth humans live and currents in the planet's oceans.

-
-
-

Answer Choices

1. Hunter-gatherers living in Siberia crossed a land bridge over the Bering Sea.
2. Many animals in the Americas were hunted to extinction by humans.
3. Melting icebergs created during warming periods altered the Gulf Stream.
4. The temperatures in Europe are warmer than in other places at comparable latitudes.
5. The last major ice age took place roughly 15,000 years in the past.
6. Humans went to New Guinea and the Americas by walking on exposed land.

Infant Imitation

How infants learn is a question child psychologists and educators have long attempted to answer. Most agree that infants learn primarily by imitating the actions of adults they witness. However, they are uncertain whether this habit of imitating is instinctive or if infants associate some type of meaning with the adults' actions. Additionally, child study experts disagree concerning the age when infants can imitate adults as well as the age when they start learning from their actions. Despite exhaustive research done on infants, child study experts still cannot say with any certainty that they know what is happening in infants' minds.

For years, most child study experts were convinced that infant imitation of adults was an innate behavior. They felt that infants are naturally inclined to imitate whatever they see. In that regard, these experts believed that infants do not learn anything through their behavior. In recent decades, however, a new theory based on certain experimental studies has gained prominence. In order better to understand infant imitation, extensive testing of infants was done in controlled situations. Many tests involved having infants observe adults' facial gestures. The reason these experiments concentrated on facial gestures is that unless infants constantly have mirrors in front of them, they cannot see their own facial gestures. Since no mirrors were involved, the infants had not formed any **imprinted** memories of their own facial gestures, which meant that when they made facial gestures similar to those of adults, they were consciously imitating the adults' actions. Most of the studies focused on mouth movements, particularly the positions of the lips and the tongue.

One result of these experiments was the creation of a new theory regarding infant imitation and learning. The leading experts in the field of child study, Andrew Meltzoff and M. Keith Moore, determined that infants are actively learning whenever they imitate adults. Their studies showed that even after several days had passed between the first time that infants saw a gesture and when they were given a chance to do it themselves, they could imitate it exactly. This led the men to conclude that the infants had observed an action, remembered it, and repeated it, which therefore indicated they had learned to do something.

Another issue concerning infant imitation that is constantly debated concerns the age infants are when they begin to learn by imitating. Previously, the majority of child study experts believed that only infants above the age of one were actively learning from imitation. But further studies by Meltzoff and Moore led them to conclude that infants as young as six weeks old could learn in this manner. In another experiment, they tested several six-week-old infants over the course of several days, again by utilizing adult facial gestures. They ascertained that those infants were actively seeking to duplicate what they were seeing—even complex actions involving the mouth and tongue—and were making their own facial gestures better the more often they saw others make their own gestures.

Meltzoff and Moore further believed that very young infants can correlate the sight of a person making a facial gesture and how the infants feel when making the same gesture. Basically, infants assume their own feelings are identical to those of the person they are imitating. In their minds, infants associate what they observe with what they are doing, they further associate their actions with their feelings, and they finally **project** their feelings onto others based upon their observations of adults' facial gestures. For instance, when an infant sees someone smiling and imitates that smile, the infant suddenly feels happy. At the same time, the infant believes the person smiling must also be happy. Thus Meltzoff and Moore arrived at the conclusion that infants are born with the ability to understand other people's mental states.

Meltzoff and Moore's theories on infant imitation were radically different from those accepted at the time, so they proved to be highly controversial with the child study community. Today, there are supporters of both theories of infant imitation. For the time being, each school of thought has its own strengths and weaknesses, and it is likely that given infants' limited ability to communicate, exactly when most infants start learning by imitating adults will never be conclusively known.

Glossary

imprinted: fixed in one's mind

project: to ascribe one's thoughts or feelings to another person

21 The word they in the passage refers to

Ⓐ child psychologists and educators

Ⓑ infants

Ⓒ the actions

Ⓓ adults

22 The word innate in the passage is closest in meaning to

Ⓐ impressive

Ⓑ immature

Ⓒ instinctive

Ⓓ insidious

23 According to paragraph 2, the tests that were implemented focused on facial gestures because

Ⓐ infants can imitate them more easily than they can copy hand gestures

Ⓑ previous studies on infants had also involved facial gestures

Ⓒ they are expressions that infants have not seen themselves make

Ⓓ most experts believe that infants can remember them fairly well

Glossary

imprinted: fixed in one's mind

Infant Imitation

How infants learn is a question child psychologists and educators have long attempted to answer. Most agree that infants learn primarily by imitating the actions of adults they witness. However, they are uncertain whether this habit of imitating is instinctive or if infants associate some type of meaning with the adults' actions. Additionally, child study experts disagree concerning the age when infants can imitate adults as well as the age when they start learning from their actions. Despite exhaustive research done on infants, child study experts still cannot say with any certainty that they know what is happening in infants' minds.

2→ For years, most child study experts were convinced that infant imitation of adults was an innate behavior. They felt that infants are naturally inclined to imitate whatever they see. In that regard, these experts believed that infants do not learn anything through their behavior. In recent decades, however, a new theory based on certain experimental studies has gained prominence. In order better to understand infant imitation, extensive testing of infants was done in controlled situations. Many tests involved having infants observe adults' facial gestures. The reason these experiments concentrated on facial gestures is that unless infants constantly have mirrors in front of them, they cannot see their own facial gestures. Since no mirrors were involved, the infants had not formed any **imprinted** memories of their own facial gestures, which meant that when they made facial gestures similar to those of adults, they were consciously imitating the adults' actions. Most of the studies focused on mouth movements, particularly the positions of the lips and the tongue.

24 In paragraph 3, why does the author mention Andrew Meltzoff and M. Keith Moore?

Ⓐ To identify the men who proposed a new theory on infant imitation

Ⓑ To criticize the methodology of the tests that they conducted on infants

Ⓒ To explain the types of gestures that they got the infants to imitate

Ⓓ To credit them for having founded the field of child psychology

25 Which of the following can be inferred from paragraph 4 about when infants begin to learn by imitating?

Ⓐ It is impossible for an infant to begin learning until the child is six months old.

Ⓑ There is some controversy concerning how old infants are when this happens.

Ⓒ An infant's intelligence plays a key role concerning when the child starts learning.

Ⓓ Most child psychologists feel that infants learn more as they become older.

3→ One result of these experiments was the creation of a new theory regarding infant imitation and learning. The leading experts in the field of child study, Andrew Meltzoff and M. Keith Moore, determined that infants are actively learning whenever they imitate adults. Their studies showed that even after several days had passed between the first time that infants saw a gesture and when they were given a chance to do it themselves, they could imitate it exactly. This led the men to conclude that the infants had observed an action, remembered it, and repeated it, which therefore indicated they had learned to do something.

4→ Another issue concerning infant imitation that is constantly debated concerns the age infants are when they begin to learn by imitating. Previously, the majority of child study experts believed that only infants above the age of one were actively learning from imitation. But further studies by Meltzoff and Moore led them to conclude that infants as young as six weeks old could learn in this manner. In another experiment, they tested several six-week-old infants over the course of several days, again by utilizing adult facial gestures. They ascertained that those infants were actively seeking to duplicate what they were seeing—even complex actions involving the mouth and tongue—and were making their own facial gestures better the more often they saw others make their own gestures.

26 The word correlate in the passage is closest in meaning to

Ⓐ associate

Ⓑ resist

Ⓒ comprehend

Ⓓ produce

27 According to paragraph 5, Meltzoff and Moore believed that infants could naturally determine people's mental states because

Ⓐ most of the infants became happy when people smiled at them

Ⓑ the infants that they tested were able to make many types of gestures

Ⓒ they were able to associate feelings with certain facial gestures

Ⓓ many of the adults reported that their own feelings had changed

28 According to paragraph 6, the author implies that the study of infant imitation

Ⓐ requires more tests in order for it to be fully understood

Ⓑ has certain aspects that people will always disagree on

Ⓒ attracts a lot of research money because of its prominence

Ⓓ is a precise science that is close to being perfected

Glossary

project: to ascribe one's thoughts or feelings to another person

[5]→ Meltzoff and Moore further believed that very young infants can correlate the sight of a person making a facial gesture and how the infants feel when making the same gesture. Basically, infants assume their own feelings are identical to those of the person they are imitating. In their minds, infants associate what they observe with what they are doing, they further associate their actions with their feelings, and they finally **project** their feelings onto others based upon their observations of adults' facial gestures. For instance, when an infant sees someone smiling and imitates that smile, the infant suddenly feels happy. At the same time, the infant believes the person smiling must also be happy. Thus Meltzoff and Moore arrived at the conclusion that infants are born with the ability to understand other people's mental states.

[6]→ Meltzoff and Moore's theories on infant imitation were radically different from those accepted at the time, so they proved to be highly controversial with the child study community. Today, there are supporters of both theories of infant imitation. For the time being, each school of thought has its own strengths and weaknesses, and it is likely that given infants' limited ability to communicate, exactly when most infants start learning by imitating adults will never be conclusively known.

29 Look at the four squares [■] that indicate where the following sentence could be added to the passage.

Likewise, an infant who sees and makes a scared face may experience a feeling of fear.

Where would the sentence best fit?

Click on a square [■] to add the sentence to the passage.

Meltzoff and Moore further believed that very young infants can correlate the sight of a person making a facial gesture and how the infants feel when making the same gesture. Basically, infants assume their own feelings are identical to those of the person they are imitating. In their minds, infants associate what they observe with what they are doing, they further associate their actions with their feelings, and they finally **project** their feelings onto others based upon their observations of adults' facial gestures. **1** For instance, when an infant sees someone smiling and imitates that smile, the infant suddenly feels happy. **2** At the same time, the infant believes the person smiling must also be happy. **3** Thus Meltzoff and Moore arrived at the conclusion that infants are born with the ability to understand other people's mental states. **4**

Glossary

project: to ascribe one's thoughts or feelings to another person

30 Directions: An introductory sentence for a brief summary of the passage is provided below. Complete the summary by selecting the THREE answer choices that express the most important ideas of the passage. Some sentences do not belong because they express ideas that are not presented in the passage or are minor ideas in the passage. **This question is worth 2 points.**

Drag your answer choices to the spaces where they belong.
To remove an answer choice, click on it. To review the passage, click on **View Text**.

There is a new theory that opposes the conventional thinking on the process of infant imitation.

-
-
-

Answer Choices

1. Tests that researchers carried out induced infants to imitate the facial gestures of adults.
2. Most researchers in the past assumed that infants did not start to learn by imitating until they were one year of age.
3. The two competing theories of infant imitation propose ideas that are very different from each other.
4. Child study experts Meltzoff and Moore felt that infants could learn from imitation when they were six weeks old.
5. Some infants project their emotions onto others, so they believe that if they are happy, others are happy, too.
6. It is sometimes possible for infants to see a facial gesture and then to remember it several days later.

The Influence of Greek and Roman Architecture

Three types of antique Greek columns and capitals

Greece and Rome were two of the greatest ancient civilizations, and both have had a lasting influence on history and culture. One area in which people in later civilizations have imitated them is in the realm of architecture. For instance, the construction techniques and architectural styles of both Greece and Rome were revived during the European Renaissance in the fifteenth and sixteenth centuries and were later heavily imitated during the Neoclassical Period in the eighteenth and nineteenth centuries.

Greek architecture evolved over a period of hundreds of years. Its heyday was the classical period of Greek history, which lasted from approximately 500 to 100 B.C. Ancient Greek architectural styles are typically divided into three separate groups: Ionic, Doric, and Corinthian. These three styles were based primarily on regional differences. The Doric style was closely associated with mainland Greece while the Ionic style was more closely associated with the Greek islands in the Aegean Sea as well as the Greek colonies located in Asia Minor in the land that is Turkey today. The Corinthian style, meanwhile, is regarded as an offshoot of the Ionic style yet is more elaborate in nature. The differences between the three styles are best observed in the columns used in Greek buildings. Doric columns are rather plain, Ionic columns are noted for their **scrolled** tops, and Corinthian columns have intricate designs. Additionally, Doric columns were short and squat while Ionic and Corinthian columns were taller and slenderer.

The Romans copied the Greeks in both the design and use of columns although some of their methods differed from the Greeks'. For example, the Romans regularly used all three styles of columns on the same building by employing a different style on each story of the structure. However, the Romans were innovators in their own right. Rome's two greatest contributions to the architectural world were the arch and the dome. Arches and domes permitted the Romans to erect much larger buildings—and with more massive interiors—than the Greeks ever did. Whereas the Greeks often built temples and other structures with open roofs, the Romans constructed domes over their large buildings. The Pantheon in Rome is the greatest example of a Roman domed building. As for arches, they permitted the Romans to build walls with large openings for doorways and windows. Arches were also used to great effect in enormous Roman **aqueducts**, some of which ran for hundreds of kilometers.

When Rome fell in 476, knowledge of both Roman and Greek architecture slowly disappeared from the West. But in Italy during the fifteenth century, a revival of Roman and Greek architecture began. During this time, Italian architects, who had previously been influenced by the Gothic style that prevailed in Western Europe, became exposed to information concerning ancient Greek and Roman building methods. This knowledge mostly came from Constantinople, the capital of the Byzantine Empire, which was located in modern-day Turkey and Greece. At that time, the Byzantine Empire was being besieged by the Ottoman Turks and was slowly losing power. Sensing its eventual defeat, many Byzantines fled to the West. While doing so, they took books and other sources of information on ancient Greece and Rome with them. In Italy, where many went, they found students eager to learn. From these refugees, Italian architects learned the secrets of Roman rounded arches and domes. They also began practicing the Roman customs of employing mathematical precision and symmetry in their building designs as they abandoned the haphazard, imprecise style of Gothic architecture. Eventually, this new style captured the imaginations of others in Europe and spread throughout the Western world during the Renaissance.

A few centuries later during the mid-eighteenth century, the Roman city of Pompeii, which had been consumed whole by ash in the eruption of Mount Vesuvius 1,700 years before, was unearthed. The city's discovery sparked another revival of interest in classical architecture. This initiated the Neoclassical Period. During the eighteenth and nineteenth centuries, many university buildings, libraries, and government buildings were designed and built to resemble ancient Greek and Roman structures. While the use of steel and the constructing of skyscrapers in the twentieth century somewhat lessened the influence of ancient Greece and Rome, their methods, styles, and concepts remain relevant to this day.

Glossary

scrolled: ornamental; fancy

aqueduct: an aboveground or belowground structure used to transport water, often long distances

31 Which of the sentences below best expresses the essential information in the highlighted sentence in the passage? *Incorrect* answer choices change the meaning in important ways or leave out essential information.

Ⓐ Greek and Roman architectural styles gained popularity during the Renaissance and lost it during the Neoclassical Period.

Ⓑ The Renaissance and the Neoclassical Period were the only two times that Europeans imitated Greek and Roman styles.

Ⓒ From the Renaissance to the Neoclassical Period, Greek and Roman architecture dominated Europe.

Ⓓ People mimicked ancient Greek and Roman architecture during the Renaissance and the Neoclassical Period.

The Influence of Greek and Roman Architecture

Greece and Rome were two of the greatest ancient civilizations, and both have had a lasting influence on history and culture. One area in which people in later civilizations have imitated them is in the realm of architecture. For instance, the construction techniques and architectural styles of both Greece and Rome were revived during the European Renaissance in the fifteenth and sixteenth centuries and were later heavily imitated during the Neoclassical Period in the eighteenth and nineteenth centuries.

32 The word heyday in the passage is closest in meaning to

Ⓐ archetype

Ⓑ creation

Ⓒ zenith

Ⓓ appearance

33 The author's description of the Ionic style in paragraph 2 mentions which of the following?

Ⓐ How it evolved through the altering of the Corinthian style

Ⓑ Where in Greece people tended to use it the most

Ⓒ Why the Greeks made columns in this style so tall and slender

Ⓓ What caused Greeks on the mainland to reject its usage

Glossary

scrolled: ornamental; fancy

[2]→ Greek architecture evolved over a period of hundreds of years. Its heyday was the classical period of Greek history, which lasted from approximately 500 to 100 B.C. Ancient Greek architectural styles are typically divided into three separate groups: Ionic, Doric, and Corinthian. These three styles were based primarily on regional differences. The Doric style was closely associated with mainland Greece while the Ionic style was more closely associated with the Greek islands in the Aegean Sea as well as the Greek colonies located in Asia Minor in the land that is Turkey today. The Corinthian style, meanwhile, is regarded as an offshoot of the Ionic style yet is more elaborate in nature. The differences between the three styles are best observed in the columns used in Greek buildings. Doric columns are rather plain, Ionic columns are noted for their **scrolled** tops, and Corinthian columns have intricate designs. Additionally, Doric columns were short and squat while Ionic and Corinthian columns were taller and slenderer.

34 In paragraph 3, why does the author mention The Pantheon?

Ⓐ To state that the Romans added arches to it after its initial construction

Ⓑ To emphasize the great size of the dome that was placed above it

Ⓒ To note that it was a temple that was constructed in ancient Rome

Ⓓ To provide the name of the ideal Roman building with a dome

35 According to paragraph 3, the Roman style of columns differed from the Greek style in that

Ⓐ the Romans made their columns higher thanks to their use of the arch

Ⓑ the Romans sometimes had all three styles on the same structure

Ⓒ the Romans incorporated domes into their buildings with columns

Ⓓ the Romans only used one style of column throughout their empire

Glossary

aqueduct: an aboveground or belowground structure used to transport water, often long distances

3→ The Romans copied the Greeks in both the design and use of columns although some of their methods differed from the Greeks'. For example, the Romans regularly used all three styles of columns on the same building by employing a different style on each story of the structure. However, the Romans were innovators in their own right. Rome's two greatest contributions to the architectural world were the arch and the dome. Arches and domes permitted the Romans to erect much larger buildings—and with more massive interiors—than the Greeks ever did. Whereas the Greeks often built temples and other structures with open roofs, the Romans constructed domes over their large buildings. The Pantheon in Rome is the greatest example of a Roman domed building. As for arches, they permitted the Romans to build walls with large openings for doorways and windows. Arches were also used to great effect in enormous Roman **aqueducts**, some of which ran for hundreds of kilometers.

36 The word haphazard in the passage is closest in meaning to

Ⓐ decorative

Ⓑ random

Ⓒ dangerous

Ⓓ sturdy

37 The author's description of the Byzantine Empire in paragraph 4 mentions all of the following EXCEPT:

Ⓐ the reason that many of its people began to depart the empire

Ⓑ the threat of destruction that the empire faced from the Turks

Ⓒ the effect on Western architecture that some of its people had

Ⓓ the styles of buildings that were constructed within its cities

[4]→ When Rome fell in 476, knowledge of both Roman and Greek architecture slowly disappeared from the West. But in Italy during the fifteenth century, a revival of Roman and Greek architecture began. During this time, Italian architects, who had previously been influenced by the Gothic style that prevailed in Western Europe, became exposed to information concerning ancient Greek and Roman building methods. This knowledge mostly came from Constantinople, the capital of the Byzantine Empire, which was located in modern-day Turkey and Greece. At that time, the Byzantine Empire was being besieged by the Ottoman Turks and was slowly losing power. Sensing its eventual defeat, many Byzantines fled to the West. While doing so, they took books and other sources of information on ancient Greece and Rome with them. In Italy, where many went, they found students eager to learn. From these refugees, Italian architects learned the secrets of Roman rounded arches and domes. They also began practicing the Roman customs of employing mathematical precision and symmetry in their building designs as they abandoned the haphazard, imprecise style of Gothic architecture. Eventually, this new style captured the imaginations of others in Europe and spread throughout the Western world during the Renaissance.

38 According to paragraph 5, one characteristic of the Neoclassical Period was

Ⓐ the usage of steel to construct libraries and government buildings

Ⓑ homes and other buildings that resembled those constructed in Pompeii

Ⓒ a return to the styles employed during ancient Greece and Rome

Ⓓ an increase in the number of university buildings constructed

5→ A few centuries later during the mid-eighteenth century, the Roman city of Pompeii, which had been consumed whole by ash in the eruption of Mount Vesuvius 1,700 years before, was unearthed. The city's discovery sparked another revival of interest in classical architecture. This initiated the Neoclassical Period. During the eighteenth and nineteenth centuries, many university buildings, libraries, and government buildings were designed and built to resemble ancient Greek and Roman structures. While the use of steel and the constructing of skyscrapers in the twentieth century somewhat lessened the influence of ancient Greece and Rome, their methods, styles, and concepts remain relevant to this day.

39 Look at the four squares [■] that indicate where the following sentence could be added to the passage.

Many even transported water centuries later during medieval times, thereby proving the superior nature of Roman engineering.

Where would the sentence best fit?

Click on a square [■] to add the sentence to the passage.

The Romans copied the Greeks in both the design and use of columns although some of their methods differed from the Greeks'. For example, the Romans regularly used all three styles of columns on the same building by employing a different style on each story of the structure. However, the Romans were innovators in their own right. Rome's two greatest contributions to the architectural world were the arch and the dome. Arches and domes permitted the Romans to erect much larger buildings—and with more massive interiors—than the Greeks ever did. Whereas the Greeks often built temples and other structures with open roofs, the Romans constructed domes over their large buildings. [1] The Pantheon in Rome is the greatest example of a Roman domed building. [2] As for arches, they permitted the Romans to build walls with large openings for doorways and windows. [3] Arches were also used to great effect in enormous Roman **aqueducts**, some of which ran for hundreds of kilometers. [4]

Glossary

aqueduct: an aboveground or belowground structure used to transport water, often long distances

40 Directions: Select the appropriate statements from the answer choices and match them to the architectural style to which they relate. TWO of the answer choices will NOT be used. **This question is worth 3 points.**

Drag your answer choices to the spaces where they belong.
To remove an answer choice, click on it. To review the passage, click on **View Text**.

Answer Choices

1. Knowledge of how to make domes enabled large buildings to be made.
2. Many of their buildings were used by the government or universities.
3. Arches were employed to make structures such as aqueducts.
4. They constructed buildings that were made of steel.
5. They employed mathematical precision in their building designs.
6. The Ionic and Corinthian styles of columns were popular.
7. The temples that they built often had open roofs.

ARCHITECTURAL STYLE

Greece

-
-

Rome

-
-
-

TOEFL® MAP

ACTUAL TEST

Reading 2

CONTINUE

Reading Section Directions

This section measures your ability to understand academic passages in English. You will have **54 minutes** to read and answer questions about **3 passages**. A clock at the top of the screen will show you how much time is remaining.

Most questions are worth 1 point but the last question for each passage is worth more than 1 point. The directions for the last question indicate how many points you may receive.

Some passages include a word or phrase that is **underlined** in blue. Click on the word or phrase to see a definition or an explanation.

When you want to move to the next question, click on **Next**. You may skip questions and go back to them later. If you want to return to previous questions, click on **Back**. You can click on **Reivew** at any time, and the review screen will show you which questions you have answered and which you have not answered. From this review screen, you may go directly to any question you have already seen in the Reading section.

Click on **Continue** to go on.

Types of Precipitation

Precipitation is any form of water that falls to the ground from clouds. Clouds are formed when evaporated water vapor rises, **condenses**, and then attaches itself to dust or salt particles in the atmosphere and subsequently joins with other particles. When a cloud contains too much condensed water, it releases that water, which falls to the ground as liquid, freezing, or frozen precipitation. The type of precipitation that falls depends upon the weather conditions and the temperature.

Liquid precipitation forms in air in which the temperature is above zero degrees Celsius. It has two basic forms: rain and drizzle. Rain is the most common form of precipitation on the planet, yet it does not fall everywhere in equal amounts because some regions get near-constant rainfall while others, such as deserts, may not receive any rainfall for decades. Rain is generally defined as water droplets larger than half a millimeter. It may fall directly from clouds, or it may fall when snow or ice crystals formed in below-freezing temperatures melt while descending through the atmosphere and then transform into rain. As for drizzle, it is comprised of water droplets smaller than half a millimeter. It is common in subtropical regions and over oceans, tends to fall from stratus clouds, which are low-lying, flat, nearly featureless clouds that often combine to form a uniform gray mass across the entire sky, and typically falls in misty and foggy weather conditions.

Freezing precipitation forms in air that has various temperatures at different layers. It comes in two forms: freezing drizzle and freezing rain. Like liquid precipitation, the type of freezing precipitation that falls is determined by the size of the droplets. Both kinds of freezing precipitation occur when snow falls from clouds high in the atmosphere. As the snow passes through warmer air, it completely melts and transforms into water droplets. However, even closer to the ground, there is a colder layer of air, which causes the water droplets to begin turning into ice crystals. There is not enough time for them to freeze completely, so they land as hard droplets of ice crystals. Upon contact with any surface, freezing drizzle and freezing rain can create thin sheets of ice. These are particularly dangerous since they can turn roads into slick surfaces and cover tree branches and power lines with heavy layers of ice. As a result, this ice can knock down branches and power lines, which may result in obstructed roads and blackouts.

Frozen precipitation comes in three main forms: sleet, hail, and snow. Sleet occurs when snow falls through a warmer layer of air but only partially thaws. Then, it reenters a colder layer of air, where the water freezes again, but this time it forms into hard ice pellets rather than snowflakes. Sleet can cause treacherous driving conditions if it covers roads. Hail is formed in large cumulonimbus clouds, which are ones that spawn thunderstorms. Inside a thunderstorm, there are drafts of air rapidly moving up and down through different temperature layers. As the water droplets rise in a thunderstorm formation, they freeze into ice pellets in cold air. The conditions in a thunderstorm cause the pellets repeatedly to ascend and descend. As they do this, they attract more water droplets, which freeze in layers in the colder air. Finally, the layers of ice become too heavy, so the pellets fall to the ground as hail. Hailstones can be heavy and large—up to twelve centimeters in diameter—and regularly damage crops, vehicles, and buildings and injure people and animals.

Snow forms when supercooled water droplets freeze in temperatures between minus eighteen degrees Celsius and thirty-one degrees Celsius. The freezing temperatures form an ice nucleus around which a **lattice** of frozen water creates a snowflake. When the snowflake becomes too heavy, it falls to the ground. Snow often falls from stratus clouds in low-lying layers when ground temperatures are just below freezing. When the clouds are relatively low in altitude, the snow has a better chance of reaching the ground without transforming into a different type of precipitation. When snow falls from clouds high in the atmosphere, it may often transform into liquid or freezing precipitation by the time it reaches the ground.

Glossary

condense: to change from a gaseous state to a liquid or solid one

lattice: a crystal-like pattern

1 According to paragraph 1, precipitation falls to the ground when

Ⓐ the local temperature begins to change

Ⓑ water vapor in the atmosphere condenses

Ⓒ there is too much water within a cloud

Ⓓ clouds form under certain circumstances

2 Why does the author mention stratus clouds in paragraph 2?

Ⓐ To state that they are usually responsible for drizzle

Ⓑ To note that they are found at low levels in the atmosphere

Ⓒ To explain why they are often located above oceans

Ⓓ To claim that they are the causes of foggy and misty weather

3 According to paragraph 2, which of the following is NOT true of rain?

Ⓐ It is one of the two types of liquid precipitation that fall.

Ⓑ Its droplets must be at least half a millimeter in size.

Ⓒ It falls in most places on the Earth but not in the same amounts.

Ⓓ It normally falls from low-altitude stratus clouds.

Glossary

condense: to change from a gaseous state to a liquid or solid one

Types of Precipitation

[1]→ Precipitation is any form of water that falls to the ground from clouds. Clouds are formed when evaporated water vapor rises, **condenses**, and then attaches itself to dust or salt particles in the atmosphere and subsequently joins with other particles. When a cloud contains too much condensed water, it releases that water, which falls to the ground as liquid, freezing, or frozen precipitation. The type of precipitation that falls depends upon the weather conditions and the temperature.

[2]→ Liquid precipitation forms in air in which the temperature is above zero degrees Celsius. It has two basic forms: rain and drizzle. Rain is the most common form of precipitation on the planet, yet it does not fall everywhere in equal amounts because some regions get near-constant rainfall while others, such as deserts, may not receive any rainfall for decades. Rain is generally defined as water droplets larger than half a millimeter. It may fall directly from clouds, or it may fall when snow or ice crystals formed in below-freezing temperatures melt while descending through the atmosphere and then transform into rain. As for drizzle, it is comprised of water droplets smaller than half a millimeter. It is common in subtropical regions and over oceans, tends to fall from stratus clouds, which are low-lying, flat, nearly featureless clouds that often combine to form a uniform gray mass across the entire sky, and typically falls in misty and foggy weather conditions.

4 The word slick in the passage is closest in meaning to

Ⓐ damp

Ⓑ slippery

Ⓒ frozen

Ⓓ oily

5 According to paragraph 3, freezing precipitation falls when

Ⓐ falling snow melts and then begins to freeze before hitting the ground

Ⓑ ice crystals fall at the same time that snow is falling to the ground

Ⓒ rain that is falling to the ground freezes completely in cold weather

Ⓓ ice in clouds high in the sky slightly melts before reaching the ground

3→ Freezing precipitation forms in air that has various temperatures at different layers. It comes in two forms: freezing drizzle and freezing rain. Like liquid precipitation, the type of freezing precipitation that falls is determined by the size of the droplets. Both kinds of freezing precipitation occur when snow falls from clouds high in the atmosphere. As the snow passes through warmer air, it completely melts and transforms into water droplets. However, even closer to the ground, there is a colder layer of air, which causes the water droplets to begin turning into ice crystals. There is not enough time for them to freeze completely, so they land as hard droplets of ice crystals. Upon contact with any surface, freezing drizzle and freezing rain can create thin sheets of ice. These are particularly dangerous since they can turn roads into slick surfaces and cover tree branches and power lines with heavy layers of ice. As a result, this ice can knock down branches and power lines, which may result in obstructed roads and blackouts.

6 The word spawn in the passage is closest in meaning to

Ⓐ produce

Ⓑ forecast

Ⓒ enable

Ⓓ enforce

7 According to paragraph 4, which of the following is true of hail?

Ⓐ It falls when there are thunderstorms in temperatures that are below freezing.

Ⓑ It is occasionally responsible for the deaths of both people and animals.

Ⓒ Stratus and cumulonimbus clouds are both able to create hailstones.

Ⓓ The pellets that form it can cause damage when they strike the ground.

8 Which of the following can be inferred from paragraph 5 about snow?

Ⓐ It accumulates at a much slower rate than rain.

Ⓑ The weather can sometimes be too cold for it to fall.

Ⓒ Only northern regions of the planet ever get snow.

Ⓓ It may fall for either long or short periods of time.

Glossary

lattice: a crystal-like pattern

4→ Frozen precipitation comes in three main forms: sleet, hail, and snow. Sleet occurs when snow falls through a warmer layer of air but only partially thaws. Then, it reenters a colder layer of air, where the water freezes again, but this time it forms into hard ice pellets rather than snowflakes. Sleet can cause treacherous driving conditions if it covers roads. Hail is formed in large cumulonimbus clouds, which are ones that spawn thunderstorms. Inside a thunderstorm, there are drafts of air rapidly moving up and down through different temperature layers. As the water droplets rise in a thunderstorm formation, they freeze into ice pellets in cold air. The conditions in a thunderstorm cause the pellets repeatedly to ascend and descend. As they do this, they attract more water droplets, which freeze in layers in the colder air. Finally, the layers of ice become too heavy, so the pellets fall to the ground as hail. Hailstones can be heavy and large—up to twelve centimeters in diameter—and regularly damage crops, vehicles, and buildings and injure people and animals.

5→ Snow forms when supercooled water droplets freeze in temperatures between minus eighteen degrees Celsius and thirty-one degrees Celsius. The freezing temperatures form an ice nucleus around which a **lattice** of frozen water creates a snowflake. When the snowflake becomes too heavy, it falls to the ground. Snow often falls from stratus clouds in low-lying layers when ground temperatures are just below freezing. When the clouds are relatively low in altitude, the snow has a better chance of reaching the ground without transforming into a different type of precipitation. When snow falls from clouds high in the atmosphere, it may often transform into liquid or freezing precipitation by the time it reaches the ground.

9 Look at the four squares [■] that indicate where the following sentence could be added to the passage.

The former tends to create ones that are smaller than those made by the latter.

Where would the sentence best fit?

Click on a square [■] to add the sentence to the passage.

Freezing precipitation forms in air that has various temperatures at different layers. It comes in two forms: freezing drizzle and freezing rain. Like liquid precipitation, the type of freezing precipitation that falls is determined by the size of the droplets. Both kinds of freezing precipitation occur when snow falls from clouds high in the atmosphere. As the snow passes through warmer air, it completely melts and transforms into water droplets. However, even closer to the ground, there is a colder layer of air, which causes the water droplets to begin turning into ice crystals. There is not enough time for them to freeze completely, so they land as hard droplets of ice crystals. [1] Upon contact with any surface, freezing drizzle and freezing rain can create thin sheets of ice. [2] These are particularly dangerous since they can turn roads into slick surfaces and cover tree branches and power lines with heavy layers of ice. [3] As a result, this ice can knock down branches and power lines, which may result in obstructed roads and blackouts. [4]

VIEW TEXT

PREVIEW

HELP

BACK

NEXT

10 Directions: Select the appropriate statements from the answer choices and match them to the type of precipitation to which they relate. TWO of the answer choices will NOT be used. **This question is worth 4 points.**

Drag your answer choices to the spaces where they belong.
To remove an answer choice, click on it. To review the passage, click on **View Text**.

Answer Choices

1. Can create layers of ice on trees and roads
2. Often falls from stratus clouds above oceans
3. Falls from the highest clouds in the atmosphere
4. May fall to the ground in the form of drizzle or rain
5. Is sometimes formed in cumulonimbus clouds
6. Falls to the ground in the form of snow
7. Happens when the temperature is above freezing
8. May fall so fast that people have difficulty seeing
9. Forms into ice crystals prior to hitting the ground

TYPE OF PRECIPITATION

Liquid Precipitation

-
-
-

Freezing Precipitation

-
-

Frozen Precipitation

-
-

The Economics of the Ayutthaya Kingdom

The temple Wat Chaiwatthanaram in Ayutthaya Province

Modern-day Thailand developed from a series of kingdoms that Europeans called Siam. The most prosperous kingdom was centered on the city of Ayutthaya, one of the world's largest cities during the seventeenth and eighteenth centuries. The Ayutthaya kingdom lasted from the middle of the fourteenth to the late eighteenth century. Its primary city began as a fortified region on a series of islands where several rivers converged. Over time, it became a powerful kingdom and maintained a great deal of influence in Southeast Asia, where it received **tribute** from many smaller, less powerful kingdoms. The people of Ayutthaya called themselves *Thai*, from whence the modern name of the country derives, and were mostly Buddhist. The Ayutthaya economy was agriculturally based and relied upon a mass of peasant farmers who grew rice and provided service labor to their local lords.

With large tracts of arable land and plentiful rainfall, the Ayutthaya region, which was slightly north of the area where Bangkok, Thailand, lies today, virtually always enabled farmers to grow enough food to feed everyone and to have a surplus. This surplus fed the lords of the land and the monks in Buddhist temples, and remaining supplies were sold elsewhere. This trade was maritime in nature and was carried out mostly by immigrant Chinese merchants as the Thai people were essentially tied to the land. They were not slaves since no one owned them, but every Thai peasant was attached to a lord. These lords counted their power in the amount of land they possessed and the number of peasants they controlled, which determined the amount of rice they cultivated. Peasants had to provide corvee labor for their lords. This was a system requiring all peasants to provide free labor for their lords wherever it was needed. This could include working on construction projects or even fighting battles. Chinese immigrants, however, had no such obligations, so they were free to move about the land and to engage in trade.

Rice was the basis of trade, so it was traded for other items, often by utilizing the barter system. There were two primary types of rice cultivation in the region. One was based on a local strain that, when cooked, was **glutinous** and stuck together. A staple of highland farming in Thailand today, this rice grows in shallow water in paddies, where irrigation systems control the amount of water it receives. However, much Ayutthaya land was in the Chao Phraya floodplain, which contains the river system that runs through modern-day Bangkok. This vast region flooded to depths of up to fifty centimeters of water, making it impossible to grow the short-grained rice. Thus sometime in the early years of the Ayutthaya kingdom, the Thais imported from the Bengal region a strain of rice called floating rice. It had longer grains, was not as glutinous as the upland rice, and, most importantly, grew well in deep-water floodplains.

One result of this was a massive alteration in agricultural practices in the Ayutthaya region. Suddenly, much more land could be cultivated and more rice grown, so the kingdom's wealth increased exponentially. Thanks to their newfound riches and their fortified city serving as a power center, the Thais became the most powerful people in Southeast Asia. Over the next several centuries, the territory they controlled grew, and many places were obligated to pay tribute to the Ayutthaya Thai rulers. This was not power based on controlling land in the geographical sense as Europeans understood it; instead, it was based on wealth, influence, and personal relationships between rulers. There were occasional rebellions, and outside powers, normally Chinese and Europeans, tried to influence the kingdom. But for more than four centuries, the Ayutthaya rulers, bolstered by their massive rice production and trade, held sway in the region.

The kingdom's downfall came in the late eighteenth century. Foreign influences, most notably European attempts to gain trade concessions, began dividing the ruling class. A series of internal rebellions, coupled with the usurping of several rulers in a short period of time, weakened the kingdom. When a Burmese army invaded in 1765, the Thais could not resist. The great city of Ayutthaya was captured and burned in 1767 as all of its wealth could still not save it.

Glossary

tribute: a payment given from one sovereign or state to another in return for security or peace

glutinous: sticky

11 According to paragraph 1, which of the following is true of the Ayutthaya kingdom?

Ⓐ It sometimes had to pay tribute to kingdoms in nearby lands.

Ⓑ It was the most powerful kingdom in the world in the 1700s.

Ⓒ It had an economy that was dependent on the farming of crops.

Ⓓ It fortified all of the rivers that flowed throughout its land.

Glossary

tribute: a payment given from one sovereign or state to another in return for security or peace

The Economics of the Ayutthaya Kingdom

[1]➔ Modern-day Thailand developed from a series of kingdoms that Europeans called Siam. The most prosperous kingdom was centered on the city of Ayutthaya, one of the world's largest cities during the seventeenth and eighteenth centuries. The Ayutthaya kingdom lasted from the middle of the fourteenth to the late eighteenth century. Its primary city began as a fortified region on a series of islands where several rivers converged. Over time, it became a powerful kingdom and maintained a great deal of influence in Southeast Asia, where it received **tribute** from many smaller, less powerful kingdoms. The people of Ayutthaya called themselves *Thai*, from whence the modern name of the country derives, and were mostly Buddhist. The Ayutthaya economy was agriculturally based and relied upon a mass of peasant farmers who grew rice and provided service labor to their local lords.

12 The author discusses corvee labor in paragraph 2 in order to

- (A) criticize this system as something that was similar to slavery
- (B) mention why Chinese immigrants were excluded from this system
- (C) explain what kind of work the lords expected from their peasants
- (D) praise the Ayutthaya rulers for the way in which they got free labor

13 According to paragraph 2, when did the people of the Ayutthaya kingdom sell their rice?

- (A) When there was enough left over after feeding every member of society
- (B) When Buddhist monks determined that it was advantageous to do so
- (C) When the rulers of the kingdom needed to raise currency from abroad
- (D) When Chinese merchants requested that they engage in trade with them

14 The author's description of immigrant Chinese merchants in paragraph 2 mentions all of the following EXCEPT:

- (A) why they were better at trading than native Thais
- (B) how wealthy they became from engaging in trade
- (C) how they transported the products that they traded
- (D) which kinds of products they typically traded

[2]→ With large tracts of arable land and plentiful rainfall, the Ayutthaya region, which was slightly north of the area where Bangkok, Thailand, lies today, virtually always enabled farmers to grow enough food to feed everyone and to have a surplus. This surplus fed the lords of the land and the monks in Buddhist temples, and remaining supplies were sold elsewhere. This trade was maritime in nature and was carried out mostly by immigrant Chinese merchants as the Thai people were essentially tied to the land. They were not slaves since no one owned them, but every Thai peasant was attached to a lord. These lords counted their power in the amount of land they possessed and the number of peasants they controlled, which determined the amount of rice they cultivated. Peasants had to provide corvee labor for their lords. This was a system requiring all peasants to provide free labor for their lords wherever it was needed. This could include working on construction projects or even fighting battles. Chinese immigrants, however, had no such obligations, so they were free to move about the land and to engage in trade.

15 According to paragraph 3, the Thais imported rice from another place because

Ⓐ the rice grew much better in the warm temperatures in their land

Ⓑ much of their land was unsuitable for cultivating the native rice

Ⓒ they realized the need to diversify the crops which they grew

Ⓓ there was a desire to raise glutinous rice all throughout the kingdom

[3]→ Rice was the basis of trade, so it was traded for other items, often by utilizing the barter system. There were two primary types of rice cultivation in the region. One was based on a local strain that, when cooked, was **glutinous** and stuck together. A staple of highland farming in Thailand today, this rice grows in shallow water in paddies, where irrigation systems control the amount of water it receives. However, much Ayutthaya land was in the Chao Phraya floodplain, which contains the river system that runs through modern-day Bangkok. This vast region flooded to depths of up to fifty centimeters of water, making it impossible to grow the short-grained rice. Thus sometime in the early years of the Ayutthaya kingdom, the Thais imported from the Bengal region a strain of rice called floating rice. It had longer grains, was not as glutinous as the upland rice, and, most importantly, grew well in deep-water floodplains.

Glossary

glutinous: sticky

16 The word bolstered in the passage is closest in meaning to

Ⓐ impressed
Ⓑ strengthened
Ⓒ approved
Ⓓ overlooked

17 Which of the following can be inferred from paragraph 4 about rice?

Ⓐ Its consumption ensured that the Thai people received enough nutrition.
Ⓑ It was the only crop that grew easily all throughout the Ayutthaya kingdom.
Ⓒ Some neighboring kingdoms offered it to the Ayutthaya as tribute.
Ⓓ It was directly related to the creation of wealth in the Ayutthaya kingdom.

18 According to paragraph 5, the Ayutthaya kingdom was defeated because

Ⓐ an army of outside invaders destroyed its major city
Ⓑ Europeans instigated armed rebellions throughout the land
Ⓒ there was a power struggle between two of its leaders
Ⓓ the Chinese and the Burmese combined forces to conquer it

4→ One result of this was a massive alteration in agricultural practices in the Ayutthaya region. Suddenly, much more land could be cultivated and more rice grown, so the kingdom's wealth increased exponentially. Thanks to their newfound riches and their fortified city serving as a power center, the Thais became the most powerful people in Southeast Asia. Over the next several centuries, the territory they controlled grew, and many places were obligated to pay tribute to the Ayutthaya Thai rulers. This was not power based on controlling land in the geographical sense as Europeans understood it; instead, it was based on wealth, influence, and personal relationships between rulers. There were occasional rebellions, and outside powers, normally Chinese and Europeans, tried to influence the kingdom. But for more than four centuries, the Ayutthaya rulers, bolstered by their massive rice production and trade, held sway in the region.

5→ The kingdom's downfall came in the late eighteenth century. Foreign influences, most notably European attempts to gain trade concessions, began dividing the ruling class. A series of internal rebellions, coupled with the usurping of several rulers in a short period of time, weakened the kingdom. When a Burmese army invaded in 1765, the Thais could not resist. The great city of Ayutthaya was captured and burned in 1767 as all of its wealth could still not save it.

19 Look at the four squares [■] that indicate where the following sentence could be added to the passage.

Among them were kingdoms located in the modern-day countries of Cambodia, Laos, and Myanmar.

Where would the sentence best fit?

Click on a square [■] to add the sentence to the passage.

One result of this was a massive alteration in agricultural practices in the Ayutthaya region. Suddenly, much more land could be cultivated and more rice grown, so the kingdom's wealth increased exponentially. Thanks to their newfound riches and their fortified city serving as a power center, the Thais became the most powerful people in Southeast Asia. Over the next several centuries, the territory they controlled grew, and many places were obligated to pay tribute to the Ayutthaya Thai rulers. [1] This was not power based on controlling land in the geographical sense as Europeans understood it; instead, it was based on wealth, influence, and personal relationships between rulers. [2] There were occasional rebellions, and outside powers, normally Chinese and Europeans, tried to influence the kingdom. [3] But for more than four centuries, the Ayutthaya rulers, bolstered by their massive rice production and trade, held sway in the region. [4]

20 **Directions:** An introductory sentence for a brief summary of the passage is provided below. Complete the summary by selecting the THREE answer choices that express the most important ideas of the passage. Some sentences do not belong because they express ideas that are not presented in the passage or are minor ideas in the passage. **This question is worth 2 points.**

Drag your answer choices to the spaces where they belong.
To remove an answer choice, click on it. To review the passage, click on **View Text**.

The Ayutthaya kingdom dominated its region for several centuries thanks primarily to its cultivation of rice.

-
-
-

Answer Choices

1. When a new strain of rice was imported, the kingdom suddenly increased its power.
2. Ayutthaya farmers grew enough rice to feed all of the people and to sell to people in other lands.
3. The Chao Phraya floodplain covers a small area of the land occupied by the Ayutthaya kingdom.
4. An army from Burma helped end the long reign of power of the Ayutthaya kingdom.
5. Neighboring kingdoms had to pay tribute to the Ayutthaya because of its strength.
6. Chinese merchants were primarily responsible for trading rice to people in foreign lands.

Honeybee Decision Making

Honeybees are a key component in their ecosystems due to their ability to spread pollen, which fertilizes flowers and tree blossoms. They live in colonies called swarms, and each of these resides in a nest called a hive. A typical swarm contains one queen bee, a few male bees, called drones, and thousands of female bees, called workers. During spring, most swarms reach a point where their hives become overpopulated. When this happens to a swarm, it divides into two. Half the honeybees remain in the hive, but they are led by a new queen bee, a daughter of the previous queen bee. The other half follows the old queen bee to locate a new nesting site. The silent manner in which honeybees find a new place for a hive demonstrates they are capable of communicating with one another in a sophisticated manner.

The process of finding a new nesting site begins when the honeybees leaving the colony gather together in a large cloud outside the hive. After a short time, they fly **en masse** to a nearby spot—typically a tree—where they remain until their new nesting location is determined. While the majority of the bees wait, dozens of scout bees depart in all directions to commence the search. When each scout returns to the swarm, it gives a report by performing something that biologists call the **waggle** dance. This ritual dance involves a honeybee moving in a figure-eight pattern in which the middle part of the movement is performed with a side-to-side motion that makes the bee appear as though it is waggling. These movements are the scout bees' way of indicating what they have found to the swarm. A scout bee performs its waggle dance in the direction it wants the swarm to move. For instance, a honeybee that wants the swarm to move north performs its waggle dance to the north of the swarm.

Observations of waggle dances seem to show that each scout divulges the quality of the location it has found through its dancing technique. When there are more movements in a waggle dance, it indicates that the bee has found a good location. Each scout bee that returns begins to perform a waggle dance until there are many bees doing it simultaneously. Then, the scout bees gradually move to where the most aggressive dancers are and start to dance in the same manner. In effect, the scout bees come to an agreement. Eventually, once all of the scouts are dancing in the same manner, the swarm follows them as they depart for the new location.

Close studies done on scout bee waggle dances through the use of video recording equipment indicate that the process of finding, deciding on, and then moving to a new nesting site typically takes around three to five days. In some cases, such as when it rains, the process may take longer since honeybees do not usually move during inclement weather. Scientists have also noted that scouts perform waggle dances for around twelve to sixteen hours a day. During the first part of the decision-making process, no potential nesting sites seem to be embraced by the majority of the scout bees. In one study, for instance, on the first day, the scout bees danced in nine different directions. However, during the middle part of the process as the waggle dances continue, some scout bees stop their dances and join a few of the most aggressively dancing scout bees. Finally, during the third stage of the decision-making process, more and more scout bees abandon their own dances to join others. In virtually every case which biologists have observed, there was ultimately a unanimous decision among the scout bees concerning which direction the swarm should fly.

What remains a mystery to biologists is the mechanism that permits honeybees to reach decisions in such a unique way. Some speculate that it may be a chemical process in the scouts which causes them to lose their eagerness for a particular site when they observe others that seem more enthusiastic about their own sites. In the end, it is nature's way of ensuring the honeybees' survival so that swarms can find locations to build new hives.

Glossary

en masse: as one; as a group

waggle: to move back and forth; to shake

21 The word component in the passage is closest in meaning to

Ⓐ element

Ⓑ leader

Ⓒ organism

Ⓓ predator

22 In paragraph 1, the author implies that honeybees

Ⓐ begin their reproduction cycles during the winter months

Ⓑ can communicate without the ability to vocalize sounds

Ⓒ live in virtually any location that has trees and flowers

Ⓓ sometimes clash with honeybees from other hives

Honeybee Decision Making

1→ Honeybees are a key component in their ecosystems due to their ability to spread pollen, which fertilizes flowers and tree blossoms. They live in colonies called swarms, and each of these resides in a nest called a hive. A typical swarm contains one queen bee, a few male bees, called drones, and thousands of female bees, called workers. During spring, most swarms reach a point where their hives become overpopulated. When this happens to a swarm, it divides into two. Half the honeybees remain in the hive, but they are led by a new queen bee, a daughter of the previous queen bee. The other half follows the old queen bee to locate a new nesting site. The silent manner in which honeybees find a new place for a hive demonstrates they are capable of communicating with one another in a sophisticated manner.

23 The word commence in the passage is closest in meaning to

Ⓐ plan

Ⓑ begin

Ⓒ reveal

Ⓓ decide on

24 In paragraph 2, which of the following is NOT true of the waggle dance?

Ⓐ It involves a bee moving in a figure eight while making other motions.

Ⓑ It indicates the location of a possible place to make a new hive.

Ⓒ It is performed by scout bees that are returning to the swarm.

Ⓓ It is done in the opposite direction the bee wants the swarm to go.

25 According to paragraph 3, what happens while the scout bees are doing the waggle dance?

Ⓐ The rest of the hive watches the bees perform.

Ⓑ Some scout bees start following other bees' movements.

Ⓒ More scout bees fly off to search for better locations.

Ⓓ All of the bees in the hive begin to dance the same way.

Glossary

en masse: as one; as a group

waggle: to move back and forth; to shake

2→ The process of finding a new nesting site begins when the honeybees leaving the colony gather together in a large cloud outside the hive. After a short time, they fly **en masse** to a nearby spot—typically a tree—where they remain until their new nesting location is determined. While the majority of the bees wait, dozens of scout bees depart in all directions to commence the search. When each scout returns to the swarm, it gives a report by performing something that biologists call the **waggle** dance. This ritual dance involves a honeybee moving in a figure-eight pattern in which the middle part of the movement is performed with a side-to-side motion that makes the bee appear as though it is waggling. These movements are the scout bees' way of indicating what they have found to the swarm. A scout bee performs its waggle dance in the direction it wants the swarm to move. For instance, a honeybee that wants the swarm to move north performs its waggle dance to the north of the swarm.

3→ Observations of waggle dances seem to show that each scout divulges the quality of the location it has found through its dancing technique. When there are more movements in a waggle dance, it indicates that the bee has found a good location. Each scout bee that returns begins to perform a waggle dance until there are many bees doing it simultaneously. Then, the scout bees gradually move to where the most aggressive dancers are and start to dance in the same manner. In effect, the scout bees come to an agreement. Eventually, once all of the scouts are dancing in the same manner, the swarm follows them as they depart for the new location.

26 Which of the sentences below best expresses the essential information in the highlighted sentence in the passage? *Incorrect* answer choices change the meaning in important ways or leave out essential information.

(A) Scientists have managed to record some of the waggle dances that the scout bees perform for the hive.

(B) Videos of waggle dances show that the entire process of locating a new hive takes a few days.

(C) It takes the scout bees anywhere from three to five days to come to an agreement after they start dancing.

(D) Once the scout bees depart the hive, they return and start doing the waggle dance after several days.

27 According to paragraph 4, which of the following is true of the waggle dance?

(A) It is performed by the scout bees no matter how bad the weather.

(B) It takes anywhere from twelve to sixteen hours to complete.

(C) It is only finished when the queen makes the ultimate decision.

(D) It is a multistage process that can take some time to complete.

4→ Close studies done on scout bee waggle dances through the use of video recording equipment indicate that the process of finding, deciding on, and then moving to a new nesting site typically takes around three to five days. In some cases, such as when it rains, the process may take longer since honeybees do not usually move during inclement weather. Scientists have also noted that scouts perform waggle dances for around twelve to sixteen hours a day. During the first part of the decision-making process, no potential nesting sites seem to be embraced by the majority of the scout bees. In one study, for instance, on the first day, the scout bees danced in nine different directions. However, during the middle part of the process as the waggle dances continue, some scout bees stop their dances and join a few of the most aggressively dancing scout bees. Finally, during the third stage of the decision-making process, more and more scout bees abandon their own dances to join others. In virtually every case which biologists have observed, there was ultimately a unanimous decision among the scout bees concerning which direction the swarm should fly.

28 According to paragraph 5, why might scout bees stop doing their own versions of the waggle dance?

Ⓐ Something in their bodies makes them more interested in another bee's dancing.

Ⓑ The scouts that dance more aggressively release pheromones that the bees sense.

Ⓒ They become exhausted after dancing for several hours, so they take a break.

Ⓓ The bees instinctively realize where the ideal spot for the new hive should be.

[5]→ What remains a mystery to biologists is the mechanism that permits honeybees to reach decisions in such a unique way. Some speculate that it may be a chemical process in the scouts which causes them to lose their eagerness for a particular site when they observe others that seem more enthusiastic about their own sites. In the end, it is nature's way of ensuring the honeybees' survival so that swarms can find locations to build new hives.

29 Look at the four squares [■] that indicate where the following sentence could be added to the passage.

One reason for this is that water on honeybees' wings can make it difficult for them to fly and to remain aloft.

Where would the sentence best fit?

Click on a square [■] to add the sentence to the passage.

1 Close studies done on scout bee waggle dances through the use of video recording equipment indicate that the process of finding, deciding on, and then moving to a new nesting site typically takes around three to five days. **2** In some cases, such as when it rains, the process may take longer since honeybees do not usually move during inclement weather. **3** Scientists have also noted that scouts perform waggle dances for around twelve to sixteen hours a day. **4** During the first part of the decision-making process, no potential nesting sites seem to be embraced by the majority of the scout bees. In one study, for instance, on the first day, the scout bees danced in nine different directions. However, during the middle part of the process as the waggle dances continue, some scout bees stop their dances and join a few of the most aggressively dancing scout bees. Finally, during the third stage of the decision-making process, more and more scout bees abandon their own dances to join others. In virtually every case which biologists have observed, there was ultimately a unanimous decision among the scout bees concerning which direction the swarm should fly.

30 **Directions:** An introductory sentence for a brief summary of the passage is provided below. Complete the summary by selecting the THREE answer choices that express the most important ideas of the passage. Some sentences do not belong because they express ideas that are not presented in the passage or are minor ideas in the passage. **This question is worth 2 points.**

Drag your answer choices to the spaces where they belong.
To remove an answer choice, click on it. To review the passage, click on **View Text**.

A honeybee swarm determines the new location of its hive according to how its scout bees perform the waggle dance.

-
-
-

Answer Choices

1. Scientists call it the waggle dance because it appears as though the scouts are dancing while they fly.
2. The scout bees move in ways that indicate the direction of the possible hive location that they have found.
3. Honeybees have an important role in the environment in that they pollinate numerous flowers and blossoms.
4. The scouting and the waggle dance can take a swarm of honeybees up to five days before they make their decision.
5. When a hive has too many bees, a new queen appears, and the old queen leads some hive members to a new location.
6. During the waggle dance, bees stop doing their own dances and begin to follow other bees doing their own dances.

TOEFL® MAP

ACTUAL TEST

Reading 2

Answers and Explanations

Actual Test 01

p.13

Answers

1 Ⓒ 2 Ⓑ 3 Ⓐ 4 Ⓓ 5 Ⓒ
6 Ⓒ 7 Ⓓ 8 Ⓐ 9 2
10 2, 4, 6

11 Ⓓ 12 Ⓒ 13 Ⓐ 14 Ⓑ 15 Ⓐ
16 Ⓓ 17 Ⓒ 18 Ⓐ 19 4
20 1, 5, 6

21 Ⓓ 22 Ⓐ 23 Ⓒ 24 Ⓑ 25 Ⓒ
26 Ⓐ 27 Ⓒ 28 Ⓐ 29 4
30 Short-Day Plant: 1, 4, 5 Long-Day Plant: 2, 3

Explanations

Passage 1

p.15

1 **Vocabulary Question** | When attempts to improve the service fell prey to a variety of problems, they were harmed by these different problems.

2 **Sentence Simplification Question** | The sentence points out that the colonists used places in port cities to have mail be delivered to from across the ocean in Europe. This thought is best expressed in the sentence in answer choice Ⓑ.

3 **Rhetorical Purpose Question** | In explaining the role of Richard Fairbanks' tavern in the Massachusetts Bay Colony, the author writes, "For instance, in the Massachusetts Bay Colony in 1639, a law calling for all incoming mail to be delivered to Richard Fairbanks's tavern in Boston was enacted. It was a popular gathering place which most local people were familiar with, so it served this purpose well. Fairbanks was permitted to collect one penny for each letter a person received as this served as a kind of early postage stamp system."

4 **Vocabulary Question** | When rates were not uniform throughout the colonies, they were not identical but were instead different.

5 **Factual Question** | The author writes, "King William took a firm hand in 1692 by setting up a colony-wide postal system when he gave a patent to Thomas Neale to serve as the postmaster general for twenty-one years."

6 **Inference Question** | When the author writes, "Serving the British crown in this manner became odious to colonists as the revolutionary spirit, which would result in the colonies rebelling against Britain, grew over time. In many towns, there was a crown post office and a colonial one, which was more popular with the Americans," it can be inferred that a large number of American colonists disliked using the crown postal system.

7 **Rhetorical Purpose Question** | The author credits George Washington with establishing what would become the United States Postal System in writing, "Then, in 1792, President George Washington signed a law establishing the United States Post Office Department, which later became the United States Postal Service."

8 **Factual Question** | About Benjamin Franklin, the passage reads, "Then, in 1753, Benjamin Franklin was appointed deputy postmaster general for the northern colonies," and, "Franklin himself was removed from office in 1774 when his association with the growing rebellion movement made the crown sour on him. When the American Revolution began in 1775, Franklin was the obvious choice to serve as the American postmaster general. A new system was enacted by the American Congress on July 25, 1775."

9 **Insert Text Question** | The sentence before the second square reads, "Postal riders traveled on long routes that were rough and, at times, dangerous, especially during inclement weather." The sentence to be added notes that some of the postal riders were attacked while others were robbed. Thus the two sentences go well together.

10 **Prose Summary Question** | The summary sentence notes that there were certain developments in the postal system in the American colonies, and these resulted in the establishment of the United States Postal Service. This thought is best described in answer choices 2, 4, and 6. Answer choices 3 and 5 are minor points, so they are incorrect answers. Answer choice 1 contains information not included in the passage, so it is also wrong.

Passage 2

p.23

11 **Factual Question** | The author writes, "Their territories are where they obtain their food sources, so without these lands, they would perish."

12 Negative Factual Question | About animals' territory, the author writes, "In Yellowstone National Park, for instance, wolf packs consisting of between five to twenty-five members claim large regions of hilly, forested land and attack any wolves from rival packs that enter their territory. Lions, which live in groups called prides, act similarly while living on the savannahs of Africa." So while wolves claim forested land, it is lions—not wolves—that claim grassy plains such as savannahs.

13 Vocabulary Question | When cats impart their scents onto various objects, they convey their scents.

14 Factual Question | About cats marking their territory, it is written, "Meanwhile, members of the cat family, from tiny domestic cats to the largest tigers, rub their faces or flanks against objects, which imparts their scents onto them and thereby marks their territory."

15 Vocabulary Question | When an animal is unmolested while in another animal's territory, it is unopposed by the animal that claims the land.

16 Factual Question | The author declares, "Yet the pride males do not always fight to the death; if they sense they are losing, they may flee and allow the unattached males to take over."

17 Rhetorical Purpose Question | In writing about cheetahs and leopards, the author points out, "Occasionally, males and females of the same species occupy different territories. Male and female cheetahs and leopards do this as they travel in small groups which are solely male or female. When cheetahs and leopards cross into another's territory, they do so for the purpose of mating."

18 Inference Question | The author writes, "In some cases, the costs of defending a territory can outweigh the benefits. Animals may expend a massive amount of energy while defending their territory. They may suffer injuries or even be killed." Since animals can use energy, suffer injuries, and be killed, the author is implying that animals do not always benefit when they defend their land.

19 Insert Text Question | The sentence before the fourth square reads, "Deer have special glands they use to secrete substances indicating their territory." The sentence to be added describes the glands that rabbits have on their bodies. It also begins with "similarly," which helps make a connection between the two sentences. Thus the two sentences go well together.

20 Prose Summary Question | The summary sentence notes that animals claim territory and then fight other animals to protect it. This thought is best described in answer choices [1], [5], and [6]. Answer choices [2] and [3] are minor points, so they are incorrect answers. Answer choice [4] contains information not mentioned in the passage, so it is also incorrect.

Passage 3

p.31

21 Vocabulary Question | When a plant propagates, it spreads to other places.

22 Factual Question | The passage reads, "However, it has now been established through extensive experimentation that short-day plants flower depending upon their level of darkness exposure while long-day plants flower based upon the amount of light they are exposed to."

23 Sentence Simplification Question | The sentence points out that the amount of sunlight plants growing at high altitude receive is determined by the season while plants growing at the equator get a constant amount of light and darkness. This thought is best expressed in the sentence in answer choice (C).

24 Inference Question | In writing, "Light exposure can also be adjusted artificially by the use of high-energy lighting systems for greater light exposure or extensive coverings to simulate darkness. These methods are regularly employed in commercial greenhouses to influence the flowering of plants that normally would not bloom under natural conditions at certain times of the year," the author implies that people can use greenhouses to grow plants in seasons when the plants would not normally grow.

25 Vocabulary Question | When the sun is concealed by clouds or an eclipse, it is covered.

26 Negative Factual Question | There is no mention in the passage of the number of hours of darkness per day that short-day plants need for their seeds to germinate.

27 Rhetorical Purpose Question | The author writes, "Some common long-day plants are asters, lettuce, wheat, poppies, spinach, and potatoes. At high latitudes, these long-day plants flower when they are exposed to more than twelve hours of sunlight."

28 Factual Question | It is written, "Another factor which influences the flowering response of long-day plants is the presence of gibberellic acid. It is a natural hormone which is found in most plants and prompts the accelerated growth of plant cells."

29 **Insert Text Question** | The sentence before the fourth square reads, "These are called day-neutral plants, and their flowering response is based on their age." The sentence to be added describes what happens to day-neutral plants as they become older. Thus the two sentences go well together.

30 **Fill in a Table Question** | Regarding short-day plants, the author writes, "At high latitudes, short-day plants mostly flower in spring and autumn, which is when daylight exposure is fewer than twelve hours," and, "In short-day plants, it has no influence whatsoever on when plants flower." The author also notes, "Short-day plants flower when exposed to fewer than twelve hours of light per day." As for long-day plants, the author writes, "Unlike with short-day plants, flashes of light during hours of darkness actually stimulate flower growth. Therefore, they flower more efficiently during the long daylight hours of late spring and summer."

Actual Test 02

p.39

Answers

1 Ⓓ 2 Ⓑ 3 Ⓑ 4 Ⓒ 5 Ⓓ
6 Ⓐ 7 Ⓓ 8 Ⓓ 9 4
10 2, 4, 6

11 Ⓑ 12 Ⓒ 13 Ⓒ 14 Ⓐ 15 Ⓓ
16 Ⓐ 17 Ⓐ 18 Ⓑ 19 2
20 2, 3, 6

21 Ⓐ 22 Ⓒ 23 Ⓑ 24 Ⓑ 25 Ⓓ
26 Ⓑ 27 Ⓒ 28 Ⓐ 29 3
30 Full-Length Portrait: 3, 6, 9 Half-Length Portrait: 1, 8 Bust-View Portrait: 2, 4

31 Ⓐ 32 Ⓑ 33 Ⓑ 34 Ⓐ 35 Ⓐ
36 Ⓓ 37 Ⓐ 38 Ⓑ 39 2
40 2, 5, 6

Explanations

Passage 1

p.41

1 **Sentence Simplification Question** | The sentence points out that plants extract nitrogen form the soil while animals can get it in two separate ways. This thought is best expressed by the sentence in answer choice Ⓓ.

2 **Vocabulary Question** | When something is subjected to industrial procedures, it is exposed to them.

3 **Factual Question** | The author writes, "These fall to the ground when it rains. Some nitrogen compounds are introduced to the atmosphere by pollution created by vehicles and factories; these too may fall to the ground when it rains."

4 **Factual Question** | During the author's description of the decay stage, it is noted, "At some point, the animals' metabolisms create organic nitrogen compounds which are expelled from the body as waste. This organic waste matter must then be broken down by bacteria, which convert it into ammonia."

5 **Negative Factual Question** | About nitrates, the passage reads, "In some instances, plant roots directly absorb ammonia from the soil, but most depend upon bacteria to create nitrates. Plants can then make use of them to grow." However, there is no mention of the manner in which the nitrates are used by plants.

6 **Factual Question** | The author declares, "Some of these nitrates can cause problems in that they are easily soluble in water and thus often enter lakes, streams, and rivers. High nitrate levels in water may result in excessive algae growth."

7 **Factual Question** | About denitrification, the author writes, "They take in nitrates and later expel them as N_2, the gaseous form of nitrogen, which then returns to the atmosphere to complete the nitrogen cycle."

8 **Vocabulary Question** | When something does not keep pace with another thing, then it occurs too slowly.

9 **Insert Text Question** | The sentence before the fourth square reads, "High nitrate levels in water may result in excessive algae growth, which can dramatically affect aquatic life." The sentence to be added mentions that fish, which are "aquatic life," get no oxygen so die in great numbers. Thus the two sentences go well together.

10 **Prose Summary Question** | The summary sentence notes that the nitrogen cycle involves the removal of

nitrogen from the air, its use by plants and animals, and then its return to the air. This thought is best described in answer choices [2], [4], and [6]. Answer choices [1], [3], and [5] are minor points, so they are incorrect answers.

Passage 2

p.49

11 **Factual Question** | The author points out, "The first business that became industrialized was the textile industry. In fact, much of the machinery built early in the Industrial Revolution was designed specifically for the making of textiles."

12 **Reference Question** | The "it" that had become the leading material used in the manufacturing of textiles was cotton.

13 **Factual Question** | It is written, "Even after the textile industry became industrialized, most clothing continued to be made by hand until the sewing machine was invented in the nineteenth century."

14 **Vocabulary Question** | When people are ingenious, they are resourceful and come up with new ideas.

15 **Rhetorical Purpose Question** | About the flying shuttle, the author mentions, "The flying shuttle, which let weavers make wider cloth much faster than before."

16 **Inference Question** | The author writes, "Numerous other cities saw factories erected in them as large parts of England became industrialized seemingly overnight." In noting that England "became industrialized seemingly overnight," the author implies that factories in England were built very quickly.

17 **Sentence Simplification Question** | The sentence points out that the machines were efficient, but many textile workers opposed using the machines and sometimes even became violent because of them. This thought is best expressed in the sentence in answer choice (A).

18 **Factual Question** | It is written, "Sheep farmers, who depended on the textile industry by selling their wool to make cloth, opposed the change to cotton and got legislation passed by Parliament that restricted its importation from foreign lands."

19 **Insert Text Question** | The sentence before the second square reads, "The ultimate invention that sent the entire textile industry propelling toward industrialization was the perfection of the steam engine in the late eighteenth century." The sentence to be added notes that James Watts was responsible for "this feat," which refers to the perfecting of the steam engine. Thus the two sentences go well together.

20 **Prose Summary Question** | The summary sentence notes that the Industrial Revolution caused many changes in the textile industry in England. This thought is best described in answer choices [2], [3], and [6]. Answer choices [1] and [5] are minor points, so they are incorrect answers. Answer choice [4] contains wrong information, so it is also incorrect.

Passage 3

p.57

21 **Inference Question** | In writing, "Centuries later during the Middle Ages and the Renaissance, portrait painting became more prominent and private. Wealthy patrons commissioned artists to paint their images, which frequently flattered the paying subject instead of displaying any unattractive details," the author implies that sometimes portraits painted in the Renaissance did not depict people as they actually looked.

22 **Vocabulary Question** | When people flaunt their status, they show off their rank to others.

23 **Negative Factual Question** | The author notes, "One famous example of a full-length portrait is Thomas Gainsborough's *The Blue Boy* (1770), which was painted in oil." The painting was therefore made in the eighteenth century, not the seventeenth century.

24 **Sentence Simplification Question** | The sentence points out that one side of a subject's face is shown since the subject is painted at an angle. This thought is best expressed by the sentence in answer choice (B).

25 **Vocabulary Question** | The enigmatic smile on the *Mona Lisa* is a mysterious one.

26 **Factual Question** | The passage reads, "This type of portrait painting became especially popular during the Renaissance, and while many artists pocketed commissions from the wealthy and powerful, they also painted everyday people by using the half-length portrait form."

27 **Rhetorical Purpose Question** | The author notes, "In the past, Dutch grandmasters did not consider works of that nature to be portrait art, but they instead called them tronies, a Dutch word meaning "faces."

28 **Factual Question** | It is written, "One is called the kit-cat portrait, which is a half-length portrait that

additionally includes the subject's hands in the work. The name is derived from the famous London gentleman's Kit Cat Club, where every single one of the club's members had their portrait done in this style."

29 **Insert Text Question** | The sentence before the third square reads, "One of the most famous bust-view portraits is *Girl with a Pearl Earring* (1665) by Dutch master Johannes Vermeer." The sentence to be added notes that Vincent van Gogh also painted a large number of bust-view portraits. Thus the two sentences go well together.

30 **Fill in a Table Question** | Regarding full-length portraits, the author writes, "This style came into vogue in Europe during the seventeenth century as individuals of means enjoyed displaying themselves in full-length portraits to flaunt their status. Of significance in full-length portraits is the harmony between the subject and the background, which tends to be fairly colorful with deep, rich backgrounds. One famous example of a full-length portrait is Thomas Gainsborough's *The Blue Boy* (1770), which was painted in oil." As for half-length portraits, the author notes, "Arguably the most famous painting in this genre is the *Mona Lisa* (1503-1506) by Leonardo da Vinci," and, "Half-length portraits depict the upper body from the waist to the head, show the subject either standing or sitting, and feature backgrounds with more muted color schemes than those that are displayed in full-length portraits." About bust-view portraits, the author writes, "In the past, Dutch grandmasters did not consider works of that nature to be portrait art, but they instead called them tronies, a Dutch word meaning "faces," and these works were often painting of common people featuring exaggerated expressions," and, "Such pictures are done with watercolors and oils as well as with pencils in sketches."

Passage 4

p.64

31 **Vocabulary Question** | When certain classes of people ensured that their children were educated, they guaranteed that they received some schooling.

32 **Negative Factual Question** | The author writes, "Despite the facts that education was stressed in the Renaissance and that many universities were founded then, most children—regardless of their social status—were educated in their homes in some manner." Thus more people learned at their homes than at universities.

33 **Rhetorical Purpose Question** | In pointing out how some children learned during the Renaissance, the author declares, "The children of wealthier merchants frequently received some formal education from private tutors in their homes as they at least learned to read, write, and do mathematics since it was expected that they would take part in their family businesses."

34 **Inference Question** | The author notes, "If they survived infancy, boys farmed the land with their fathers or learned their fathers' trades." In writing "if they survived infancy," the author implies that many peasant children died when they were young.

35 **Vocabulary Question** | When children were educated in all facets of life, they learned about all of its many aspects.

36 **Factual Question** | The author writes, "A few were occasionally trained to become members of the clergy at either churches or monasteries, but, for the most part, only upper-class youths received this type of education. During the Renaissance, merchants and noblemen with many sons usually sent their youngest to receive religious training."

37 **Inference Question** | The author notes, "University students were expected to study the works of the ancient Greeks and Romans, particularly those of Aristotle." By singling out Aristotle by name as a person whose works were studied, the author implies that Aristotle was greatly respected during the Renaissance.

38 **Factual Question** | It is written, "The emergence of nation-states and the onset of democracy during these two centuries led reformers to push for mass education for all children regardless of their social status."

39 **Insert Text Question** | The sentence before the second square reads, "These children began their studies at young ages, were trained in Latin and sometimes Greek, and learned the Bible as well as the ceremonial aspects of church life." The sentence to be added notes that these children later became priests as adults. The word "consequently" creates a cause-effect relationship between the two sentences. Thus the two sentences go well together.

40 **Prose Summary Question** | The summary sentence notes that all classes of people were affected by the education methods of the European Renaissance for centuries. This thought is best described in answer choices [2], [5], and [6]. Answer choices [3] and [4] are minor points, so they are incorrect answers. Answer choice [1] contains information not mentioned in the passage, so it is also incorrect.

Actual Test 03

p.73

Answers

1 Ⓓ	2 Ⓒ	3 Ⓒ	4 Ⓐ	5 Ⓒ
6 Ⓓ	7 Ⓐ	8 Ⓑ	9 4	
10 2, 3, 5				
11 Ⓒ	12 Ⓓ	13 Ⓐ	14 Ⓓ	15 Ⓓ
16 Ⓒ	17 Ⓓ	18 Ⓐ	19 2	
20 2, 4, 5				
21 Ⓐ	22 Ⓑ	23 Ⓓ	24 Ⓐ	25 Ⓒ
26 Ⓐ	27 Ⓑ	28 Ⓒ	29 1	
30 Cause: 3, 4, 5 Effect: 2, 7				

Explanations

Passage 1

p.75

1 **Vocabulary Question** | An untamed region is a place that is wild and that has little or no signs of human civilization.

2 **Factual Question** | About the primitive tribes, the author writes, "Consequently, large numbers of the people who live in these areas lead a virtual Stone Age existence, and some South American tribes have not yet even made contact with the outside world." Since some have not made contact with the outside world, then they know nothing about modern civilization.

3 **Inference Question** | The author mentions, "While their simple lives may seem ideal to some, there remains an undercurrent of violence between some tribes, and many practiced headhunting well into the twentieth century." In noting that there is "an undercurrent of violence between some tribes," the author implies that tribes sometimes go to war against one another.

4 **Rhetorical Purpose Question** | The author provides a description of the Waroa in writing, "One tribe, the Waroa, lives around the delta of the Orinoco River in Venezuela and has around 20,000 members. The Waroa were a viable community prior to the Spanish arrival in the 1500s and have been able to maintain much of their cultural identity up to the present day."

5 **Negative Factual Question** | About the Assurini, the author comments, "They occupy one small region that lies between tributaries of the Amazon River and survive by growing crops, fishing, and hunting." The author mentions that they grow crops, but there is no mention of which crops they grow.

6 **Negative Factual Question** | The author writes, "The Europeans drove lots of tribes away from their homelands and into the jungles. There, the people learned to survive and how to make do with whatever resources they could find." The Europeans forced the natives to live in the jungle but did not teach them how to survive there.

7 **Vocabulary Question** | When the tribes tried to ward off the developers encroaching on their lands, they tried to fight them off in order to keep them away.

8 **Factual Question** | The author notes, "However, in recent decades, the lands and the rights of these tribes have gradually come to be protected by the law. Most South American countries have made efforts to protect their native tribes. In Brazil, for instance, there are many tribal reservations—mostly in the Amazon Rainforest—where the lands of the tribes are protected."

9 **Insert Text Question** | The sentence before the fourth square reads, "The Assurini have avoided disappearing by intermarrying with people from other tribes." The sentence to be added notes that this—the intermarrying—is common for small tribes in South America. Thus the two sentences go well together.

10 **Prose Summary Question** | The summary sentence notes that large numbers of primitive tribes live throughout South America. This thought is best described in answer choices 2, 3, and 5. Answer choices 4 and 6 are minor points, so they are incorrect answers. Answer choice 1 contains wrong information, so it is also incorrect.

Passage 2

p.83

11 **Vocabulary Question** | When sulfur has hues, it has different shades or colors.

12 **Negative Factual Question** | In paragraph 1, the author only names Io as one of the four Galilean moons. Throughout the entire passage, the names of two others—Europa and Ganymede—are given, but the name of the fourth moon is only provided in the Insert Text question.

13 **Vocabulary Question** | An orbital track that is eccentric

is peculiar.

14 **Factual Question** | The author writes, "Io's own rotational period is such that one side of it continually faces Jupiter. This is similar to the manner in which the moon orbits Earth."

15 **Inference Question** | The passage notes, "Its orbital eccentricity is a result of powerful gravitational forces from Jupiter as well as from the two nearest Galilean moons, Europa and Ganymede. Io is caught in between the gravitational effects of these heavenly bodies, so its orbital path is affected, and there are a large number of tidal effects on its interior as well." The author points out that Io is between Jupiter on one side and Europa and Ganymede on the other, so Io must orbit more closely to Jupiter than the other two moons.

16 **Rhetorical Purpose Question** | The author writes, "What astronomers agree on is that Io's interior is extremely active. This is due to a process called tidal heating, which is the result of the effects of the gravitational pull of Jupiter and some nearby moons. Because of tidal heating, Io is highly volcanically active with a surface that has numerous active and extinct volcanoes."

17 **Factual Question** | It is mentioned, "The explanation for its lack of impact craters soon became evident. The incessant volcanic activity has resulted in Io's surface being constantly reshaped since the volcanic eruptions either fill in or cover up any impact craters on the moon."

18 **Negative Factual Question** | In describing the material ejected by Io's volcanoes, the author comments, "Even more of this material—at a rate of about one ton a second—gets sucked up by Jupiter's magnetic field. This material is mainly comprised of ionized elements such as sulfur, oxygen, and chlorine." Thus the material that is ionized is sucked up by Jupiter's magnetic field; it does not fall back to the moon's surface.

19 **Insert Text Question** | The sentence before the second square reads, "Of its seventy-nine moons, most are small, but four are rather sizable as they are nearly as large as some of the solar system's smaller planets." The sentence to be added notes that Ganymede is bigger than Mercury and almost the same size as Mars. Those are two of the solar system's smaller planets. Thus the two sentences go well together.

20 **Prose Summary Question** | The summary sentence notes that the volcanic activity on Jupiter's moon Io contributes to its features. This thought is best described in answer choices [2], [4], and [5]. Answer choices [3] and [6] are minor points, so they are incorrect answers. Answer choice [1] contains information not mentioned in the passage, so it is also incorrect.

Passage 3

p.90

21 **Vocabulary Question** | When London was primed to be the center of unprecedented growth, it was positioned to grow.

22 **Factual Question** | The author notes, "But the fall of the Roman Empire in the fifth century resulted in the Roman abandonment of Britain, so, for some time, London was virtually empty."

23 **Rhetorical Purpose Question** | It is written, "During the mid and late Middle Ages, London expanded as both a town and economic center when the European world became more connected due to increased shipbuilding and maritime trade."

24 **Factual Question** | About mercantilism, the author writes, "At that time, mercantilism was the reigning economic philosophy in Britain. It called for the protecting of British trade between the home island and its colonies. The government accordingly enacted laws imposing taxes on imports and protecting British trade. The main objectives were to attain a trade surplus and to amass gold and silver."

25 **Inference Question** | The passage reads, "One result of this mercantilist philosophy was that extraordinary wealth poured into London. At the center of British economic activity, London grew rapidly and expanded in size and population." In noting that London gained much wealth and was at the center of British economic activity, it can be inferred that much of Great Britain also benefitted financially from mercantilism.

26 **Reference Question** | The "It" that was based in London was the British East India Company.

27 **Vocabulary Question** | When investors were given capital, they were provided with funds from investors.

28 **Negative Factual Question** | The only mention of wars in the paragraph is, "Unfortunately, the onset of World War I in 1914 brought this entire system to a halt." This war was in the twentieth century, not the nineteenth.

29 **Insert Text Question** | The sentence before the first square reads, "It was based in London, so treasures from India made their way there." The sentence to be

added notes that the company conducted business in other British colonies. The important word that connects the two sentences is "also." Thus the two sentences go well together.

30 **Fill in a Table Question** | Regarding the causes of the economic development of London, the author writes, "The British East India Company, for instance, was granted a monopoly on trade in India. It was based in London, so treasures from India made their way there. The company had to raise money for its initial ventures, so it sold shares of stock that gave investors pieces of the wealth it was amassing. This helped establish the London Stock Exchange, which had its humble beginnings in London's coffee shops, where merchants gathered to trade stocks and to learn global financial news," and, "At that time, mercantilism was the reigning economic philosophy in Britain. It called for the protecting of British trade between the home island and its colonies." The author also writes, "Located on the Thames River with easy access to the North Sea, London became a shipping and commerce center." As for the causes of the economic development of London, the author notes, "The development of fast steamships, the telegraph, and the telephone in the nineteenth century connected London with the entire world, so it became the world's financial center," and, "During the mid and late Middle Ages, London expanded as both a town and economic center when the European world became more connected due to increased shipbuilding and maritime trade. London was poised to take advantage of this thanks to its geographical location and political power. The city continued to grow in size and wealth throughout the medieval period as well as during the Renaissance."

Actual Test 04

p.97

Answers

1 (C) 2 (A) 3 (C) 4 (D) 5 (B)
6 (C) 7 (D) 8 (A) 9 [1]
10 [4], [5], [6]

11 (A) 12 (D) 13 (A) 14 (C) 15 (A)
16 (A) 17 (B) 18 (D) 19 [3]
20 [1], [2], [4]

21 (B) 22 (D) 23 (B) 24 (B) 25 (B)
26 (B) 27 (B) 28 (B) 29 [3]
30 Optical Telescope: [3], [5], [6] Radio Telescope: [1], [4]

31 (B) 32 (D) 33 (C) 34 (B) 35 (B)
36 (A) 37 (C) 38 (D) 39 [4]
40 [2], [4], [6]

Explanations

Passage 1

p.99

1 **Vocabulary Question** | As the life of the longleaf pine tree encompasses several stages, it includes these various stages.

2 **Vocabulary Question** | Animals partial to eating the seeds are fond of consuming them.

3 **Negative Factual Question** | The author mentions nothing about how high the longleaf pine tree may grow.

4 **Rhetorical Purpose Question** | The paragraph about the grass stage focuses on the first stage of growth of the longleaf pine tree and what happens during it.

5 **Factual Question** | The passage notes, "The trees experience a growth spurt and often become a meter or two higher in merely a few months' time." Since the trees experience a growth spurt, they grow faster than normal.

6 **Sentence Simplification Question** | The sentence points out that longleaf pines more than 2.5 meters high and in the sapling stage have tough bark, so they are almost never killed in forest fires. This thought is best expressed in the sentence in answer choice (C).

7 **Inference Question** | The author mentions, "Longleaf pines do not fully mature until they have been alive for

around three decades. At that point, the mature stage begins, and they produce cones with fertile seeds." Since the seeds are fertile, it is implied that they can reproduce.

8 **Factual Question** | The author declares, "There are longleaf pine nurseries in which trees are raised and then reintroduced to forests whenever they are healthy enough to survive in the wild."

9 **Insert Text Question** | The sentence before the first square reads, "Most longleaf pines live to be around 300 years old, yet there are documented cases of some living for nearly 500 years." The sentence to be added notes that the trees can die for various reasons prior to reaching that age. The phrase "of course" is the key phrase that joins the two sentences. Thus the two sentences go well together.

10 **Prose Summary Question** | The summary sentence notes that there are several unique stages in the life of the longleaf pine tree. This thought is best described in answer choices 4, 5, and 6. Answer choices 1 and 2 are minor points, so they are incorrect answers. Answer choice 3 contains wrong information, so it is also incorrect.

Passage 2 p.107

11 **Factual Question** | The author notes, "Sometime around 1200 B.C., the Bronze Age civilization in the region by the eastern Mediterranean Sea collapsed entirely. The dominant people there—the Mycenaeans—occupied mainland Greece, Crete, and other islands, but their civilization was overwhelmed, so Greece and the nearby area entered a 400-year-period which saw little progress."

12 **Sentence Simplification Question** | The sentence points out that historians know when the Mycenaeans developed as a culture and have learned about them by discovering their relics in Greece. This thought is best expressed by the sentence in answer choice (D).

13 **Inference Question** | The passage reads, "It is commonly believed that many of the later Greek gods, including Athena and Poseidon, and a large number of Greek myths were adopted from the Mycenaeans by the Greeks. Among these stories was that of the Trojan War, which was detailed in Homer's *Iliad* and other epic poems." Since the *Iliad* may have been inspired by a Mycenaean story, the author implies that the Mycenaeans may have been the conquerors of Troy that Homer wrote about.

14 **Vocabulary Question** | The people who hailed from the Balkans originated there.

15 **Negative Factual Question** | The seafarers mentioned by the author came from an unknown place. While they attacked Egypt, they did not originate there.

16 **Vocabulary Question** | A conundrum is a mystery or puzzle.

17 **Factual Question** | The author writes, "Although there is little evidence to support the natural disaster theory, it could explain how the militarily strong Mycenaeans could not successfully defend their land."

18 **Vocabulary Question** | A bleak period in a country's history is a miserable time.

19 **Insert Text Question** | The sentence before the third square reads, "The Dorians are thought to have hailed from the Balkans, an area north of Greece." The sentence to be added notes that the Dorians would have been able to reach Greece from their homeland easily. Thus the two sentences go well together.

20 **Prose Summary Question** | The summary sentence notes that historians have several theories on what caused the end of the Mycenean civilization and the beginning of the Greek Dark Ages. This thought is best described in answer choices 1, 2, and 4. Answer choices 3 and 5 are minor points, so they are incorrect answers. Answer choice 6 contains information not mentioned in the passage, so it is also incorrect.

Passage 3 p.115

21 **Vocabulary Question** | When images are distorted, they appear fuzzy.

22 **Factual Question** | The passage reads, "As lenses and mirrors increase in size, they become able to gather more light and thus can enable a person to see farther into space while simultaneously providing fairly clear images."

23 **Factual Question** | The author mentions, "From the Earth's surface, only a limited part of the electromagnetic spectrum can be observed. Radio waves and visible light can be observed, yet X-rays and gamma rays cannot since they are mostly absorbed by the atmosphere."

24 **Reference Question** | The "it" that had repairs

conducted on it was its (the HST's) mirror.

25 **Rhetorical Purpose Question** | It is written, "One of its most impressive achievements is the Hubble Ultra-Deep Field photograph, which shows a section of the universe where many galaxies and other objects are clearly visible. It is the farthest that any human has ever looked into deep space."

26 **Inference Question** | The author comments, "Radio astronomy and radio telescopes were first conceived in the United States in the 1930s, and the first radio telescope became operational in 1937." It can therefore be inferred that the first radio telescope was built in the United States.

27 **Vocabulary Question** | Sophisticated mirrors, lenses, and apertures are advanced pieces of equipment.

28 **Rhetorical Purpose Question** | The passage reads, "Scientists hope that all of the various types of advanced telescopes will combine to provide information about the universe's mysteries, among them black holes, dark energy, and dark matter."

29 **Insert Text Question** | The sentence before the third square reads, "Optical telescopes were typically built on mountaintops far from the bright lights of cities." The sentence to be added notes where radio telescopes can be built. The key phrase is "in contrast," so the two sentences make a contrast between optical and radio telescopes. Thus the two sentences go well together.

30 **Fill in a Table Question** | Regarding optical telescopes, the author writes, "One of the largest and most advanced space-based optical telescopes is the Hubble Space Telescope (HST)," and, "All optical telescopes gather light in order to produce an image that the eye can see. They can accomplish this in two ways: by passing light through a lens or by reflecting it off a mirror." The author also writes, "Optical telescopes were typically built on mountaintops far from the bright lights of cities. Still, even high in the atmosphere, there was some distortion of visible light." As for radio telescopes, the author notes, "Radio telescopes differ from optical telescopes in that they require no lens or mirror. Instead, they have large parabolic antennae which pick up radio signals from space. Some operate as individual telescopes while others are grouped together to improve their capabilities," and, "Radio astronomy and radio telescopes were first conceived in the United States in the 1930s, and the first radio telescope became operational in 1937."

Passage 4

p.122

31 **Negative Factual Question** | The passage reads, "Over time though, cameras and the photographic process were refined. Cameras became lighter and smaller, and celluloid film replaced the heavy plates that had previously been used." Celluloid was not used in photography's early days as it was a later development.

32 **Rhetorical Purpose Question** | About the two men, the author comments, "Two Frenchmen, Joseph Niepce and Louis Daguerre, are credited with inventing photography during the 1830s."

33 **Factual Question** | The author explains, "They conducted experiments with chemicals which proved that a polished metal plate covered in silver nitrate would, when exposed to light, leave a latent image on the plate. Once the image was exposed to some other chemicals, it could be fixed to the plate."

34 **Sentence Simplification Question** | The sentence points out that pictures were taken inside and that people were put in positions where they did not have to move. This thought is best expressed by the sentence in answer choice Ⓑ.

35 **Vocabulary Question** | Durable material is sturdy and hard to break or damage.

36 **Factual Question** | About Eastman's camera, the author notes, "Eastman's camera was revolutionary for a couple of reasons. First, the heavy plates used by daguerreotypes and other similar cameras were no longer required, nor were long exposure times necessary anymore."

37 **Rhetorical Purpose Question** | About the Kodak Brownie, the passage reads, "Then, in 1901, he introduced yet another new camera, the Kodak Brownie, which was cheap and simple to use. This camera was mass produced and marketed to the general public, thereby enabling anyone to take pictures. This set the stage for photography for practically the entire century as people took pictures and then sent the film away to be processed." So the author focuses on how it changed the world of photography.

38 **Negative Factual Question** | The author mentions how photography changed the world of art, but there is no mention of people considering photography to be an art form.

39 **Insert Text Question** | The sentence before the fourth

square reads, "The later inventing of 35mm film, colored film, and highly sophisticated cameras throughout the 1900s allowed photography to become an art form." The sentence to be added mentions that these inventions were what let people such as Ansel Adams become known as great artists. Thus the two sentences go well together.

40 **Prose Summary Question** | The summary sentence notes that there were many changes in the first few decades of photography, and those changes make it easy for the general public to take pictures. This thought is best expressed in answer choices [2], [4], and [6]. Answer choices [1], [3], and [5] are minor points, so they are incorrect answers.

Actual Test 05

p.129

Answers

1 (B)	2 (A)	3 (D)	4 (A)	5 (A)
6 (B)	7 (C)	8 (A)	9 **2**	
10 [1], [3], [5]				
11 (B)	12 (D)	13 (A)	14 (A)	15 (C)
16 (B)	17 (A)	18 (C)	19 **2**	
20 [4], [5], [6]				
21 (C)	22 (B)	23 (A)	24 (D)	25 (B)
26 (B)	27 (A)	28 (A)	29 **2**	
30 Cause: [2], [6], [7]	Effect: [1], [4]			

Explanations

Passage 1

p.131

1 **Negative Factual Question** | Constantinople was a part of the Eastern Roman Empire, so no attacks on Rome ever came from there.

2 **Vocabulary Question** | Something that is infallible is perfect.

3 **Inference Question** | About the plague, it is written, "One cause of this decline was a plague of some sort that swept through the city and killed more than a thousand people a day in the late second century." Since it was a "plague of some sort," it can be inferred that no one knows what disease caused the plague.

4 **Factual Question** | The author notes, "Additionally, during that period, there was an economic crisis that limited internal trade within the empire and made the provinces more independent from Rome's rule."

5 **Factual Question** | It is written, "Yet Rome's decline continued when Diocletian divided the empire into two and created an eastern and western empire. He ruled the eastern empire and appointed an emperor for the western empire, which was secondary in power and importance."

6 **Factual Question** | The author writes, "During the fifth century, the Western Roman Empire finally collapsed. Germanic tribes from the north invaded the Italian peninsula, and they sacked Rome three times during that century."

7 **Rhetorical Purpose Question** | The author compares Rome with Venice and Genoa in writing, "For the next 1,000 years, Rome was practically a ghost town, especially when compared to its previous glory years. The northern provinces and city-states such as Venice and Genoa became the new centers of Italian life during the Middle Ages and Renaissance."

8 **Factual Question** | About Rome's population, the author declares, "Then, during the Industrial Revolution in the eighteenth century, Rome's population slowly began edging upward."

9 **Insert Text Question** | The sentence before the second square reads, "Following Diocletian, Emperor Constantine I built his capital city of Constantinople in the east." The sentence to be added notes how long it took to make Constantinople and when it was finished. Thus the two sentences go well together.

10 **Prose Summary Question** | The summary sentence notes that there were many reasons that Rome's population declined greatly. This thought is best described in answer choices [1], [3], and [5]. Answer choices [4] and [6] are minor points, so they are incorrect answers. Answer choice [2] contains wrong information, so it is also incorrect.

Passage 2

p.139

11 **Factual Question** | The author writes, "As a result, countless animals have evolved so that they can live

in either cold or hot environments, in wet and humid tropical regions, and in the extreme dry heat of deserts. They can survive on account of certain mechanisms in their bodies and by making use of various external means."

12 **Negative Factual Question** | The author mentions, "Warm-blooded animals produce heat through an internal process which allows them to control their body temperatures even in extremely cold conditions." Warm-blooded animals can control their body temperatures, so they are not affected by the local temperature.

13 **Rhetorical Purpose Question** | The author focuses on the animals' adaption in mentioning, "Additionally, many animals in the Polar Regions have thick fur or feathers to help them preserve their body heat and to keep their bodies dry in snowy or icy conditions. Some, such as polar bears and walruses, have thick layers of fat that stop their bodies from getting too cold."

14 **Vocabulary Question** | When an animal shivers, it trembles or shakes.

15 **Negative Factual Question** | The author notes that camels may sweat in very hot weather but does not mention what temperature that happens at.

16 **Vocabulary Question** | When reptiles appear sluggish, they seem to be lethargic because they move very little.

17 **Sentence Simplification Question** | The sentence points out that reptiles and other animals have ways to cool themselves in hot weather. This thought is best expressed by the sentence in answer choice (A).

18 **Factual Question** | The passage reads, "At night, when desert temperatures may plunge, snakes, lizards, and other reptiles often lie on rocks that were exposed to the sun's rays during the day to absorb their heat."

19 **Insert Text Question** | The sentence before the second square reads, "Consequently, they can survive without eating anything far longer than mammals can." The sentence to be added notes that as an example, the anaconda, does not need to eat for weeks or months. Thus the two sentences go well together.

20 **Prose Summary Question** | The summary sentence notes that animals have internal and external means of being able to live in hot or cold places. This thought is best described in answer choices [4], [5], and [6]. Answer choices [1], [2], and [3] are minor points, so they are incorrect answers.

Passage 3

p.146

21 **Vocabulary Question** | When plants propagate, they reproduce.

22 **Factual Question** | The author mentions, "Seeds need to move away from their parent plants to be able to grow into new plants, but many merely fall to the ground because of gravity when their connections to their parent plants are terminated."

23 **Sentence Simplification Question** | The sentence points out that seeds have to compete with their parent plants and others in the ground located next to their parent plants. This thought is best expressed by the sentence in answer choice (A).

24 **Factual Question** | The author declares, "The seeds of apple, orange, and peach trees that get buried beside their parent trees are likely never to grow into adult trees because they will have to compete with their parent tree for vital resources."

25 **Rhetorical Purpose Question** | In noting how the wind can affect seeds, the author writes, "Some plants have seeds so tiny and lightweight that they are easily picked up by the wind and transported great distances. In many cases, evolution has made seeds more aerodynamic, which lets even light breezes lift and move them. For example, the dandelion has hair-like growths on its seeds that give them the appearance of helicopter blades"

26 **Vocabulary Question** | When animals ingest seeds, they swallow the seeds.

27 **Inference Question** | The passage notes, "Yet when seeds germinate, they must compete with plants that are already growing. Crowded forests, places with poor soil, and regions that receive little rainfall are not always the best locations for seeds to germinate." In mentioning "crowded forests" as places that are not good for seeds to germinate, the author implies that seeds may not grow well in them.

28 **Factual Question** | The author writes, "Additionally, due to the lack of other plants—especially tall trees—growing, young plants are practically guaranteed access to abundant sunlight."

29 **Insert Text Question** | The sentence before the second square reads, "Seeds usually only germinate when the conditions for their survival are optimal, and many remain dormant to avoid dangers such as frost, which

can kill them." The sentence to be added notes that the weather can suddenly drop below freezing in spring in some places. This is what happens when a frost takes place. Thus the two sentences go well together.

30 **Fill in a Table Question** | Regarding causes of seed dispersal, the author writes, "Seeds wrapped inside fleshy fruits and nuts are commonly dispersed by animals, which eat the fruits and the nuts and thereby simultaneously ingest the seeds. Later, the animals defecate, so the seeds, which are not digested inside their bodies, are deposited somewhere else," and, "Humans also play a role in the scattering of seeds by cultivating fruits and nuts and transporting them great distances, where some fall into the soil and then grow." The author also writes, "Some plants have seeds so tiny and lightweight that they are easily picked up by the wind and transported great distances. In many cases, evolution has made seeds more aerodynamic, which lets even light breezes lift and move them." As for effects of seed dispersal, the author notes, "This enables them to grow quickly and to become strong and healthy plants, which is one reason why areas destroyed by forest fires and floods typically recover so swiftly," and, "Resultantly, the best way for seeds to become mature plants is to disperse far from their parent plants."

Actual Test 06

p.153

Answers

1 Ⓒ 2 Ⓓ 3 Ⓒ 4 Ⓐ 5 Ⓑ
6 Ⓓ 7 Ⓓ 8 Ⓑ 9 ❷
10 [1], [2], [4]

11 Ⓑ 12 Ⓓ 13 Ⓓ 14 Ⓐ 15 Ⓑ
16 Ⓒ 17 Ⓐ 18 Ⓐ 19 ❷
20 [1], [3], [6]

21 Ⓐ 22 Ⓒ 23 Ⓒ 24 Ⓐ 25 Ⓑ
26 Ⓐ 27 Ⓒ 28 Ⓑ 29 ❷
30 [2], [3], [4]

31 Ⓓ 32 Ⓒ 33 Ⓑ 34 Ⓓ 35 Ⓑ
36 Ⓑ 37 Ⓓ 38 Ⓒ 39 ❹
40 Greece: [6], [7] Rome: [1], [3], [5]

Explanations

Passage 1

p.155

1 **Vocabulary Question** | When taxes are levied, they are charged to people.

2 **Factual Question** | The author claims, "Due to the nature of transportation then, news was usually at least six months old when it reached the most isolated places in the colonies."

3 **Rhetorical Purpose Question** | In describing newspapers, the author notes, "In 1721, the first truly American newspaper, *The New-England Courant*, was published by James Franklin, Benjamin Franklin's older brother, in Boston, Massachusetts."

4 **Sentence Simplification Question** | The sentence points out that the anti-British letters in American newspapers helped make colonists turn against the British. This thought is best expressed by the sentence in answer choice Ⓐ.

5 **Factual Question** | The passage reads, "No pamphlet played a greater role than *Common Sense*, which was written by Thomas Paine and printed in 1776 after the first shots of the revolution had already been fired."

6 **Vocabulary Question** | When the momentum for an armed rebellion became unstoppable, the impetus for the revolution could not be halted.

7 **Inference Question** | It is noted, "Consequently, many colonists only received news by word of mouth, so some information could not be trusted in its entirety." Thus the author implies that the colonists mistrusted some of the news that they heard.

8 **Factual Question** | Concerning the importance of newspapers and pamphlets, the author declares, "While measuring the importance of newspapers, pamphlets, and other means of conveying information to the success of the revolution is not easy, it is safe to state that without them, the revolution itself likely would never have occurred. It was, after all, the newspapers and the pamphlets which printed the material that helped unite the American colonists against the British."

9 **Insert Text Question** | The sentence before the second square reads, "Fighting between the British and American colonists started in Massachusetts in spring of 1775." The sentence to be added provides more specific information, namely the exact date and the towns where

the fighting happened. Thus the two sentences go well together.

10 **Prose Summary Question** | The summary sentence notes that newspapers and pamphlets played a role in uniting American colonists and starting the American Revolution. This thought is best described in answer choices [1], [2], and [4]. Answer choices [3] and [5] are minor points, so they are incorrect answers. Answer choice [6] contains information not mentioned in the passage, so it is also incorrect.

Passage 2

p.163

11 **Negative Factual Question** | There is no mention in the passage of how frequently major ice ages happen on the Earth.

12 **Vocabulary Question** | When the Earth's average temperatures plummet, they plunge or drop very much.

13 **Rhetorical Purpose Question** | The author points out, "A land bridge appeared between Indonesia and New Guinea, so people subsequently moved south to New Guinea."

14 **Inference Question** | The author notes, "When the land bridge appeared in the Bering Sea around 15,000 years ago, many tribespeople in Siberia followed wandering herds of animals across to Alaska." The author implies that the tribespeople needed the herds of animals for food by mentioning that they followed the animals across the land bridge.

15 **Factual Question** | It is written, "However, many animal species became extinct because of overhunting."

16 **Factual Question** | The author writes, "For instance, during these warming periods, huge icebergs around Europe and North America broke off from gigantic sheets of ice and flowed into the Atlantic Ocean. As they moved southward, the icebergs began to melt, releasing large amounts of fresh water into the saltwater ocean. This altered the salinity levels of the Atlantic Ocean and may have played a role in determining the course and strength of the Gulf Stream, the most important current in the Atlantic."

17 **Sentence Simplification Question** | The sentence points out that research in Greenland shows that during times of warming, less snow and ice fell. This thought is best expressed by the sentence in answer choice (A).

18 **Factual Question** | About the rocks, the author notes, "These rocks are consistent with others found only in certain land masses in Northern Europe. The presence of these rocks in the middle of the ocean led scientists to conclude they had been carried there on icebergs. As the ice sheets advanced, they carved up the land and gathered rocks that were then buried in the ice. When icebergs broke off from these ice sheets and later melted in the ocean, the rocks fell to the bottom."

19 **Insert Text Question** | The sentence before the second square reads, "Eventually, humans in North America made their way south, departed the glacial zone, and found warmer lands filled with animals that had never seen humans before." The sentence to be added names some of the new animals that had not ever seen humans before. Thus the two sentences go well together.

20 **Prose Summary Question** | The summary sentence notes that ice ages have affected where humans live and ocean currents. This thought is best described in answer choices [1], [3], and [6]. Answer choices [2], [4], and [6] are minor points, so they are incorrect answers.

Passage 3

p.171

21 **Reference Question** | The "they" that are uncertain whether this habit of imitating is instinctive or if the infants associate some type of meaning with the adults' actions are child psychologists and educators.

22 **Vocabulary Question** | Innate behavior by infants is instinctive.

23 **Factual Question** | The author notes, "The reason these experiments concentrated on facial gestures is that unless infants constantly have mirrors in front of them, they cannot see their own facial gestures. Since no mirrors were involved, the infants had not formed any imprinted memories of their own facial gestures, which meant that when they made facial gestures similar to those of adults, they were consciously imitating the adults' actions."

24 **Rhetorical Purpose Question** | The author stresses that the two men were responsible for proposing a new theory in writing, "One result of these experiments was the creation of a new theory regarding infant imitation and learning. The leading experts in the field of child study, Andrew Meltzoff and M. Keith Moore, determined that infants are actively learning whenever they imitate adults."

25 Inference Question | The passage reads, "Another issue concerning infant imitation that is constantly debated concerns the age infants are when they begin to learn by imitating. Previously, the majority of child study experts believed that only infants above the age of one were actively learning from imitation. But further studies by Meltzoff and Moore led them to conclude that infants as young as six weeks old could learn in this manner." The author implies that there is a controversy over age in mentioning what each theory states.

26 Vocabulary Question | When young infants correlate two separate activities, they associate the activities with each other.

27 Factual Question | The author claims, "Meltzoff and Moore further believed that very young infants can correlate the sight of a person making a facial gesture and how the infants feel when making the same gesture. Basically, infants assume their own feelings are identical to those of the person they are imitating."

28 Inference Question | The author notes, "For the time being, each school of thought has its own strengths and weaknesses, and it is likely that given infants' limited ability to communicate, exactly when most infants start learning by imitating adults will never be conclusively known." Thus the author implies that experts will never agree on some things since certain things about infants "will never be conclusively known."

29 Insert Text Question | The sentence before the second square reads, "For instance, when an infant sees someone smiling and imitates that smile, the infant suddenly feels happy." The sentence to be added notes what will happen to the infant upon making a scared face. The important word is "likewise," which helps connect the two sentences by making a comparison. Thus the two sentences go well together.

30 Prose Summary Question | The summary sentence notes that a new theory on infant imitation opposes the conventional thinking on it. This thought is best described in answer choices 2, 3, and 4. Answer choices 1, 5, and 6 are minor points, so they are incorrect answers.

Passage 4

p.178

31 Sentence Simplification Question | The sentence points out that the Renaissance and the Neoclassical Period were times when people imitated Greek and Roman architecture. This thought is best expressed by the sentence in answer choice D.

32 Vocabulary Question | A heyday is a period of time when something reaches its zenith.

33 Factual Question | About the Ionic style, the author declares, "The Ionic style was more closely associated with the Greek islands in the Aegean Sea as well as the Greek colonies located in Asia Minor in the land that is Turkey today."

34 Rhetorical Purpose Question | About the Pantheon, the author writes, "The Pantheon in Rome is the greatest example of a Roman domed building."

35 Factual Question | The passage notes, "For example, the Romans regularly used all three styles of columns on the same building by employing a different style on each story of the structure."

36 Vocabulary Question | A haphazard style is one that is random and chaotic in nature.

37 Negative Factual Question | There is no mention of the styles of the buildings that were constructed in the cities of the Byzantine Empire.

38 Factual Question | The author points out, "The city's discovery sparked another revival of interest in classical architecture. This initiated the Neoclassical Period. During the eighteenth and nineteenth centuries, many university buildings, libraries, and government buildings were designed and built to resemble ancient Greek and Roman structures."

39 Insert Text Question | The sentence before the fourth square reads, "Arches were also used to great effect in enormous Roman aqueducts, some of which ran for hundreds of kilometers." The sentence to be added notes that the aqueducts were transporting water even during the Middle Ages. Thus the two sentences go well together.

40 Fill in a Table Question | Regarding Greece, the author writes, "Ancient Greek architectural styles are typically divided into three separate groups: Ionic, Doric, and Corinthian," and, "Whereas the Greeks often built temples and other structures with open roofs." As for Rome, the author notes, "Rome's two greatest contributions to the architectural world were the arch and the dome. Arches and domes permitted the Romans to erect much larger buildings—and with more massive interiors—than the Greeks ever did. Whereas the Greeks often built temples and other structures with open roofs, the Romans constructed domes over their large buildings," and, "Arches were also used to great effect in enormous Roman aqueducts, some of which ran for hundreds of kilometers." The author also writes, "They also began practicing the Roman customs of employing mathematical precision and symmetry in their building designs as they abandoned the haphazard, imprecise style of Gothic architecture."

Actual Test 07

p.187

Answers

1 (C) 2 (A) 3 (D) 4 (B) 5 (A)
6 (A) 7 (D) 8 (B) 9 **2**
10 Liquid Precipitation: [2], [4], [7] Freezing Precipitation: [1], [9] Frozen Precipitation: [5], [6]

11 (C) 12 (C) 13 (A) 14 (B) 15 (B)
16 (B) 17 (D) 18 (A) 19 **1**
20 [1], [2], [5]

21 (A) 22 (B) 23 (B) 24 (D) 25 (B)
26 (B) 27 (D) 28 (A) 29 **3**
30 [2], [4], [6]

Explanations

Passage 1

p.189

1 **Factual Question** | The passage reads, "When a cloud contains too much condensed water, it releases that water, which falls to the ground as liquid, freezing, or frozen precipitation."

2 **Rhetorical Purpose Question** | The author writes, "As for drizzle, it is comprised of water droplets smaller than half a millimeter. It is common in subtropical regions and over oceans, tends to fall from stratus clouds." So the author mentions stratus clouds to note that drizzle usually falls from them.

3 **Negative Factual Question** | According to the passage, drizzle, not rain, falls from stratus clouds.

4 **Vocabulary Question** | When surfaces are slick, they are slippery.

5 **Factual Question** | About freezing precipitation, it is written, "Both kinds of freezing precipitation occur when snow falls from clouds high in the atmosphere. As the snow passes through warmer air, it completely melts and transforms into water droplets. However, even closer to the ground, there is a colder layer of air, which causes the water droplets to begin turning into ice crystals. There is not enough time for them to freeze completely, so they land as hard droplets of ice crystals."

6 **Vocabulary Question** | When certain clouds spawn thunderstorms, they produce them or cause them to form.

7 **Factual Question** | The author writes, "Hailstones can be heavy and large—up to twelve centimeters in diameter—and regularly damage crops, vehicles, and buildings and injure people and animals."

8 **Inference Question** | The passage reads, "Snow forms when supercooled water droplets freeze in temperatures between minus eighteen degrees Celsius and thirty-one degrees Celsius." It can therefore be inferred that temperatures below minus eighteen degrees Celsius may be too cold for snow to fall.

9 **Insert Text Question** | The sentence before the second square reads, "Upon contact with any surface, freezing drizzle and freezing rain can create thin sheets of ice." The sentence to be added refers to the former, which is freezing drizzle, and the latter, which is freezing rain, and notes how large the ice sheets created by each are. Thus the two sentences go well together.

10 **Fill in a Table Question** | Regarding liquid precipitation, the author writes, "It is common in subtropical regions and over oceans," and, "Liquid precipitation forms in air in which the temperature is above zero degrees Celsius. It has two basic forms: rain and drizzle." As for freezing precipitation, the author notes, "Upon contact with any surface, freezing drizzle and freezing rain can create thin sheets of ice. These are particularly dangerous since they can turn roads into slick surfaces and cover tree branches and power lines with heavy layers of ice," and, "However, even closer to the ground, there is a colder layer of air, which causes the water droplets to begin turning into ice crystals. There is not enough time for them to freeze completely, so they land as hard droplets of ice crystals." And as for frozen precipitation, the author points out, "Hail is formed in large cumulonimbus clouds, which are ones that spawn thunderstorms," and, "Frozen precipitation comes in three main forms: sleet, hail, and snow."

Passage 2 p.196

11 Factual Question | The author writes, "The Ayutthaya economy was agriculturally based."

12 Rhetorical Purpose Question | In writing about corvee labor, the author notes, "Peasants had to provide corvee labor for their lords. This was a system requiring all peasants to provide free labor for their lords wherever it was needed. This could include working on construction projects or even fighting battles." Thus the author focuses on the kind of work that peasants had to do.

13 Factual Question | The passage notes, "With large tracts of arable land and plentiful rainfall, the Ayutthaya region, which was slightly north of the area where Bangkok, Thailand, lies today, virtually always enabled farmers to grow enough food to feed everyone and to have a surplus. This surplus fed the lords of the land and the monks in Buddhist temples, and remaining supplies were sold elsewhere."

14 Negative Factual Question | There is no mention of how much money the immigrant Chinese merchants earned from engaging in trade.

15 Factual Question | The author writes, "Thus sometime in the early years of the Ayutthaya kingdom, the Thais imported from the Bengal region a strain of rice called floating rice. It had longer grains, was not as glutinous as the upland rice, and, most importantly, grew well in deep-water floodplains."

16 Vocabulary Question | When the rulers were bolstered by the rice production and trade, they were strengthened by these two factors.

17 Inference Question | In writing, "Suddenly, much more land could be cultivated and more rice grown, so the kingdom's wealth increased exponentially," the author implies that rice was directly connected with the creation of wealth.

18 Factual Question | The passage notes, "When a Burmese army invaded in 1765, the Thais could not resist. The great city of Ayutthaya was captured and burned in 1767 as all of its wealth could still not save it."

19 Insert Text Question | The sentence before the first square reads, "Over the next several centuries, the territory they controlled grew, and many places were obligated to pay tribute to the Ayutthaya Thai rulers." The sentence to be added names some of the places that had to pay tribute. Thus the two sentences go well together.

20 Prose Summary Question | The summary sentences notes that rice cultivation helped the Ayutthaya kingdom dominate its area for centuries. This thought is best described in answer choices [1], [2], and [5]. Answer choices [4] and [6] are minor points, so they are incorrect answers. Answer choice [3] contains incorrect information, so it is also wrong.

Passage 3 p.204

21 Vocabulary Question | When honeybees are a key component of their ecosystems, they are considered an important element of them.

22 Inference Question | The author writes, "The silent manner in which honeybees find a new place for a hive demonstrates they are capable of communicating with one another in a sophisticated manner." Since honeybees can communicate in a "silent manner," it can be inferred that they communicate without vocalizing sounds.

23 Vocabulary Question | When the search commences, it begins.

24 Negative Factual Question | The scout bees do the waggle dance in the direction they want the hive to go. They do not do it in the opposite direction.

25 Factual Question | It is noted, "Each scout bee that returns begins to perform a waggle dance until there are many bees doing it simultaneously. Then, the scout bees gradually move to where the most aggressive dancers are and start to dance in the same manner."

26 Sentence Simplification Question | The sentence points out that video recordings of the waggle dance have showed that, from start to finish, everything takes a few days to complete. This thought is best expressed by the sentence in answer choice (B).

27 Factual Question | The author writes, "Scientists have also noted that scouts perform waggle dances for around twelve to sixteen hours a day. During the first part of the decision-making process, no potential nesting sites seem to be embraced by the majority of the scout bees. In one study, for instance, on the first day, the scout bees danced in nine different directions. However, during the middle part of the process as the waggle dances continue, some scout bees stop their dances and join a few of the most aggressively dancing scout bees. Finally, during the third stage of the decision-making process, more and more scout bees abandon their own dances to join others."

28 **Factual Question** | The author notes, "Some speculate that it may be a chemical process in the scouts which causes them to lose their eagerness for a particular site when they observe others that seem more enthusiastic about their own sites."

29 **Insert Text Question** | The sentence before the third square reads, "In some cases, such as when it rains, the process may take longer since honeybees do not usually move during inclement weather." The sentence to be added notes that honeybees have difficulty flying and staying aloft when water gets on their wings. Thus the two sentences go well together.

30 **Prose Summary Question** | The summary sentence notes that honeybee scouts do the waggle dance, and then the swarm determines the location of its new hive. This thought is best described in answer choices [2], [4], and [6]. Answer choices [1], [3], and [5] are minor points, so they are incorrect answers.

TOEFL® MAP

ACTUAL TEST

New TOEFL® Edition

Michael A. Putlack
Stephen Poirier

Reading 2

Translations

TOEFL® MAP ACTUAL TEST

New TOEFL® Edition

Reading 2

Translations

Actual Test 01

Passage 1 • History p.15

미국 우체국의 초기 역사

미국이 식민지였던 17세기와 18세기 당시 주요 커뮤니케이션 수단은 글이었다. 문자는 선박에 의해 혹은 육로로 전달되었고, 종종 친구나 여행자들에 의해 전해졌으며, 거리와 자연의 위력 때문에 지연 및 손실 문제가 일어날 수 있었다. 17세기 후반이 되기 전까지는 정부의 체계적인 우편 서비스가 존재하지 않았고, 우편 서비스를 향상시키기 위한 초창기의 노력들은 대부분 여러 가지 문제들로 인해 성과를 이루지 못했다.

미국 식민지들의 지리적인 크기와 인구가 증가함에 따라 우편물의 양도 늘어났지만, 초기에는 우체국이나 우편 배달부가 존재하지 않았다. 유럽에서 대서양을 건너오는 우편물의 양이 증가하자 곧 식민지 주민들은 항구 도시의 특정 시설들을, 선박으로 도착하는 우편물을 처리하는, 우편물 보관 장소로 사용하기로 결정했다. 예를 들어 1639년 매사추세츠만 식민지에서는 도착하는 모든 우편물을 보스턴에 있는 리처드 페어뱅크스의 선술집으로 보내도록 한 법이 제정되었다. 이곳은 사람들이 많이 모이는 곳으로 대부분의 지역 주민들에게 친숙한 장소였기 때문에 그러한 임무를 잘 수행했다. 페어뱅크스에게는 한 사람이 받는 편지 한 통당 1페니를 징수하는 것이 허용되었는데, 이것이 초기 우표 시스템의 한 가지 유형이 되었다. 이와 비슷한 우편물 보관소들이 다른 식민지에도 세워졌다. 보통은 한 동네에 사는 주민 중 한 명이 이웃 사람들에게 도착한 우편물이 있는지를 확인하기 위해 매일 보관소를 방문하곤 했다.

시간이 지나면서 영국 왕실은 특별한 목적을 지닌 우체국을 설립하고, 배달부를 갖춘 우편 경로를 설정하고, 우편물 배달 요금을 징수함으로써 영국에서 사용되는 것과 유사한 식민지 우편 시스템을 만들기 위해 노력했다. 윌리엄 왕은 1692년 식민지 전역에 우편 시스템을 도입하기 위한 확고한 조치를 취하여 토마스 닐에게 21년간 우정 장관으로 일할 수 있는 특권을 부여했다. 닐은 우체국 설립과 우편 경로 설정, 그리고 우편 요금 책정에 관한 협약을 각 주들과 체결했다. 식민지 전체의 우편 요금은 통일되지 않았는데, 그 이유는 주마다 자체적인 지불 시스템을 협상을 통해 정했기 때문이었다.

윌리엄 왕의 새로운 우편 서비스는 이후 미국 우편 시스템의 설립으로 이어진 출발점으로 간주된다. 하지만 시스템의 모든 점이 완벽한 것은 아니었다. 우편 시스템에서 일할 사람을 모집하는 일은 항상 문제였다. 우편 배달부는 거칠고, 특히 악천후 시 때때로 위험하기도 한, 긴 경로를 이동해야 했다. (또한 그들 중 일부는 적대적인 미 원주민들로부터 공격을 받기도 했고, 때때로 노상 강도들에게 강탈을 당하기도 했다.) 일부 도시에는 우체국이 없었기 때문에 식민지의 우체국장들은 우편물을 보관할 장소로 자신의 집이나 가게를 내어 줄 사람들을 고용했다. 시간이 지남에 따라, 결국 식민지들로 하여금 영국을 상대로 반란을 일으키게 만든 혁명 정신이 고취되자, 이러한 방식으로 영국 왕실에게 서비스를 제공하는 것은 식민지 주민들에게 혐오스럽게 느껴졌다. 여러 도시에 왕실 우체국과 식민지 우체국이 있었지만, 미국인들에게는 식민지 우체국이 더 인기가 많았다. 식민지의 우편 시스템을 보다 잘 관리하기 위한 하나의 시도로서 1711년 영국 의회는 우편 시스템을 재정비하는 법안을 통과시켰다. 이후 뉴욕 시가 우편 시스템의 중심이 되었고, 기타 모든 우체국들이 그 아래에 놓이게 되었다. 또한 우편 요금도 인상되었는데, 이는 왕실 우편 시스템에 대한 식민지 주민들의 반감을 더욱 증가시켰다.

영국 왕실의 시스템은 식민지와 함께 확대되었지만, 편지가 배달되는데 몇 주가 — 때로는 몇 달이 — 걸렸기 때문에 결코 효율적이지 못했다. 이후 1753년에 벤자민 프랭클린이 북부 식민지의 우정 장관 대리로 임명되었다. 프랭클린은 16년 동안 펜실베니아 필라델피아의 우체국장으로 일했기 때문에 우편 업무 경력을 가지고 있었다. 그는 즉시 시스템을 개혁하기 시작했다. 우편 경로를 개선시키고, 배달 시간을 단축시켰으며, 그리고 우편 시스템의 부채를 상환했다. 하지만 식민지 전역에 퍼져 있던, 우편 서비스를 통해 돈이 영국 왕실로 흘러 들어가고 있다는 소문은 여전히 시스템에 문제가 되었다. 프랭클린이 거세지는 반란 운동과 연관되어 있었기 때문에 영국 왕실과 그의 관계는 악화되었고 그는 1774년 자리에서 물러났다. 1775년 미국 혁명이 시작되자 프랭클린은 미국의 우정 장관 자리에 대한 확실한 선택이 되었다. 새로운 시스템은 1775년 7월 25일 미 의회에 의해 법으로 정해졌다. 이후 1792년에 조지 워싱턴 대통령이, 이후 미국 우정 공사가 된, 미국 우정청을 설립하는 법안에 서명했다.

WORD REMINDER

be subject to ~의 대상이다 fall prey to ~이 먹이가 되다, ~에 의해 피해를 입다 establishment 기관, 업체 drop-off point 배달품 전달 장소 enact (법을) 제정하다 purpose-built 특별한 목적을 지닌 take a hand 손을 대다, 조치를 취하다 patent 특허 postmaster general (미국의) 우정 장관 inclement weather 악천후 odious 혐오스러운 rebel 반란을 일으키다 subordinate 종속된 sour 불쾌하게 만들다, (관계를) 악화시키다 rumbling 소문 plague 역병; 성가시게 하다

Passage 2 • Zoology p.23

동물의 세력권 행동

동물계의 일부 종들은 격렬하게 세력권을 보호하려고 한다. 이러한 행동은 다른 생물보다 곤충, 조류, 그리고 포유류에게서 흔히 나타난다. 전형적으로 이들 동물들은 특정 지역이 자신의 세력권임을 주장하고 목숨을 잃으면서까지 이를 지키려고 한다. 영역은 먹이를 구하는 곳이기 때문에 이러한 지역이 없으면 죽음을 맞이하게 될 것이다. 또한 영역은 번식지 역할을 하기도 하며, 동물이 새끼를 기르는 거처를 포함하고 있을 수도 있다. 동물들은 여러 가지 방법으로 영역 표시를 하면서 영역을 지키는데, 신체의 분비물을 이용해 영역의 경계를 표시하는 방법도 여기에 포함된다. 이러한 경계를 넘는 경우 공격을 받을 수 있고, 어떤 침입자는 죽음을 맞이할 수 있다.

동물의 영역은 어떤 지형으로도 이루어질 수 있다. 예를 들면 옐로우 스톤 국립 공원에서는 다섯에서 스물 다섯 마리 사이의 늑대 무리들이 언덕과 숲으로 이루어진 넓은 지역을 영역으로 삼고, 경쟁 관계의 늑대 무리 중 어떤 늑대라도 자신들의 영역을 침범하면 공격을 한다. 프라이드라는 무리를 짓고 살아가는 사자들도 아프리카의 대초원에서 서식하면서 비슷한 행동을 한다. 하마들은 강둑과 호숫가 근처에 펼쳐진 지역을 영역으로 삼으면서, 인간을 포함하여, 자신의 영역에 들어온 위협적으로 느껴지는 생물에게 공격을 가한다. 바다코끼리들도 마찬가지로 자기 영역이라고 생각하는 해변가 지역을 격렬하게 방어한다. 몇몇 동물의 경우, 영역의 크기가 작을 수도 있다: 작은 개미총이나 벌집의 주변 지역에 국한될 수도 있다. 하지만, 예컨대 늑대나 아프리카 및 아시아의 커다란 고양잇과 동물의 경우, 그 영역이 수 킬로미터에 이르는 광활한 지역에 걸쳐 있을 수도 있다.

세력권 습성을 보이는 대부분의 동물들은 냄새로 영역의 경계를 표시한

다. 이러한 냄새는 동물의 배설물, 소변, 혹은 특별한 분비선에서 나온다. 개와 늑대는 소변을 이용하여 영역 표시를 한다. 영역 내에 있는 나무, 수풀, 그리고 기타 물체에 소변을 뿌린다. 소변 냄새는 다른 동물들에게, 특히 동일한 종의 다른 동물들에게, 그 지역이 자신의 영역임을 알려 준다. 이러한 동물의 소변에는 오랫동안 냄새를 지속시키는 화학 물질이 포함되어 있다. 반면, 크기가 작은 애완용 고양이로부터 가장 큰 호랑이에 이르기까지, 고양잇과에 속하는 동물들은 얼굴이나 옆구리를 사물에 문지르는데, 이로써 그들의 냄새가 전달되어 영역 표시가 이루어진다. 사슴은 특별한 분비선을 가지고 있어서 이를 이용해 영역을 표시하는 물질을 분비한다. (마찬가지로 몇몇 토끼들의 경우 분비물을 만들어 낼 수 있는 분비선이 턱 근처에 있다.) 기타 영역 표시 방법으로 색깔을 나타내거나 경고음을 사용하는 방법이 있다. 예를 들어 새들은 침입자들을 쫓아내기 위해 날개를 퍼덕일 수 있으며, 자신이 어떤 지역을 차지하고 있다는 점을 다른 새에게 알리기 위해 특정한 소리를 낼 수도 있다.

때때로 이러한 신호에도 불구하고 어떤 동물이 다른 동물의 영역을 침범할 수도 있다. 이러한 경우에는 몇 가지 결과가 발생할 수 있다. 동물이 잠깐만 머무는 경우에는 공격을 받지 않거나 심지어는 발견이 되지 않은 상태로 떠날 수도 있다. 또한 경고를 받고 달아날 수도 있고, 혹은 떠나지 않는 경우에는 싸움이 일어날 수도 있다. 만일 그곳에 계속 남아 있겠다는 의도를 보인다면 그 지역을 차지하고 있는 동물들의 주의를 끌게 될 것이다. 늑대들은 자신의 영역을 침범한 다른 늑대들에게 재빨리 싸움을 걸어 공격한 후, 침입자들이 죽을 때까지 싸움을 한다. 사자들도 비슷한 행동을 하는데, 특히 짝을 찾지 못한 수컷들이 암컷을 차지하기 위해 무리를 공격하는 경우에 그러하다. 하지만 무리에 속한 수컷들이 항상 죽을 때까지 싸우는 것은 아니다. 자신이 패배할 것이라고 판단을 하면 도주를 해서 짝이 없는 수컷들이 무리를 차지하도록 내버려 둔다. 패배한 수컷들은, 극히 드문 경우이긴 하지만, 다른 수컷을 물리칠 때까지 혼자서 돌아다닌다.

때때로 동일한 종의 수컷과 암컷이 다른 영역을 차지하는 경우도 있다. 수컷과 암컷 치타 및 표범이 이러한 행동을 하는데, 이들은 수컷이나 암컷으로만 구성된 소규모 무리를 지어 돌아다닌다. 치타와 표범이 남의 영토를 침범하는 때는 짝짓기를 하기 위한 경우이다. 짝짓기를 한 후에는 흩어지며, 새끼가 태어나면 암컷들이 새끼를 기르고 이들에게 사냥하는 법을 가르친다.

일부 경우, 영역을 지키는 대가가 보상보다 더 클 수도 있다. 동물은 영역을 지키느라 엄청난 양의 에너지를 소모할 수도 있다. 부상을 입을 수도 있고, 심지어 목숨을 잃을 수도 있다. 하지만 생존 경쟁에서 자신의 먹이를 지키고 서식지와 무리를 보호하는 일은 동물들에게 똑같이 중요한 일이다. 결국에는 최강자만이 살아남는다.

WORD REMINDER

territorial 세력권의 습성을 갖는 stake a claim ~에 대한 권리를 주장하다 secretion 분비물 perpetrator 가해자 pack 떼, 무리 savannah 대초원 stretch 길게 펼쳐진 지역 deem ~이라고 여기다 walrus 바다코끼리 anthill 개미총 feces 배설물 urine 소변 gland 분비선, 분비 기관 flank (동물의) 옆구리 impart 전달하다 unmolested 공격을 받지 않는 unattached 결혼을 하지 않은 vanquish 완파하다

Passage 3 • **Botany** p.31

단일 식물과 장일 식물

식물은 매일 노출되는 빛과 어둠의 양에 반응한다. 이러한 현상은 광주기 현상으로 알려져 있다. 식물에 있어서 노출되는 빛과 어둠의 양에 대한 주요 메커니즘은 꽃을 피우는 능력인 개화이다. 꽃에는 식물의 생식 기관이 포함되어 있기 때문에 개화 과정은 식물의 번식 능력에서 핵심적이다. 꽃에서는 꿀이 생산되며, 이는 색깔과 향기와 함께 새, 벌, 그리고 기타 곤충들을 유인하는데, 이들은 식물의 수분에 있어서 중요한 역할을 한다. 일부 식물들은 빛이 적고 어둠이 많은 환경에 노출될 때 보다 효과적으로 꽃을 피우기 때문에 단일 식물로 알려져 있다. 빛이 많고 어둠이 적은 환경에 노출되는 경우 그에 대한 반응으로 꽃을 더 잘 피우는 식물들은 장일 식물이라고 불린다. 노출되는 빛과 어둠의 양에 상관없이 꽃을 피우는 식물들도 있다. 이들은 중성 식물이라 불리며, 이들의 개화 반응은 연령에 기반한다. (일반적으로 이러한 식물들은 연령이 높을 수록 더 많은 꽃을 피운다.)

모든 식물들은 잎에 피토크롬이라고 불리는 색소를 가지고 있는데, 피토크롬은 빛과 어둠의 주기를 감지하여 식물의 개화 시기에 영향을 미칠 수 있다. 오랫동안 과학자들은 모든 식물의 개화에 가장 큰 영향을 미치는 것이 낮 동안의 햇빛과 흡수되는 햇빛의 양이라고 생각했다. 하지만 광범위한 실험을 통해 현재 단일 식물은 노출되는 어둠의 정도에 따라, 장일 식물은 노출되는 빛의 양에 기반하여 개화를 한다고 알려져 있다. 이러한 점 때문에 특정한 양의 빛과 어둠에 영향을 받는 식물들은 때때로 장야 식물과 단야 식물이라는 용어로도 알려져 있다.

식물이 빛과 어둠에 노출되는 시간의 길이는 하루 12시간 이상인지 혹은 12시간 이하인지를 기준으로 삼는다. 단일 식물은 빛에 노출되는 시간이 하루 12시간 이하일 때 개화하며, 장일 식물은 하루 12시간 이상 빛을 받을 때 개화한다. 자연 환경에서 이러한 노출량은 보통 기울어진 지구 자전축에 의해 일어나는 계절 변화의 영향을 받는다. 북쪽과 남쪽의 고위도에서 성장하는 식물들은 계절에 따라 햇빛에 노출되는 시간이 더 적을 때도 있고 낮 동안 햇빛에 더 많이 노출되는 경우도 있는 반면, 적도 근처의 식물들은 빛과 어둠에 노출되는 정도에 있어서 계절 변화의 영향을 매우 적게 받는다. 또한 빛에 대한 노출의 정도는 더 많은 빛에 노출시키기 위한, 혹은 커다란 차양막으로 어두운 환경을 조성하기 위한 고에너지 조명 시스템을 사용함으로써 인공적으로 조절될 수 있다. 이러한 방법은, 보통 1년 중 특정 시기의 자연 조건에서는 꽃을 피우지 않는, 식물의 개화에 영향을 미치기 위해 상업적인 온실에서 주로 사용된다.

흔히 볼 수 있는 단일 식물에는 국화, 포인세티아, 벼, 콩, 양파, 딸기, 그리고 면이 포함된다. 고위도 지방에서 단일 식물은 주로 봄과 가을에 꽃을 피우는데, 이때 낮 동안 햇빛에 노출되는 시간은 12시간 이하이다. 개화는 밤에 이루어지지만 지속적으로 어두워야 하기 때문에 항상 그런 것은 아니다. 따라서 천둥이 칠 때의 번개와 같이 번쩍이는 빛이 있으면 그러한 과정이 방해를 받을 수도 있다. 반면에 낮 동안 어두운 경우, 예컨대 짙은 구름이 해를 가리거나 일식이 일어나는 경우, 개화 과정은 부정적으로든 긍정적으로든 영향을 받지 않는다.

흔히 볼 수 있는 장일 식물로 과꽃, 상추, 밀, 양귀비, 시금치, 그리고 감자가 있다. 고위도에서 이들 장일 식물은 12시간 이상 햇빛에 노출될 때 꽃을 피운다. 따라서 늦봄과 여름의 긴 낮 시간에 보다 효과적으로 꽃을 피운다. 단일 식물의 경우와 달리 어두울 때 치는 번개는 사실상 꽃의 성장을 자극한다. 또한 낮 동안 해가 비치는 도중에 어둠이 찾아오면 꽃의 성장에는 영향이 미치지 않는다. 장일 식물의 개화 반응에 영향을 미치는 또 다른 요인은 지베

렐린산의 존재 유무이다. 이는 대부분의 식물에서 발견되는 자연적인 호르몬으로서 식물 세포의 성장을 촉진시킨다. 장일 식물에서 지베렐린산은 개화에 적극적인 역할을 담당하지만, 단일 식물의 개화 시기에는 어떠한 영향도 끼치지 않는다.

WORD REMINDER

photoperiodism 광주기성 propagate 번식시키다 reproductive organ 생식 기관 nectar (꽃의) 꿀, 과즙 pigment 색소, 안료 phytochrome 피토크롬 absorption 흡수 tilt 기울기 axis 축 latitude 위도 equator 적도 artificially 인공적으로 simulate 모의 실험을 하다, 시뮬레이션을 하다 chrysanthemum 국화 poinsettia 포인세티아 conceal 숨기다, 감추다 solar eclipse 일식 stimulate 자극하다

Actual Test 02

Passage 1 • Environmental Science p.41

질소 순환

질소는 아미노산, 단백질, 그리고 식물이 광합성에 활용하는 엽록소의 일부를 구성하고 있기 때문에 지구상의 모든 생명체들에게 필수적인 성분이다. 질소가 없다면 지구에는 생명체가 존재하지 못할 것이다. 질소는 지구 대기의 78% 정도를 차지하고 있지만, 기체 상태로 있는 경우에는 식물과 동물에게 쓸모가 없다. 식물은 토양으로부터 고정 상태의 질소를 흡수해야 하는 반면, 동물은 자신에게 필요한 질소를 식물에서 직접적으로 얻거나 식물을 섭취한 다른 동물을 먹음으로써 간접적으로 얻는다. 질소가 대기에서 지면으로, 그리고 다시 대기로 되돌아가는 과정이 질소 순환이다. 이 과정은 네 가지의 주요 단계, 즉 질소 고정, 부해, 질수 하합, 그리고 탈질소 과정으로 이루어진다.

질소 고정은 질소가 대기에서 지면으로 이동하는 것과 관련이 있으며, 여러 가지 방법으로 일어날 수 있다. 번개가 대기 중의 질소 분자를 분해시킬 수도 있는데, 이들은 산소와 결합하여 질소 화합물을 만들어 낸다. 이 화합물은 비가 내릴 때 지면으로 떨어진다. 자동차나 공장에서 생성되는 오염 물질에 의해 대기에 유입되는 질소 화합물들도 있다. 이들 역시 비가 내릴 때 지면으로 떨어질 수 있다. 또한 질소를 대기에서 추출하여 이를 농부들이 농장에서 사용하는 화학 비료, 예컨대 암모니아 및 질산 암모니아로 바꾸는 산업 공정에 질소가 이용될 수도 있다. 질소 고정의 또 다른 방법으로서 토양에 존재하는 박테리아에 의해 이루어지는 자연적인 과정을 들 수 있다. 이들 박테리아는 일부 식물들과 공생 관계를 맺고 있는데, 이를 통해 박테리아가 식물에게 필요한 질소 화합물을 만들어 낼 수 있다. 이러한 식물들 중 대부분은 콩과 식물로, 대두와 자주개자리가 여기에 포함된다.

분해 단계는 식물 및 동물이 질소를 흡수한 뒤 이를 노폐물로 변환시키는 과정과 관련이 있으며, 이때 질소가 암모니아로 변할 수 있다. 질소가 토양에 유입되면 식물은 뿌리를 통해 이를 흡수한다. 동물들은 이러한 식물을 섭취함으로써 질소를 체내로 흡수한다. 어느 시점에 이르면 동물들의 신진대사를 통해 유기 질소 화합물이 생성되고, 이들은 노폐물로서 몸 밖으로 배출된다. 이러한 유기 노폐물은 이후 박테리아에 의해 분해되어야 하는데, 박테리아는 이를 암모니아로 바꾸어 놓는다. 이 과정은 노폐물에서도 이루어지지만 동물이 죽는 경우에도 일어난다. 사체가 부패하면 유기 물질은 결국 암모니아로 변한다.

질소 순환의 세 번째 단계, 즉 질소 화합 단계는 암모니아를 두 가지 질소 화합물로 변화시키는 특별한 박테리아와 관련이 있다. 암모니아는 두 개의 질산염, 즉 이산화질소로 알려진 NO_2와 NO_3로 변화한다: 일부 경우, 식물 뿌리가 토양으로부터 암모니아를 직접 흡수하기도 하지만, 대부분은 질산염을 만들어 내는 박테리아에 의존한다. 그러면 식물은 질산염을 이용해 성장할 수 있다. 이러한 질산염 중 일부는 물에 쉽게 용해되어 호수, 시내, 그리고 강으로 유입된다는 점에서 문제를 일으킬 수 있다. 물속의 질산염 수치가 증가하면 해조류가 과도하게 증식될 수 있는데, 이는 수중 생물들에게 심각한 영향을 끼칠 수 있다. (기본적으로 물고기들이 산소를 빼앗기기 때문에 다수의 물고기들이 죽게 된다.)

질소 순환의 마지막 단계는 탈질소화이다. 이 단계에서 질산염은 특별한 박테리아에 의해 다시 질소로 바뀌어 대기로 들어가게 된다. 이 박테리아는 토양, 습지, 그리고 바다의 특정 지역과 같은 산소 공급이 제한적인 환경에서

서식한다. 산소가 없기 때문에 박테리아는 산소 대신 질소로 호흡하도록 진화했다. 이들은 질소를 흡입한 후 이를 기체 형태인 N_2로 배출하는데, 이것이 대기로 되돌아가면 질소 순환이 완료된다.

현대적인 농법으로 인하여 토양과 수계에 지나치게 많은 질소가 유입되고 탈질소화 과정이 그에 부합하는 속도를 내지 못함으로써 토양과 수중에 질소가 지나치게 많아질 것이라는 우려가 현재 존재한다. 농사를 많이 짓는 지역과 인접해 있는 일부 바다의 경우, 다량의 질산염이 물속에 유입되어 바닷속 해조류의 양이 증가하고 있다. 이러한 해조류는 수중의 산소를 다량으로 소비함으로써 죽음의 해역을 만들어 내는데, 이로써 대부분의 해양 생물들의 생존 가능성에 제약이 생긴다. 그 결과, 이러한 죽음의 해역에서는 생명체가 거의 없기나 전혀 없을 수 있다. 이러한 상황이 계속된다면 조만간 전 세계 바다의 많은 부분이 매우 작은 생명체 이외에는 어떤 생명체도 살 수 없는 장소가 될 것이다.

WORD REMINDER

chlorophyll 엽록소 molecule 분자 symbiotic 공생하는 alfalfa 자주개자리 (옥수수과 식물) assimilate 동화시키다, 흡수하다 metabolism 신진대사 nitrate 질산염 soluble 녹는, 녹기 쉬운 survivability 생존 가능성

Passage 2 • Economics p.49

산업 혁명 당시 영국의 섬유 무역

산업 혁명으로 전 세계의 많은 지역이 시골 중심의 농경 사회에서 도시 중심의 산업 기반 사회로 바뀌었다. 산업 혁명은 1700년대 중반 영국에서 시작되었다. 최초로 산업화된 분야는 섬유 산업이었다. 실제로 산업 혁명 초기에 제작된 다수의 기기들은 섬유 제작을 위해 특별히 설계된 것들이었다. 하지만 가내 수공업 방식의 섬유 산업에서 기계를 이용하고 노동자들을 고용하는 공장제 산업으로 변화하는 과정은 순탄하지 않았으며, 변화에 대한 저항도 심했다. 그러나 시간이 흐르면서 공장의 수는 증가했고, 일자리를 찾는 사람들이 공장 주변으로 모였으며, 작은 마을은 거대한 도시로 성장했다.

섬유 산업은 생필품인 옷을 만드는데 사용되는 천을 생산한다. 18세기 초 모든 직물들은 천연물로 만들어졌다. 이들 중 영국에서 가장 널리 사용된 두 가지는 양털과 아마였는데, 양털이 지배적으로 사용되었다. 하지만 면이 점점 더 흔해지자 18세기가 끝날 무렵에는 면이 직물 제조의 주원료가 되었다. 당시 직물은 각 가정에서 사람들의 작업을 통해 만들어졌기 때문에 가내 수공업 형태로 제작되었다. 종종 가족 전체가 원재료를 준비하고 이를 실패로 만드는 작업에 참여했다. 그 후 이러한 실은 손으로 작동되는 베틀에서 커다란 필의 천으로 직조되었다. 실을 준비하고 천을 직조하는 일 모두 같은 집에서 이루어지는 경우가 많았다. 이후 필 형태의 직물은 — 또 다시 각 가정에서 — 모든 작업을 손으로 하는 침모와 재봉사들에 의해 옷으로 만들어졌다. 심지어 섬유 산업이 산업화된 이후에도 19세기에 재봉틀이 발명되기 전까지는 대부분의 옷이 수작업으로 만들어졌다.

18세기 중반 가내 수공업을 중심으로 한 섬유 산업에서 공장제 섬유 산업으로의 변화에 유일하게 준비가 되어 있던 곳은 영국이었다. 농법의 혁신으로 식량 생산량과 인구가 증가했지만, 동시에 농장에서는 노동력에 대한 필요성이 감소했다. 따라서 영국에는 공장에서 활용할 수 있는 잉여 노동력이 생겨났다. 게다가 영국 및 기타 기역의 재능 있는 사람들이 천연 소재를 준비하고 직물을 직조하는 과정의 속도를 향상시키는 기기를 만들어 냈다. 이에 대한 몇 가지 예로 수력 및 그 이후에 등장한 증기로 작동하는 개량된 베틀과, 직공들로 하여금 예전보다 더 빠른 속도로 폭이 넓은 직물을 만들 수 있게 해 준 플라잉셔틀, 그리고 한 사람이 보다 짧은 시간에 더 많은 실을 생산할 수 있도록 한 다축방적기를 들 수 있다. 섬유 생산은 계속해서 더욱 산업화되었고, 이 과정에서 기업들은 직원들을 건물에 모아 놓았는데, 이러한 건물은 기기에 동력을 공급해 주는 낙수가 존재하는 곳 근처에 위치한 경우가 많았다.

섬유 산업 전반의 산업화를 촉진시킨 가장 중요한 발명은 18세기 후반에 완성된 증기 기관이었다. (이러한 업적에 가장 큰 역할을 한 사람이 제임스 와트였다.) 섬유 기계에 증기 기관이 결합되자 물이 떨어지는 곳 근처에 공장을 세울 필요가 없어졌다. 대신 어느 곳에나 공장을 세울 수 있었고, 실세로 그렇게 되었다. 영국의 섬유 산업의 경우, 셀 수 없이 많은 공장들이 맨체스터 시의 북부에 생겨났다. 하지만 영국에서 산업화가 된 지역은 이곳만이 아니었다. 수많은 다른 도시에서도 공장들이 세워졌고, 영국의 많은 지역이 하룻밤 사이에 산업화된 것처럼 보였다.

하지만 섬유 산업의 급성장에 대한 저항이 심했다. 수 세기 동안 영국의 특정 가문과 도시들이 가내 수공업 방식의 섬유 제조에 있어서 중심적인 역할을 했다. 작업 속도가 빠르고 보다 적은 노동력을 필요로 하는 새로운 기계가 등장하기 시작하자 많은 섬유 노동자들이 이러한 기계의 사용을 거부했고, 그 중 일부는 폭동을 일으켜 때때로 기계를 부수기도 했다. 직물 제조에 사용되는 양털을 판매함으로써 섬유 산업에 의존했던 목양업자들은 섬유 산업이 면 중심으로 바뀌는 것을 반대해 영국 의회로 하여금 해외로부터의 면 수입을 제한하는 법안을 제정하도록 만들었다. 하지만 섬유 산업의 산업화는 계속되었고, 섬유 공장에서 사용된 방법은 다른 산업의 본보기가 되었다. 이러한 과정에서 영국은 산업화로 막대한 이익을 얻었고, 19세기에 영국은 전 세계에서 가장 부유한 국가가 되었다.

WORD REMINDER

agrarian 농경의 flax 아마 bolt (판에 감아 놓은) 직물 한 필, 묶음 loom 베틀 seamstress 여자 재봉사 sewing machine 재봉틀 ingenious 독창적인 spinning jenny 다축방적기 burgeoning 급성장하다

Passage 3 • Art p.57

초상화

초상화는 한 인물이나 인물들을 묘사하며, 가장 일반적인 형태의 미술 중 하나이다. 사람을 대상으로 한 그림은 고대부터 그려져 왔지만, 수천 년 전에 그려진 그림이 현재까지 남아 있는 경우는 거의 없다. 고대 이집트, 그리스, 그리고 로마의 초상 미술은, 그림이나 프레스코화가 아닌 석상 형태로 통치자 및 종교인들의 초상이 공용 공간에 전시되었기 때문에, 사적이라기보다는 공적인 성격을 띠었다. 수 세기 후 중세 시대와 르네상스 시대에 초상화는 보다 널리 알려지고 사적인 성격을 띠게 되었다. 부유한 후원자들은 화가들에게 자신의 이미지를 그려 줄 것을 의뢰했는데, 이러한 그림은 종종 매력적이지 않은 세세한 부분을 보여 주기 보다 돈을 지불하는 대상을 돋보이게 해 주는 경우가 많았다. 이 당시, 초상화의 크기에 따른 세 가지 주요 양식의 초상화들이 발전했다.

전신 초상화는 자세히 표현된 배경과 함께 그림의 대상 전체를 보여 주었다. 재력가들이 자신의 지위를 자랑하기 위해 전신을 나타내는 것을 선호함에 따라 이러한 양식은 17세기 유럽에서 유행했다. 전신 초상화에서는 대상과 배경 사이의 조화가 중요하며, 배경은 상당히 다채롭고 깊고 풍부한 색을 나타내는 경향이 있다. 전신 초상화 중 유명한 사례가 토머스 게인즈버러의 유화인 *파란 옷을 입은 소년*(1770)이다. 이 초상화는 파란색 비단 옷을 입은 어린 아이가 한 손을 엉덩이에 대고 서서 확고한 표정을 짓고 있는 모습을 보여 준다. 배경색은 짙은 갈색과 초록색이며, 나무로 덮인 산이 두드러진 특징이다. 미술사가들은 이 인물이 부유한 상인의 아들을 나타낸다고 생각한다. 하지만 이에 대한 명확한 근거는 부족하다. 실제로 대상의 초점이 어린 아이의 사치스러운 복장에 맞춰진 것은 아니기 때문에, 이 작품은 부유함을 나타냈다기보다 의복을 자세히 그린 그림이라고 할 수 있다.

반신 초상화는 머리부터 허리까지의 신체 윗부분을 나타내고, 대상이 서 있거나 앉아 있는 모습을 보여 주며, 전신 초상화에서 볼 수 있는 것보다 덜 화려한 색 배합을 사용한 배경이 특징이다. 이 그림들은, 대부분이 수채화로 그려지거나 캔버스 위에 유화로 그려지는데, 대상의 얼굴 모양에 더 큰 비중을 둔다. 대상의 얼굴은 보통 관찰자와 일정한 각도를 이루어 그려지며, 이로써 얼굴의 한쪽 면이 보다 두드려지게 된다. 이러한 유형의 초상화는 르네상스 시대에 특히 인기가 많았고, 많은 화가들이 부유하고 권력을 가진 사람들로부터 수수료를 받기도 했지만 반신 초상화 형태를 이용해 평범한 사람들의 모습을 그리기도 했다. 아마도 이러한 장르의 그림 중에서 가장 유명한 것이 레오나르도 다빈치의 *모나리자*(1503-1506)일 텐데, 이 작품은 묘사의 대상인 여성을, 특히 알 수 없는 미소를 강조하고 있는 반면 배경의 중요성은 훨씬 낮게 두고 있다.

흉상 초상화는 대상의 얼굴 표정을 강조해 대상의 머리와 어깨만을 묘사하며, 그 배경은 거의 전적으로 중요시되지 않는다. 따라서 흉상 초상화는 대상의 얼굴을 극도로 자세하게 보여 준다. 이러한 그림은 수채화 물감이나 유화 물감으로 그려지며, 또한 스케치 북에 연필로도 그려진다. 가장 유명한 흉상 초상화 중 하나는 네덜란드의 거장 요하네스 베르메르가 그린 *진주 귀걸이를 한 소녀*(1665)이다. (19세기에 활동했던 네덜란드의 빈센트 반 고흐 역시 이러한 양식이 적용된 다수의 자화상을 그렸다.) 베르메르의 작품은 캔버스에 유화 물감으로 그려졌고, 진주 귀걸이와 동양적인 터번으로 보이는 것을 착용한 여자 아이의 옆모습을 보여 준다. 과거에 네덜란드의 거장들은 이러한 특징을 지닌 작품들을 초상화로 생각하지 않았고 대신 이를 네덜란드어로 얼굴을 의미하는 트로니라고 불렀는데, 이러한 작품들은 과장된 표정을 지은 평범한 사람들을 그린 경우가 많았다.

초상화의 주요 카테고리에 부차적인 유형들도 존재한다. 그 하나가 킷캣 초상화로 불리는 것으로, 이는 반신 초상화에 그림 대상의 양손이 추가적으로 포함되어 있는 것이다. 이러한 명칭은 유명한 영국 신사들의 킷캣 클럽에서 유래했는데, 이곳 클럽 회원들 중 미혼인 모든 회원들이 이러한 스타일로 자신의 초상화를 그리게 했다. 미술사가들은 또한 대상의 얼굴이 향하고 있는 방향과 관찰자와 대상의 얼굴이 이루는 각도에 따라 초상화를 분류하기도 하는데, 이는 논란이 되는 작품을 분류할 때 사용되는 방법이다.

WORD REMINDER

commission 위임하다, 위탁하다 flatter 아첨하다; (실물보다) 돋보이게 하다 come into vogue 유행하다 means 재력 flaunt 과시하다 extravagant 낭비하는, 사치스러운 mute 약화시키다 prominence 두드러짐, 현저함 pocket 호주머니에 넣다; 돈을 벌다 enigmatic 수수께끼의 subordinate 종속된, 부수적인

Passage 4 • Education p.64

르네상스 시대의 교육

15세기와 16세기에 유럽은 르네상스라고 알려진 시기를 겪고 있었다. 당시 유럽에서 어린이가 받았던 교육은 보통 아이의 가문의 사회적 지위에 의해 좌우되었다. 대부분의 유럽인들은 가난한 농부였기 때문에 이들의 아이들은 정식 교육을 받지 못했으나, 부유한 상인 및 귀족들은 자신의 아이들로 하여금 반드시 교육을 받도록 하는 경우가 많았다. 르네상스 시기에 교육이 강조되었다는 점과 그 당시에 많은 대학들이 설립되었다는 사실에도 불구하고, 대부분의 아이들은 — 사회적 지위와 상관없이 — 몇 가지 방식으로 가정에서 교육을 받았다.

르네상스 시기 농민 가정에서 태어난 대부분의 아이들에게 삶은 혹독했다. 남자아이들은 죽지 않고 유아기를 넘기면 아버지와 함께 토지를 경작하거나 아버지가 하던 장사를 배웠다. 운이 좋은 아이들은 장인의 견습생으로 받아들여져 그들로부터 특별한 기술을 배웠다. 여자아이들의 경우, 대부분은 훌륭한 아내가 되는 법과 아이를 기르는 법을 배웠다. 보다 부유한 상인 집안의 아이들은 종종 가정 교사로부터 정식 교육을 받는 경우가 많았는데, 이들은 가업에 참여할 것으로 기대되었기 때문에 최소한 읽고, 쓰고, 수학적인 계산을 하는 법을 배웠다.

귀족들은 종종 인생의 모든 측면에서 아이들을 교육시키기 위해 많은 노력을 기울였다. 귀족 남자아이들은 기본적인 읽기, 쓰기, 그리고 몇몇 언어 이외에도 승마, 무기를 사용하는 무술, 그리고 춤을 배웠다. 일부는 군사 훈련을 받거나 기초적인 공학을 배우기도 했다. 귀족 여자아이들은 남자아이들에 비해 교육을 덜 받기는 했지만, 이들 역시 읽기와 쓰기뿐만 아니라 언어, 음악, 그리고 춤을 배웠다. 미술과 음악의 시대였던 르네상스 시기에 특히 그러했는데, 많은 남녀 아이들이 특히 이탈리아의 전문 학교에서 이러한 과목들을 배웠다.

유년 시절 이후 농민 가정의 아이들이 교육을 받을 기회는 거의 존재하지 않았다. 교회나 수도원 중 한 곳에서 성직자가 되기 위한 교육을 받는 아이들이 소수 있었지만, 대부분의 경우 상류층의 아이들만이 이러한 교육을 받았다. 르네상스 기간 동안 많은 아들을 둔 상인들과 귀족들은 보통 가장 어린 아들을 내보내 종교적인 교육을 받게 했다. 이 아이은 어린 나이에 공부를 시작했고, 라틴어 및 때로는 그리스어로 교육을 받았으며, 성경뿐만 아니라 교회의 의식에 대해서도 배웠다. (그 결과 이들은 성인이 되면 성직자가 되었다.) 귀족 집안의 몇몇 여자아이들은 수녀원으로 보내져 교육을 받고 수녀가 되기도 했다. 보통 이러한 일은 집안에 딸이 많은 경우에 일어났는데, 그렇게 해야 딸이 결혼할 때 내는 상당 금액의 지참금을 아낄 수 있었기 때문이었다.

상인 및 귀족의 아들들이 십대가 되면 아버지의 사업에 참여하거나, 궁중 생활을 하거나, 군인이 되거나, 혹은 대학에 진학했다. 대학은 중세 시대에 처음 등장했지만, 교육이 중시되었던 르네상스 시기에 보다 많은 대학들이 설립되었다. 그럼에도 불구하고, 학생들이 다닐 수 있었던 대학들은 지역에 따라 수준이 달랐다. 게다가, 비록 대부분의 대학들이 다양한 과목의 수업을 제공하기는 했지만, 한 가지 분야에 특화된 대학들도 있었다. 전형적인 분야로 천문학, 의학, 철학, 수사학, 역사학, 수학, 논리학, 그리고 문법이 있었다. 르네상스 시기에 고대 그리스어 및 라틴어 문헌이 재발견되고 그 결과 휴머니즘 철학이 발달함으로써 대학 교육은 상당한 영향을 받게 되었다. 대학생들은 고대 그리스와 로마의 저작물들, 특히 아리스토텔레스의 저작물에 대해 공부할 것으로 기대되었다.

르네상스 당시에 생겨난 학습법은 여러 해 동안 유럽을 지배했다. 하지만 교육에 관한 르네상스 이념은 점차 수정되어 18세기와 19세기에 결국 교체

되었다. 이 두 세기 동안 민족 국가의 출현과 민주주의의 등장으로 개혁가들은 사회적인 지위에 상관없이 모든 아이들이 대중 교육을 받을 것을 요구했다. 하지만 국가가 비용을 지불하는 기본 교육을 받더라도, 대부분의 남자아이들은 계속해서 아버지의 뒤를 따랐고, 대부분의 여자아이들은 아내 및 어머니가 되는 법을 배웠다. 대학은 르네상스 시대 때와 변함이 없었다. 이곳은 남학생들이 지배하는 부유층과 특권층을 위한 장소였다. 유럽에서 르네상스 모델이 사라지고 지위나 성에 상관없이 모든 사람들에게 대학 교육이 가능해 진 것은 20세기 후반에 이르러서였다.

WORD REMINDER

peasant 소작농 apprentice 견습생 clergy 성직자 convent 수녀원 nun 수녀 dowry (신부의) 혼인 지참금 be obliged to ~할 의무가 있다 rhetoric 수사학 profound 심오한, 상당한 emergence 출현, 발생 privilege 특권

Actual Test 03

Passage 1 • Anthropology p.75

원시 남미의 문화

남미 대륙에는 현재 수많은 현대적 도시들이 위치해 있으며, 이곳의 많은 사람들은 비교적 높은 수준의 삶을 영위하고 있다. 하지만 대륙의 상당 부분은, 특히 아마존 강의 내륙 분지와 그곳의 수많은 지류는 여전히 야생 상태 그대로이다. 그 결과 이러한 지역에 살고 있는 많은 사람들은 사실상 석기 시대의 생활 방식을 따르고 있으며, 남미 지역의 일부 부족들은 지금까지도 외부 세계와 접촉을 하지 않고 있다. 이러한 원시 사회에 살고 있는 사람들의 생활 방식은 초기 인류의 생활 방식과 유사하다. 즉 화전 농업, 수렵 채집, 혹은 이 두 가지를 모두 하면서 살고 있다. 몇몇 사람들에게는 이들의 단순한 삶이 이상적인 것으로 보일 수도 있지만, 일부 부족 간에는 폭력적인 기류가 흐르고 있으며 20세기까지 사람을 사냥했던 부족들도 많았다. 오늘날 부족 구성원들은 자신들의 문화를 보존하기 위해 애를 쓰면서도 현대 사회의 혜택을 누리기 위한 노력을 기울이고 있다.

현재 남미에 살고 있는 아메리카 원주민의 부족 수는 200여 개가 넘는다. 유럽인들이 이곳에 도착했을 때 2,000여 개 이상의 부족이 존재했을 것으로 추정되지만, 대부분이 여러 가지 이유로 사라졌다. 오늘날까지 살아남은 부족들은 규모, 거주지, 그리고 생활 양식에서 서로 차이가 있다. 한 부족인 와로아 족은 베네수엘라의 오리노코 강 삼각주 지역에 살고 있으며, 부족원은 20,000명 정도이다. 1500년대에 스페인인들이 도착하기 전 와로아 부족은 활기 찬 사회를 이루었고, 오늘날까지 자신들의 문화적 정체성을 상당 부분 유지시켜 왔다. 반면 아마존 밀림의 앗수리니 부족은 1971년까지 외부 세계에 알려지지 않았다. 이들은 아마존 강의 지류들 사이에 있는 작은 지역을 차지하고 곡물 재배, 낚시, 그리고 사냥을 하면서 살고 있다. 이 부족은 규모가 컸던 적이 없고 오늘날에도 그 인원이 100명을 조금 넘을 뿐이다. 앗수리니 부족은 다른 부족과의 혼인을 통해 멸종을 피할 수 있었다. (이는 남미 지역에서 살아가는 다수의 소규모 부족들에게 흔한 일이다.)

안타깝게도 이러한 많은 부족들에 대한 이야기들이 사라졌다. 1500년대 초반 스페인인들과 포르투갈인들이 도착하면서 남미 지역에서의 삶의 균형은 영구적으로 무너졌다. 몇몇 부족들은 유럽에서 온 질병으로 전멸한 반면, 전쟁에서 패배한 부족들도 있었다. 정복당한 땅을 버리고 멀리 대륙 안쪽으로 들어간 부족들도 있었다. 일부 문화 인류학자들은 소수의 부족들이 과거에 훨씬 더 수준 높은 삶을 살았으며, 아마 거대한 도시에서 살고, 무역에 종사하고, 도자기를 빚고, 비교적 발전된 형태의 농사법을 이용했을 것이라고 추측한다. 하지만 땅을 정복하고, 사람들을 노예로 삼고, 원주민들에게 전통적인 샤머니즘 종교 대신 가톨릭을 믿을 것을 강요하는데 열중한 유럽인들이 많은 부족들을 고향에서 쫓아내 밀림으로 내몰았다. 그곳에서 원주민들은 생존하는 법과, 그들이 찾을 수 있는 어떤 것이든, 그것을 가지고 견뎌낼 수 있는 법을 알게 되었다. 따라서 선택이 아니라 필요에 의해서 더 원시적이 되었다. 수 세기 후 외부인들에게 다시 발견되었을 때, 이들 부족의 역사는 이미 오래 동안 잊혀져 있었다.

오늘날 대부분의 부족민들은 남미의 다른 사람들과 함께 사는 삶에 적응해 왔다. 부족간의 전쟁은 대부분 과거의 유산에 불과하며, 부족간의 교류와 통합이 가속화되고 있다. 심지어 부족간의 올림픽 경기도 있는데, 다양한 부족의 참가자들이 달리기, 창 던지기, 그리고 궁술과 같은 전통적인 활동을 통해 자신의 기량을 뽐내기 위해 모인다. 게다가 많은 부족들은 부족의 원시적

인 생활 방식에 호기심을 보이는 많은 관광객들에게 전통 의상, 도자기, 바구니, 그리고 기타 수공예품들을 판매하면서 외부 경제 활동, 특히 관광 산업에 종사하고 있다. 과거에는 그들이 버는 대부분의 돈이 영토 침범을 노리는 개발자들을 내쫓기 위해 사용되었는데, 그 이유는 개발자들이 부족의 영토 내에 있는 자원을 착취하려고 했기 때문이었다.

하지만 최근 수십 년간 이들 부족의 영토와 권리는 점차 법에 의해 보호를 받게 되었다. 남미 지역 대부분의 국가들은 원주민 부족을 보호하려고 노력해 왔다. 예를 들어 브라질에는 — 주로 아마존 밀림에 — 부족들을 위한 많은 보호 구역이 존재하며, 이곳 부족들의 영토는 보호를 받는다. 타인에 대한 폭력성을 제외하면, 원주민들의 전통적인 생활 방식은 브라질 법에 의해 보호된다. 그 결과 앗수리니와 같은 부족들은 수 세기 동안 살았던 것처럼 계속해서 살아갈 수 있다.

WORD REMINDER

tributary 지류 untamed 야생 그대로의 parallel 유사한 slash-and-burn 화전 농업 undercurrent 내면적 의향, 저의 viable 생명력이 있는, 활기가 있는 eradicate 근절하다, 박멸하다 conjecture 추측하다 make do with ~으로 임시변통하다 relic 유물 prowess 기량 ward off 막다, 물리치다 encroach 침범하다 reservation (원주민을 위한) 보호 구역

Passage 2 • Astronomy p.83

목성의 위성 이오

목성은 토성을 제외하고 태양계 내의 다른 어떤 행성보다 많은 위성을 가지고 있다. 79개의 목성 위성 중 대부분은 크기가 작지만 4개는 상당히 커서 태양계의 비교적 작은 행성들과 크기가 비슷하다. (실제로 가장 큰 위성인 가니메데는 수성보다 크고 화성과 비슷한 크기이다.) 목성 가까이를 돌고 있는 이 4개의 위성들은 1610년 이탈리아의 과학자 갈릴레오 갈릴레이에 의해서 발견되었기 때문에, 이들에게는 갈릴레이 위성이라는 이름이 붙여졌다. 네 개의 위성들 중 아마도 이오가 가장 특이할 것이다. 이오는 태양계 전체에서 가장 지리학적으로 활발한 위성으로 광범위한 화산 활동이 일어나는 곳인데, 이로써 다양한 색조의 유황으로 이루어진 산악 지대 및 평원 지대가 만들어졌다. 뿐만 아니라 이오의 화산 활동은 수많은 분화구가 형성된 원인이기도 하며, 궤도의 형태가 독특하게 된 부분적인 원인이기도 하다.

이오는 목성과 다섯 번째로 가까운 위성으로, 갈릴레이 위성들 중에서는 목성과 가장 가까운 곳에 있다. 목성의 위성들 중 세 번째로 크기가 커서 지구의 달과 그 크기가 비슷하다. 이오가 목성 주위를 도는데 걸리는 시간은 대략 52시간으로, 이는 거대한 행성의 주위를 매우 빠른 시간 안에 도는 것이다. 이오의 자전 주기도 그와 같기 때문에 이오의 한쪽 면만이 계속해서 목성을 향해 있다. 이는 달이 지구를 도는 방식과 유사하다. 이오의 공전 궤도는 완벽한 원형이 아니라는 점에서 특이하다. 공전 궤도가 특이한 것은 목성의 중력뿐만 아니라 가장 가까운 곳에 있는 갈릴레이 위성, 즉 유로파와 가니메데의 중력이 강하기 때문이다. 이오는 이러한 천체들의 중력이 미치는 영향권 안에 있기 때문에 공전 궤도에 영향을 받으며, 또한 내부에서는 많은 조석 현상이 일어난다.

이오의 내부는 규산염질 암석, 철, 그리고 막대한 양의 황으로 이루어져 있다. 이오의 성분은 외부 우주에서 이루어진 관찰에 기반한 것이어서 이오가 지구와 마찬가지로 맨틀과 핵으로 이루어진 시스템을 갖추고 있는지에 대해서는 의견이 일치하지 않는다. 천문학자들이 동의하고 있는 부분은 이오의 내부가 극도로 활동적이라는 점이다. 이는 조수 가열이라는 과정 때문인데, 조수 가열은 목성 및 몇몇 인근 위성의 중력이 작용한 결과이다. 조수 가열로 인해 이오의 화산 활동은 매우 활발하며, 그 표면에는 수많은 활화산들과 사화산들이 존재한다. 인공 위성 한 대가 저공 비행을 하는 동안 최소 아홉 개의 활화산이 관측되었다. 이러한 화산들은 종종 수백 킬로미터 상공에 있는 이오의 옅은 대기권으로 엄청난 양의 황과 기타 물질들을 뿜어낸다. 이러한 현상의 한 가지 결과로서 위성의 표면에 황으로 구성된 넓은 평원이 존재한다. 평원들은 대부분 노란색과 흰색을 띠지만, 일부는 다양한 황 동소체로 이루어져 있기 때문에 붉은색, 오렌지색, 그리고 녹색을 띠기도 한다.

많은 천문학자들을 놀라게 한 것은 20세기 후반 최초의 인공 위성들이 이오에 도달했을 당시 이들이 지구로 보낸 이오의 영상에는 충돌 분화구가 없다는 점이었다. 지구의 달이나 태양계의 여러 다른 천체와는 달리 이오의 표면은 비교적 평탄하다. 충돌 분화구가 없는 이유는 곧 명백해졌다. 끊임없는 화산 활동으로 이오의 표면이 계속해서 형태를 바꾸기 때문인데, 화산 분출로 위성에 있는 충돌 분화구는 그 내부가 채워지거나 덮이게 된다.

이오에서 화산이 폭발하는 경우, 위성 내부로부터 분출된 대부분의 물질은 먼저 위성 위로 높이 솟아오른 다음 다시 표면으로 떨어진다. 하지만 그 중 일부는 표면 위 높은 곳에 머물러 있는데, 이로 인하여 이오 주변에는 옅은 대기가 형성된다. 또한 이 물질 중 상당량은 우주로 빠져 나가 이오 반경의 여섯 배 거리에 이오를 둘러싼 구름을 만들어 낸다. 이 물질 중 훨씬 더 많은 양은 — 초당 1톤 정도의 비율로 — 목성의 자기장에 갇히게 된다. 이러한 물질은 주로 황, 산소, 그리고 염소와 같은 이온화된 원소들로 구성된다. 이들 입자들이, 천문학자들이 원환면이라고 이름을 붙인, 목성 주위의 넓은 자기장 띠를 형성한다. 이오에서 생긴 이 입자들은 평균적으로 40일 동안 목성의 원환면에 머무른 후 목성의 자기권 내로 들어가는데, 이는 원환면의 크기가 비정상적으로 큰 이유를 설명해 준다.

WORD REMINDER

Galilean moons 갈릴레이 위성 (목성의 4대 위성) hue 색조, 모습 eccentric 기이한 flyby 저공 비행 spew 분출되다 allotrope 동소체 incessant 끊임 없는, 쉴새 없는 radius 반경 ionize 이온화하다 dub 별명을 붙이다 chlorine 염소 torus 원환면 whereupon 그래서, 그 때문에 magnetosphere 자기권

Passage 3 • Economics p.90

런던의 경제 발전

오늘날 런던은 영국의 정치 중심지이자 금융 중심지이다. 하지만 런던은 로마의 요새로 처음 만들어졌고, 로마인들이 철수한 후에는 앵글로-색슨 족에 의해, 그 후에는 노르만 족에 의해 지배되었다. 런던은 중세 시대에 크게 성장하여 16세기에는 전례 없던 성장의 중심지가 되었다. 이러한 성장은 대부분 런던의 경제적 발전 덕분이라 할 수 있다. 북해로의 접근이 용이한 템즈강 인근에 위치해 있기 때문에 런던은 해운업과 상업의 중심지가 되었다. 대기업들은 그곳에 본사를 두었는데, 이로써 보다 많은 부가 유입되었다. 마침내 산업 혁명이 시작되자 런던은 더욱 크게 바뀌었고, 19세기 무렵에는 세계 금융의 중심지가 되었다.

로마인들은 서기 43년 영국을 정복한 뒤 — 그들이 론디니움이라고 불렀

던 — 주둔지로서 런던을 만들었고, 이곳은 곧 해상 무역의 중심지가 되었다. 런던의 위치는 이상적이었다. 해안에서 멀리 떨어진 템즈 강 가운데에 자리 잡고 있었으나, 선박이 강의 상류로 들어오지 못할 만큼 깊은 내륙에 있지는 않았다. 따라서 런던은 로마 시대 영국 무역의 중심지가 되었고, 인구가 가장 많을 때에는 인구가 60,000명에 이르렀다. 하지만 15세기 로마 제국이 멸망하면서 로마인들이 영국에서 철수하자 런던은 한동안 사실상 비어있는 상태에 있었다. 앵글로-색슨 족의 침략으로 다시 점령되었지만, 바이킹의 공격과 수십 년 간의 불안정한 정세로 지역 경제는 거의 성장하지 못했다. 1066년 프랑스에서 온 노르만 족이 침략했을 때 그들은 정부의 중심지로 런던을 선택했는데, 이때 도시의 부흥이 시작되었다.

중세 시대의 중후반 기간 동안 조선업과 해상 무역의 발달로 유럽의 각 지역이 보다 긴밀한 관계를 맺게 되자 런던은 도시로서, 그리고 경제적 중심지로서 확대되었다. 런던은 지리적 위치와 정치적 힘 때문에 이러한 상황을 활용할 준비가 되어 있었다. 런던은 중세 시대뿐만 아니라 르네상스 시대에도 크기와 부를 계속 확장시켰다. 16세기 영국이 미 대륙과 그 밖의 지역에 식민지를 확보하기 시작하자 엄청난 양의 돈이 영국으로 모이기 시작했다.

당시 영국에서는 중상주의가 지배적인 경제 철학이었다. 중상주의는 본국과 식민지 간에 이루어지는 영국의 무역을 보호해야 한다고 주장했다. 이에 따라 정부는 수입품에 관세를 부과하고 영국의 무역을 보호하는 법을 제정했다. 주요 목적은 무역 흑자를 달성하는 것과 금과 은을 축적하는 것이었다. 이러한 중상주의 철학의 한 가지 결과로서 영국에는 엄청난 양의 부가 유입되었다. 영국의 경제 활동의 중심지로서 런던은 급격히 성장했고, 크기와 인구가 증가했다.

이와 동시에 거대한 기업과 기관들이 설립되면서 런던이 세계 무역 및 금융의 중심지가 될 수 있는 발판이 마련되었다. 예를 들어 동인도 회사는 인도에서 무역에 대한 독점권을 부여 받았다. 이 회사는 런던에 본사를 두고 있었기 때문에 인도에서 나온 재물들은 런던으로 가게 되었다. (이곳은 또한 영국의 다른 많은 식민지에서도 사업을 했다.) 이 회사는 사업상의 초기 모험에 필요한 재원을 마련해야 했기 때문에 벌어들인 부의 일부를 투자자에게 나누어 주는 주식을 판매했다. 이는 런던의 한 커피 전문점에서 초라하게 시작된 런던 증권 거래소의 설립에 도움을 주었으며, 상인들은 이곳에 모여 주식을 거래했고 전 세계의 금융 소식을 들을 수 있었다. 잉글랜드 은행과 런던 로이즈 보험 회사와 같은 기타 중요한 기관들도 이 시기에 출범했다.

18세기 산업 혁명으로 인해 영국의 경제 철학은 중상주의로부터 자본주의로 바뀌었다. 공장에 투자한 사람들이 부유해지기 시작하자 해외 식민지와의 무역은 중요성이 낮아졌다. 영국은 자유 무역 정책을 실시하고, 세계 시장을 구축했으며, 구매를 원하는 사람이면 누구든지 그들과 제조업체에서 만든 상품을 거래했다. 런던은 이러한 경제 활동의 중심이었다. 19세기 쾌속 증기선, 전신, 그리고 전화가 개발되면서 런던은 전 세계와 연결될 수 있었고, 이로써 런던은 전 세계의 금융 중심지가 되었다. 그곳의 은행들은 자금을 전 세계로 유통시키는데 이용되었고, 금융 기관들은 투자가들에게 자본을 공급해 주었으며, 부두와 창고는 전 세계로부터 들어온 원재료 및 상품들로 가득 찼다. 안타깝게도 1914년 제1차 세계 대전이 발발하자 이러한 시스템 전체가 작동을 멈추었다.

WORD REMINDER

stronghold 성채, 요새 garrison 주둔지, 요새 seaborne 해상 수송의 incursion 급습, 급작스러운 등장 fabulous 엄청난, 경이적인 mercantilism 중상주의 enact 제정하다 amass 축적하다

Actual Test 04

Passage 1 • Botany p.99

왕솔나무

미국의 수많은 소나무 종 중에서 기다란 솔잎 때문에 가장 눈에 잘 띄는 나무 중 하나가 왕솔나무이다. 이 나무는 몇 가지 독자적인 단계로 이루어진 독특한 방식으로 자란다. 왕솔나무는 목재의 품질이 뛰어나서 오랫동안 가치가 높았는데, 이 때문에 미 남서부의 방대한 지역에서 벌목이 이루어졌다. 하지만 현재 일부 주에서 이 나무를 다시 도입하기 위한 조치들이 취해지고 있다.

왕솔나무의 원산지는 미국 남동부이고, 서식지는 서쪽으로 텍사스의 동부 지역에서 동쪽으로 버지니아주의 대서양 해안 지역까지 걸쳐 있다. 왕솔나무가 발견되는 산림에는 매우 다양한 생물들이 발견되는데, 그 이유는 주로 많은 동물들이 왕솔나무의 크고 영양가 많은 씨앗들을 즐겨 먹기 때문이다. 하지만 대부분의 다른 소나무들과는 달리 왕솔나무는 극히 느린 속도로 자라는데, 일반적인 왕솔나무는 100년에서 150년 사이가 되어야 최대 높이에 도달한다.

왕솔나무의 씨는 가을이 한창일 때 대부분 땅에 떨어지며, 몇 주 후에 싹이 난다. 그 후에는 풀 단계에 진입하는데, 이 시기의 왕솔나무는 덤불처럼 보이고 나무처럼 보이지는 않는다. 풀 단계에 있는 왕솔나무의 한 가지 이점은 때때로 서식지에 영향을 미치는 산불로부터 보호를 받는다는 점이다. 약간의 솔잎이 탈 수는 있겠지만, 나무 자체는 불길로부터 안전하다. 게다가, 풀 단계의 나무가 지면으로부터 높은 곳까지 성장하지는 않더라도, 뿌리는 결국 대략 2-3미터까지 자라게 된다. 풀 단계는 보통 1-7년 정도 지속되지만, 일부 나무들은 약 20년 동안 이 단계에 머무르기도 한다.

풀 단계가 끝나면 병솔나무 단계에 진입하는데, 이로써 지면으로부터 보다 높은 곳까지 성장한다. 이 나무들은 급격한 성장 단계를 거쳐 불과 몇 개월 동안에 1-2미터 이상 성장한다. 이 시기에 밖으로 뻗어나가는 나뭇가지들이 자라지 않아서 마치 병솔나무와 같은 모습을 보이기 때문에 이 단계의 이름이 그렇게 정해졌다. 빠른 성장 덕분에 최대한 많은 양의 햇빛을 받을 수 있지만, 나무의 껍질은 다른 부분에 비해 성장 속도가 느려서 산불에는 다소 취약한 상태에 놓이게 된다.

마침내 가지가 옆으로 뻗기 시작하는 단계가 바로 묘목 단계인데, 이때 왕솔나무는 2-3미터 정도의 높이로 성장한다. 나무 줄기와 껍질이 두꺼워지고 매년 1미터 정도씩 자란다. 묘목 단계에서는 껍질이 단단해져 다시금 산불에 잘 견디는 상태가 되기 때문에 높이가 2.5미터 이상의 왕솔나무들은 대부분 실제로 산불이 발생한다 하더라도 결코 죽지 않는다.

왕솔나무는 대략 30년이 지나야 완전히 성장한다. 이러한 시점에서 성숙기가 시작되며, 나무에서는 씨앗이 들어있는 솔방울이 생긴다. 100년 정도 이 단계에 머무른 후에는 노숙림 단계에 진입한다. 대부분의 왕솔나무들은 약 300년 정도 살지만, 거의 500년 동안 살았던 나무들에 대한 기록도 존재한다. (물론 많은 나무들이 이러한 수령에 도달하기 전에 자연 재해나 질병으로 죽는다.) 왕솔나무가 목재로서 상당한 가치를 갖는 때가 바로 이러한 마지막 두 단계에 있을 때이다. 미국이 식민지였을 때 발견된 이후로, 높고 곧게 자란 이 나무들은 선박의 돛대를 만드는데 사용되었다. 현재 왕솔나무 목재는 종이, 인조견, 테레빈유, 그리고 심지어는 플라스틱을 생산하는 경우에도 사용된다.

왕솔나무는 인간에게 가치가 높기 때문에 매우 빠른 속도로 벌목되어 개체수를 다시 회복할 수 있을 정도로 번식이 빠르게 이루어질 수 없었다. 과도한 벌목으로 인해 왕솔나무 산림의 97%가 더 이상 존재하지 않는다고 생각된다. 다행히도 현재에는 왕솔나무의 가치가 인정을 받고 있다. 플로리다 주, 조지아 주, 그리고 앨라바마 주를 포함하여 왕솔나무를 주의 나무로 지정한 많은 주에는 왕솔나무를 기르는 묘목장이 있으며, 야생에서 충분히 건강하게 자랄 수 있을 때가 되면 묘목들은 다시 숲으로 보내진다. 운이 좋다면 차후 미국 남동부 지역의 왕솔나무의 개체수는 증가할 것이다.

WORD REMINDER

encompass 포함하다 partial 몹시 좋아하는 germinate 싹트다 clump 덤불, 수풀 singe 태우다 taproot 곧은 뿌리, 직근 bottlebrush 병솔나무 sapling 묘목 impervious 견디는 mast 돛대 replenish 보충하다, 다시 채우다

Passage 2 • History p.107

그리스 암흑기의 시작

약 기원전 800년경에 시작되었던 그리스사의 고전기 이전에는 역사 학자들이 그리스 암흑기라고 부르는 시기가 있었다. 기원전 1200년 무렵에 지중해 동부 인근 지역의 청동기 문명이 완전히 몰락했다. 이곳을 지배했던 사람들은 — 즉 미케네인들은 — 그리스 본토, 크레타 섬, 그리고 기타 섬들을 점령하고 있었지만, 이들의 문명이 몰락하자 그리스와 인근 지역은 이후 발전이 거의 없었던 400년 간의 시기에 진입했다. 역사학자들에게 이러한 몰락의 정확한 원인은 알려져 있지 않지만, 가능성 있는 설명을 제시하는 몇몇 이론들이 존재한다.

미케네 문명은, 그 영향력에도 불고하고, 사실상 거의 알려져 있지 않다. 미케네 문명은 기원전 1600년경에 등장했으며, 이 문명의 도자기, 무기, 의복, 그리고 기타 유물들이 그리스 본토 유적지에서 발굴됨으로써 역사학자들은 미케네인들과 그들의 문화에 대해 어느 정도 알게 되었다. 또한 프레스코화가 그려져 있는 몇몇 미케네 건물의 유적이 발굴되어 역사학자들은 고대 문화에 대해 더 많이 알게 되었다. 미케네인들은 작은 도시 국가에 살았고 다수의 신들을 숭배했다는 점이 밝혀졌다. 아테나와 포세이돈을 포함하여 이후의 많은 그리스 신들과 다수의 그리스 신화들은 그리스인들이 미케네인들로부터 차용한 것이라는 견해가 일반적이다. 이러한 신화 중에는 호머의 *일리아드* 및 기타 서사시에 상세히 기술되어 있는 트로이 전쟁도 있다. 고대 트로이를 파괴했던 사람들이 실제로 미케네인들이었는지는 알 수 없지만, 그들은 상당히 호전적이었고, 강력한 군대를 보유하고 있었으며, 크레타 섬을 침략하여 그곳에 살고 있던 미노아인들을 정복했다.

하지만 기원전 1200년경 미케네이들의 문명을 몰락시킨 사건이 일어났다. 전해오는 이야기에 따르면 도리아인들이 미케네인들의 영토를 침범했다. 도리아인들은 그리스의 북쪽에 있는 지역인 발칸 반도 출신일 것으로 생각된다. (따라서 이들이 자신의 고국을 출발하여 그리스에 도달하기는 수월했을 것이다.) 또 다른 이론에 따르면 해상 침략 세력 때문에 미케네인들이 몰락했다고 한다. 이 시기에 해상 침략 세력이 이집트 및 기타 지중해 지역의 삶을 파괴했다는 역사적인 증거는 존재하지만, 그들이 어디서 왔는지, 목적이 무엇인지는 시간이 흐르면서 사라졌다. 어떤 경우이든 미케네 문명이 전반적으로 몰락했다는 증거는 존재하며, 수많은 폐허, 예술품 및 저작물의 부재, 그리고 이 시기에 만들어진 금속품 및 도자기의 품질이 낮다는 점은 그들이 외부 침입자에게 패배를 당했다는 점을 암시한다.

일부 역사학자들은 두 사건이 모두 일어났다고 주장한다. 도리아인들이 그리스를 침략한 후 남아 있다가 해상 세력들이 침략했을 때 그들이 도리아인들을 공격했다고 주장한다. 하지만 역사학자들은 난제에 직면해 있는데, 도리아인들이 미케도니아인들을 이길 수 있을 정도로 강하지는 않았기 때문에 그리스 문명이 그처럼 급격히 쇠퇴한 이유는 의문으로 남아 있다. 해상 침략 세력이 먼저 공격을 했고, 이로써 보다 미개했던 도리아인들이 그리스 본토를 침략할 수 있는 분위기가 조성되었을 것으로 생각하는 학자들도 있다. 해상 침략자들이 떠난 후 도리아인들이 미케네인의 영토로 이주하여 남아 있던 사람들과 동화되었다는 이론을 제시하는 학자들도 있다.

최근 수십 년 동안 제기되고 있는 세 번째 가능성은 자연 재해가 발생했다는 것이다. 몇몇 사람들은 그 지역을 강타한 강력한 지진으로 미케네 문명의 상당 부분이 파괴되어 생존자들이 쇠퇴기를 겪었을 가능성이 높다고 생각한다. 또한 가뭄으로 발생할 수도 있는 기후 변화 때문에 농사에 커다란 지장이 생기자 미케네인들이 이를 극복하지 못하고 그 결과 쇠약해진 상태에서 다른 세력에게 패배를 당했을 것이라고 생각하는 사람도 있다. 자연 재해 이론을 뒷받침하는 증거는 거의 존재하지 않지만, 이 이론은 군사적으로 강력했던 미케네인들이 지진이나 가뭄 때문에 영토를 성공적으로 방어할 수 없었다는 점을 설명할 수 있다.

그리스 암흑기의 원인이 무엇인지에 대해서는 논란의 여지가 있지만, 이 때가 그리스 역사에서 절망적인 시기였다는 사실은 명백하다. 기원전 1200년부터 이후 4세기 동안 발전이 거의 이루어지지 않았고, 당시의 문서 기록도 남아 있지 않기 때문에 이 지역에 대한 역사의 많은 부분이 알려져 있지 않다. 기원전 800년경이 되어서야 그리스 본토의 사람들이 암흑기에서 벗어나 도시 국가를 세우고 오늘날까지 전 세계에 영향을 끼치게 될 문명을 창조하기 시작했다.

WORD REMINDER

overwhelm 압도하다, 제압하다 plausible 타당한 것 같은, 그럴듯한 excavate 발굴하다 aggressive 공격적인 hail from ~의 출신이다 maraud 약탈하다, 습격하다 metallurgy 야금술 conundrum 난제 seafarer 뱃사람 bleak 암울한, 절망적인

Passage 3 • Astronomy p.115

첨단 망원경

현대의 광학 망원경은 과거에 사용되던 망원경에 비해 상당히 발전한 형태이다. 모든 광학 망원경은 눈으로 볼 수 있는 영상을 만들어 내기 위해 빛을 수집한다. 이는 두 가지 방법으로, 즉 렌즈에 빛을 투과시키거나 거울에 빛을 반사시킴으로써 실행할 수 있다. 렌즈와 거울의 크기가 커지면서 보다 많은 빛을 수집할 수 있게 되었고, 그 결과 우주의 더 먼 곳을 볼 수 있게 되었으며 동시에 꽤 뚜렷한 이미지가 제공되고 있다. 20세기 전에는 비교적 크기가 큰 렌즈와 거울의 제작이 사실상 불가능했다. 하지만 오늘날 렌즈와 거울 제작 기술의 발전 덕분에 현대적인 망원경들은 어느 때보다 먼 곳까지 볼 수 있다. 그러나 이러한 망원경들은 지구의 대기로 인해 여전히 왜곡된 영상을 보여 주는 문제를 가지고 있다. 이러한 문제는 훨씬 더 우수한 망원경들의 발명으로 해결되었는데, 이들 모두가 우주에 대한 인류의 식견을 크게 넓혀

주었다.

우주에 대한 정보를 수집하기 위해, 망원경은 전자기파 스펙트럼으로부터 정보를 얻으며, 이 스펙트럼에는 가시 광선, 전파, 감마선, 그리고 엑스선이 포함되어 있다. 지구 표면에서는 전자기파 스펙트럼의 제한적인 부분만 관측이 가능하다. 전파와 가시 광선은 관측이 가능하나 엑스선과 감마선은 주로 대기에 흡수되기 때문에 관측이 불가능하다. 하지만 우주에서는 전자기파 스펙트럼의 모든 부분에 대한 정보를 어떠한 왜곡 없이 얻을 수 있다. 1950년대 시작된 우주 시대 이전에는 사실상 단 두 종류의 망원경, 즉 광학 망원경과 전파 망원경만이 존재했다. 광학 망원경은 도시의 밝은 빛으로부터 멀리 떨어져 있는 산 꼭대기에 주로 설치되었다. (반면 전파 망원경은 어디에서나 설치가 가능해서 심지어 해수면 아래에도 설치할 수 있었다.) 하지만 대기 높은 곳에서도 가시 광선이 왜곡되는 현상은 발생했다. 그러나 우주 시대가 시작되자 망원경은 지구 궤도를 도는 인공 위성에 설치될 수 있다.

가장 크고 가장 발전된 형태의 우주 광학 망원경은 허블 우주 망원경(HST)이다. 1980년에 제작되어 1990년 우주 왕복선을 통해 우주 궤도에 진입했다. 곧바로 거울과 관련된 몇 가지 기술적인 문제가 발생해서 NASA는 우주 왕복선 승무원들에게 이를 수리하는 훈련을 시켜야만 했는데, 이는 결국 성공했다. 이때부터 HST는 우주에 관한 막대한 양의 자료를 지구로 전송했다. 가장 인상적인 성과 중 하나는 허블 울트라 딥 필드 사진으로, 이 사진은 다수의 은하계와 기타 천체들이 깨끗하게 보이는, 우주의 일부를 보여 준다. 이곳은 지금까지 인류가 관측한 우주 중 가장 멀리 떨어져 있는 곳이다. HST는 여전히 작동 중으로 2040년 경까지 사용될 예정이며, 다른 망원경들 또한 지구 궤도를 돌고 있고 기획 단계에 있는 망원경들도 있다.

전파 망원경에 대해 이야기하면, 이들은 전파 천문학에서 활용된다. 이 천문학 분야는 은하, 퀘이서, 그리고 펄서를 포함하여, 우주 물체에서 방출되는 전파를 탐지한다. 전파 천문학과 전파 망원경은 1930년대 미국에서 처음 고안되었고, 최초의 전파 망원경은 1937년에 작동되었다. 전파 망원경은 렌즈와 거울을 필요로 하지 않는다는 점에서 광학 망원경과 다르다. 대신 우주에서 나오는 전파 신호를 수집하는 커다란 접시형 안테나를 갖추고 있다. 개별적으로 작동하는 망원경들도 있지만, 성능을 향상시키기 위해 그룹으로 함께 작동하는 망원경들도 있다. 전파 망원경 덕분에 퀘이서, 펄서, 그리고 우주 배경 복사의 존재에 관한 몇 가지 발견이 이루어졌고, 이를 통해 과학자들은 우주의 나이를 계산하는데 도움을 얻을 수 있었다.

광학 망원경과 전파 망원경이 가장 일반적인 두 가지 유형이지만, 이들만 존재하는 것은 아니다. 감마선 망원경과 엑스선 망원경도 존재하는데, 이들 모두 우주에 있는 인공 위성에 설치되어야 한다. 이들은 감마선과 엑스선을 감지할 수 있는 정밀한 거울, 렌즈, 그리고 조리개를 사용한다. 과학자들은 천체로부터 나오는 감마선과 엑스선의 이미지를 활용하여, 특히 엄청나게 멀리 떨어져 있는, 별의 현상을 더 잘 이해할 수 있다. 예를 들어 감마선 망원경은 먼 은하에서 발생하는 감마선 폭발에 대한 상세 이미지와 데이터를 제공해 준다. 이는 짧은 시간 동안 지속되는 고에너지 폭발로, 우주에서 관측된 에너지 폭발 중 가장 강력한 것이다. 과학자들은 모든 종류의 첨단 망원경이 합쳐지면 블랙홀, 암흑 에너지, 그리고 암흑 물질과 같은 우주의 수수께끼에 대한 정보를 얻게 될 것이라고 기대한다.

WORD REMINDER

optical 광학의 distort 왜곡시키다 decommission 퇴역시키다, 사용을 중지하다 conceive 고안하다 parabolic 포물선 형태의, 접시 모양의 mount 싣다 aperture 조리개 outburst 폭발

Passage 4 • Art

p.122

사진의 발달

현대의 디지털 카메라는 즉시 볼 수 있는 깨끗하고 선명한 사진을 찍을 수 있다. 하지만 사진의 초창기 시절, 카메라는 그다지 발전된 형태가 아니었다. 사진술은 1800년대 중반에 프랑스에서 시작되었지만, 그 당시 사진 제작은 시간이 오래 걸리는 힘든 작업이었고 카메라 자체도 무겁고 커서 대부분의 사진 촬영은 스튜디오에서 이루어졌다. 하지만 시간이 지나면서 카메라와 사진 현상 기술이 발달했다. 카메라는 보다 가볍고 작아졌으며, 셀룰로이드 필름이 이전에 사용되던 무거운 판을 대체했다. 1900년대 초반에는 거의 모든 사람들이 사용할 수 있는 카메라와 필름을 기업들이 생산하고 있었다.

두 명의 프랑스인 조제프 니예스와 루이 다게르가 1830년대에 사진술을 발명한 것으로 인정되고 있다. 이들은 화학 물질을 이용하여 실험을 했는데, 이 실험에서 광택을 낸 금속판에 질산은을 덮고 빛에 노출시키켠 판에 잠상이 만들어진다는 점이 입증되었다. 잠상을 다른 화학 물질에 노출시키면 잠상이 판에 고정될 수 있었다. 이러한 방식으로 최초의 사진이 만들어졌다. 이 과정과 그 결과로 생긴 사진은 발명가 중 한 명의 이름을 따서 다게레오타입(은판 사진술)이라고 불렸다. 시간이 흐르면서 다른 사람들이 은판 사진술을 발전시켰지만, 이와 관련된 주요 문제점은 사진을 촬영하는데 필요한 시간이었다. 몇몇 경우, 선명한 사진을 얻기 위해서는 15분에서 30분 동안 판을 밝은 빛에 노출시켜야 했다.

그 결과 사진의 대상이 되는 사람은 절대로 움직이지 말아야 했는데, 그렇지 않으면 사진이 흐리게 나올 수 있었다. 그래서 대부분의 사진 촬영이 스튜디오에서 이루어졌고, 이곳에서 사진의 대상이 되는 사람은 움직이지 말아야 하는 긴 시간 동안 의자에 앉거나 몸을 지탱해 주는 스탠드에 기대는 자세를 취했다. 이러한 제약에도 불구하고 초기의 사진술은 상당히 인기가 높았고, 많은 사람들이 이를 이용하여 초상 사진을 찍었다. 사진술이 도래하기 이전, 모든 초상화는 화가들이 그렸지만 대부분의 사람들에게는 이를 맡길 돈이 없었다. 하지만 사진 촬영 비용은 훨씬 저렴했기 때문에 사진은 초상화보다 감당하기 쉬운 옵션이 되었다.

은판 사진술 및 이후 이와 비슷한 기법들에 있었던 또 다른 문제는 사진의 결과물을 쉽게 복제할 수 없었다는 점이었다. 이러한 문제는 1884년 미국인 조지 이스트먼이 화학적으로 처리된 종이를 사용하여 사진을 찍고 그로부터 복제물을 만들어 낼 수 있는 방법을 개발할 때까지 수십 년 동안 계속되었다. 이후 이스트먼의 종이 필름은 셀룰로이드로 대체되었는데, 셀룰로이드는 보다 잘 휘고 내구성이 강한 재료였다. 1888년에 이스트먼은 필름 한 통을 사용하여 현상하기 전에 여러 장의 사진을 찍을 수 있는 카메라를 발명하기도 했다. 필름을 카메라에 넣으면 사진사는 렌즈를 열어 빛에 필름을 노출시키는 버튼만 누르면 되었다.

이스트먼의 카메라는 두 가지 이유로 혁신적이었다. 첫째, 은판 사진기와 그와 비슷한 카메라에서 사용되던 무거운 판이 필요하지 않았고, 장시간의 노출 시간도 더 이상 필요하지 않았다. 뿐만 아니라 사진사는, 한때는 그랬지만, 사진을 인화하는데 필요한 화학적인 과정을 다루는 전문가가 될 필요도 없었다. 대신 사진사들은 필름을 꺼내 이를 코닥 회사에 보내기만 했는데, 그러면 이 회사가 필름을 인화한 후 사진사에게 되돌려 주었다.

이스트먼의 방식은 표준이 되었고 전 세계가 이를 따랐다. 이후 1901년에 그는 또 다른 새로운 카메라인 코닥 브라우니를 선보였는데, 이는 저렴할 뿐만 아니라 사용법도 간단했다. 이 카메라는 대량 생산되어서 일반 대중들에게 판매되었고, 이로 인해 누구든지 사진을 찍을 수 있게 되었다. 이로써 사진을 위한, 거의 100년 동안 지속된 무대가 마련되어 사람들은 사진을 찍

고 필름을 보내 사진을 현상했다. 그 후 1900년대에 35밀리 필름, 컬러 필름, 그리고 상당히 정교한 카메라들이 발명되면서 사진은 하나의 예술이 되었다. (이로 인해 안셀 애덤스와 같은 사진 작가들은 위대한 예술가로 인정을 받았다.)

사진의 발달은 여러 가지 중요한 결과를 가져왔다. 첫째, 1800년대 말 초상화가 급격히 쇠퇴했다. 둘째, 화가들이 사진 이미지를 캔버스에 그대로 옮겨 놓으려는 시도를 함에 따라 사진술은 프랑스의 사실주의와 같은 몇몇 미술 양식에 영향을 주었다. 셋째, 이스트먼의 카메라와 같이 대량 생산된 카메라 덕분에 사진은 전문가의 영역에서 벗어났고, 사진을 찍는 사람들은 어디든 가서 어떤 것이든 찍을 수 있는 자유를 누리게 되었다.

WORD REMINDER

bulky 부피가 큰 celluloid 셀룰로이드 latent 잠재하는 blurry 흐릿한 advent 도래, 출현 set the stage for ~을 위한 장을 마련하다

Actual Test 05

Passage 1 • History p.131

고대 로마의 인구 감소

고대에서 가장 인구가 많았던 도시는 로마였다. 로마 공화정 및 로마 제국 기간 동안, 티베르 강 유역에 위치했던 활기 없던 이 도시는 서기 200년 무렵 마침내 백만 명 정도의 인구를 보유한 도시로 성장했다. 하지만 이후 로마의 인구가 급격하게 감소하기 시작해서 서기 500년 경에는 인구가 60,000명 정도였다. 이러한 일은 여러 가지 요인에 의해 일어났다. 여기에는 수 차례에 걸친 야만인들의 침공, 내전, 전염병, 그리고 제국의 권력이 로마에서 동로마 제국의 콘스탄티노플로 이동한 점 등이 포함된다. 수 세기에 걸쳐 로마는 존재했지만 이는 예전 로마의 껍질에 불과했고, 19세기 이탈리아가 통일되어 로마가 이탈리아의 수도로 지정된 이후에야 그곳 인구는 로마 제국 전성기 당시의 인구 수준을 회복했다.

현대의 역사가들이 이 도시에 들어온 곡물의 양에 관한 남아 있는 기록을 토대로 로마의 인구를 계산했다. 결점이 없는 것은 아니지만 이러한 방법을 통해 학자들은 그곳에 거주했던 사람들의 수를 대략적으로 계산할 수 있다. 가장 그럴듯한 추측은 로마의 전성기 당시 백만 명의 사람들이 — 아마도 그보다 더 많은 사람들이 — 로마에 거주했다는 것이다. 하지만 자유 시민의 수와 노예의 수를 구분하는 일은 쉽지 않다. 그러나 로마의 인구가 2세기 말에 정점을 찍은 후 감소하기 시작했다는 점은 알려져 있다. 이러한 인구 감소의 한 가지 원인은 2세기 후반 도시 전체를 휩쓸고 하루에 천 명 이상의 사람들을 죽음에 이르게 한 일종의 역병이었다.

몇 년이 지난 3세기 초, 로마의 인구는 잇따른 재해로 인해 더욱 감소했다. 알렉산데르 세베루스 황제의 통치에 불만을 품은 로마의 군인들이 235년 그를 암살했다. 이로써 장기간의 내전이 발생했고, 보다 많은 사람들을 죽음에 이르게 한 새로운 역병과 함께, 로마 인구를 더욱 감소시킨 불안정 시기가 시작되었다. 게다가 이 기간 동안 경제적인 위기로 인하여 제국 내에서의 거래가 제한되었고 속주들은 로마의 지배로부터 보다 독립적이 되었다. 이 때문에 세수가 줄어들고 수도로 보내지는 농작물의 양도 감소해서 로마는 많은 인구를 부양할 여력이 없었다. 3세기 말에는 아마도 로마의 인구가 50만 명으로 감소했을 것이다.

3세기 말 디오클레티아누스 황제가 권력을 잡으면서 내전이 종식되었다. 그러나 디오클레티아누스가 제국을 둘로 나누어 동로마와 서로마 제국을 건설하자 로마의 쇠퇴는 계속되었다. 그는 동로마 제국을 통치하면서 서로마 제국의 황제를 별도로 임명했는데, 서로마 제국의 황제는 권력과 중요성에 있어서 부수적인 존재였다. 디오클레티아누스의 뒤를 이은 콘스탄티누스 1세는 동로마 제국에 수도인 콘스탄티노플을 건설했다. (대규모 건설 공사는 6년 동안 진행되었고 330년에 공사가 완료되었다.) 디오클레티아누스가 동로마로 권력을 이동시키기 시작했고, 콘스탄티누스는 그 일을 계속하면서 관료와 군사를 그곳에 집중시키는 일에 초점을 맞추었다. 콘스탄티노플이 규모와 중요성의 측면에서 성장함에 따라 로마는 쇠락했다.

5세기에 서로마 제국은 결국 멸망했다. 북쪽에서 온 게르만 부족들이 이탈리아 반도를 침범했고, 5세기 동안 세 차례 로마를 약탈했다. 그 결과 도시는 막대한 피해를 입었고, 막대한 인명 피해가 발생했으며, 로마의 인구는 극적으로 감소했다. 시내에 깨끗한 물을 공급해 주던 수로교 체계가 심각한 손상을 입고 식량 수송도 사실상 중단되었기 때문에, 도시에 살던 대부분의 사람들이 살아남기 위해 탈주를 했다. 5세기 말에는 60,000명 정도의 사람들

만이 그곳에 남아있었을 것이다.

그 후 1,000년 동안 로마는, 특히 예전의 영광스러웠던 시기와 비교하면, 사실상 유령 도시였다. 북쪽 지방과 베니스 및 제노아와 같은 도시 국가들이 중세 시대와 르네상스 시대 이탈리아의 새로운 삶의 중심지가 되었다. 이후 18세기 산업 혁명 기간 동안에 로마의 인구가 서서히 증가하기 시작했다. 마침내 19세기에 독립적이었던 이탈리아의 여러 주들이 통일됨으로써 근대 민족 국가로서의 이탈리아가 건국되었다. 로마는 이탈리아의 수도로 지정되었고, 이탈리아 제1의 도시로서의 위상을 되찾았으며, 인구는 최종적으로 현재의 약 280만 명으로 증가했다.

WORD REMINDER

populous 인구가 조밀한 precipitous 가파른, 황급한 epidemic 전염병 infallible 전혀 틀림이 없는 plague 역병 trigger 유발하다 revenue 수입 bureaucracy 관료제 sack 약탈하다 aqueduct 수로교 reclaim 되찾다

Passage 2 • Zoology p.139

동물이 극한의 기온에 적응하는 법

생명체는 어느 정도 온도에 영향을 받으며, 많은 생물들은 생존을 위해 온도 변화에 적응해야만 한다. 그 결과, 수많은 동물들이 춥거나 더운 환경, 축축하고 습한 열대 지역, 그리고 극도로 건조한 사막의 열기 속에서 살아갈 수 있도록 진화했다. 체내에 있는 특별한 메커니즘 덕분에, 그리고 다양한 외적인 수단들을 활용함으로써 생존이 가능하다. 전체적으로 볼 때, 이러한 점 때문에 동물들은 과열되지도 않고 너무 차가워지지도 않는다.

모든 동물은 온혈 동물 아니면 냉혈 동물이다. 온혈 동물에는 사실상 모든 포유류와 조류가 포함되는 반면, 대다수의 파충류, 양서류, 그리고 어류는 냉혈 동물이다. 온혈 동물은 체내의 과정을 통해 열을 생산하여 극도로 추운 환경에서도 체온을 조절할 수 있다. 음식을 섭취함으로써 그럴 수가 있는데, 이들의 신체는 음식을 연료로 활용하여 열을 발산시킨다. 하지만 냉혈 동물은 체온을 조절할 수 없다. 그 대신 이들의 체온은 주변의 기상 상태로부터 직접적인 영향을 받는다. 온도가 낮으면 냉혈 동물의 체온도 낮아지고, 날씨가 더우면 이들의 체온도 높아진다. 이러한 차이점 때문에 일부 환경에서는 온혈 동물이나 냉혈 동물 중 하나가 대다수의 종을 구성한다. 예를 들어 북극에서는, 몹시 추운 환경에서는 냉혈 동물들이 쉽게 죽기 때문에, 대부분의 생물들이 온혈 동물이다.

진화를 통해 동물들은 극한의 날씨에도 적응할 수 있는 신체 조건을 갖추게 되었다. 매우 추운 지역의 포유류들은 작고 둥그런 체형을 가지고 있으며 팔다리가 짧다. 이로써, 소중한 체온을 팔다리로 보내지 않고, 장기가 있는 곳에 체열을 집중시킬 수 있다. 게다가 북극 지방의 많은 동물들은 체열을 보존해 주고 눈과 얼음이 있는 환경에서 몸이 젖지 않도록 해 주는 두꺼운 털이나 깃털을 가지고 있다. 북극곰이나 바다코끼리와 같은 몇몇 동물들은 신체가 너무 차가워지는 것을 방지해 주는 두터운 지방층을 가지고 있다. 또한 포유류들은 몸을 떨 수도 있는데, 이로써 날씨가 너무 추운 경우 팔다리에서 열이 발생한다.

매우 더운 환경에서 포유류들은 몸을 식히기 위해 땀을 흘리거나 거칠게 숨을 쉬지만, 지나치게 날씨가 더우면 너무 많은 수분을 잃게 되어 결국 죽을 수도 있다. 따라서 낙타와 같은 동물들은 사막 환경에서 살아 남기 위해 적응해 왔다. 낙타는 등에 한 개나 두 개의 혹을 가지고 있다. 낙타는 이 혹에 지방을 저장하여 필요한 경우 지방을 에너지나 물로 바꿀 수 있다. 또한 한 번에 상당히 많은 양의 물을 마실 수 있고, 소변이나 대변을 볼 때 어느 경우이던 수분을 거의 잃지 않는다. 낙타는 기온이 매우 높을 때를 제외하면 땀을 흘리지 않으며, 그러한 상황에서도 그들의 신체는 다량의 수분을 보유할 수 있다.

파충류와 양서류에 대해 말하자면 이들에게는 털과 깃털이 없는데, 털과 깃털은 이들이 주로 서식하는 사막과 열대 지역에 적합하지 않다. 그 대신 이들은 비늘이 있는 질긴 피부를 가지고 있다. 악어와 같은 일부 파충류의 경우 피부가 상당히 두껍기 때문에 체내 온도가 과도하게 상승하는 것을 방지할 수 있다. 파충류는 또한 먹이를 이용하여 열을 만들어 낼 필요가 없기 때문에 신진대사의 속도가 느리다. 결과적으로 이들은 아무 것도 먹지 않고 포유류들보다 더 오래 살 수 있다. 이 때문에 파충류는 사막과 같이 먹이가 그다지 많지 않은 환경에서도 살 수 있다. (예를 들어 남미산 뱀의 일종인 아나콘다는 아무것도 먹지 않은 채 몇 주 혹은 심지어 몇 달을 버틸 수도 있다.) 느린 신진대사 덕분에 더운 기후에 서식하는 대부분의 파충류들은 거의 하루 종일 움직이지 않으며 이로 인해 종종 둔해 보이기도 한다.

이러한 적응에도 불구하고 파충류 및 기타 동물들은 여전히 극심한 더위에 취약하기 때문에, 외부 온도가 너무 높이 올라갈 때 체온을 낮출 수 있는 외부적인 수단을 찾아야만 한다. 사막에서 하루 중 가장 더운 때 동물들은 그늘을 찾거나 땅 속으로 들어간다. 밤이 되어 사막의 기온이 떨어지면 뱀, 도마뱀, 그리고 기타 파충류들은 낮 동안 햇빛에 노출되었던 바위 위에 엎드려 열을 흡수한다. 열대 지방에서는 많은 동물들이 하루 중 가장 더운 때에 물가나 누워 있을 수 있는 진흙이 있는 장소를 찾는다. 마지막으로 파충류 및 다람쥐와 곰을 포함한 많은 포유류들은 겨울의 추운 날씨를 피하기 위해 몇 달 동안 겨울잠을 잔다.

WORD REMINDER

frigid 몹시 추운 squat 땅딸막한 pant 숨을 헐떡이다 wind up (어떤 상황에) 처하게 되다 hump (낙타 등의) 혹 scaly 비늘로 뒤덮인 plunge 급락하다

Passage 3 • Botany p.146

식물이 새로운 곳으로 확산되는 방법

모든 생물과 마찬가지로 식물에게도 강력한 번식 욕구가 있다. 꽃식물의 주된 번식 방법은 새로운 지역으로 씨앗을 퍼뜨리는 것이다. 씨앗이 식물로 자라기 위해서는 땅 속에 묻힌 후 싹을 틔워야 한다. 씨앗이 다른 지역으로 퍼져 나가는 방법은 수없이 많으며, 여기에는 중력, 바람, 물, 그리고 사람 및 기타 동물들에 의해 전파되는 방법들이 포함된다. 씨앗은 불과 1미터만 이동할 수도 있고, 수천 킬로미터를 이동할 수도 있다. 또한 다른 종들이 이미 정착한 지역으로도 퍼져 나갈 수도 있고, 성장 환경이 충족되면 완전히 새로운 곳에서도 대량 번식할 수 있으며, 심지어 자연 재해로 피해를 입은 생태계를 회복시키는데 도움을 줄 수도 있다.

식물의 씨앗은 형태와 크기가 다양하다. 많은 씨앗들이 견과류의 겉껍질이나 과일의 부드러운 과육 속에 숨겨져 있고, 너무 작아서 눈에 거의 보이지 않는 씨앗들도 있다. 씨앗은 식물의 번식 과정의 최종 결과물이다. 이들이 식물로 성장하기 시작하면 원래 식물의 번식 과정은 마무리된다. 씨앗이 새로

운 식물로 성장하기 위해서는 어미 식물로부터 멀리 떨어져야 하지만, 다수의 씨앗은, 어미 식물과의 연결이 끊어지는 경우, 중력으로 인해 땅으로 떨어질 뿐이다.

어미 식물과 가장 가까이에 있는 지면이 씨앗에게 항상 이상적인 곳은 아닌데, 그 이유는 보통 다른 식물들이 — 어미 식물을 포함하여 — 그곳에서 구할 수 있는 토양, 물, 그리고 햇빛을 이미 이용하고 있기 때문이다. 예를 들어 사과, 오렌지, 그리고 복숭아 씨앗들이 어미 나무 옆에 묻히면 생명에 필수적인 자원을 두고 어미 나무와 경쟁을 해야 하기 때문에 이들이 성목으로 자라지 못할 가능성이 매우 커진다. 결과적으로 씨앗이 완전한 식물로 성장할 수 있는 가장 좋은 방법은 어미 식물로부터 멀리 떨어진 곳으로 퍼져 나가는 것이다.

씨앗이 퍼져 나가는 가장 흔한 방법 중 하나는 바람에 의한 것이다. 몇몇 식물의 씨앗은 매우 작고 가벼워서 바람에 의해 쉽게 먼 곳까지 날아간다. 많은 경우 씨앗은 진화 과정을 통해 기체 역학적이 되었는데, 이로써 약한 바람에도 공중으로 날아올라 이동할 수가 있다. 예를 들어 민들레의 씨앗에는, 헬리콥터의 날처럼 생긴, 털과 같이 부분이 있다. 물에 뜨는 씨앗들도 있는데, 이들은 시냇물이나 강물에 떠내려가서 새로운 장소의 물가에 도달하게 된다. 코코넛과 같은 몇몇 식물들의 씨앗은 넓은 바다를 떠다니다가 멀리 떨어져 있는 섬에 도달하기도 한다.

과일의 과육이나 견과류 내부에 들어 있는 씨앗은 동물들에 의해 퍼져 나가는데, 동물들은 과일이나 견과류를 먹을 때 씨앗도 같이 삼킨다. 그 후 동물이 배변을 하면 체내에서 소화되지 않은 씨앗은 다른 곳에 떨어지게 된다. 동물의 배설물은 훌륭한 비료가 되기 때문에 이들 씨앗 중 다수가 싹을 틔워서 새로운 식물로 성장한다. 호두와 도토리를 포함하여, 다람쥐나 새와 같은 동물에 의해 저장되는 씨앗들도 있다. 이러한 동물들은 대개 씨앗을 땅 속에 저장해 두지만, 때때로 견과류를 은닉해 놓은 장소를 잊어버려서 일부가 싹을 틔워 식물로 성장하기도 한다. 인간 또한 과일과 견과류를 경작하고 이를 먼 곳까지 이동시킴으로써 씨앗의 확산에 일정한 역할을 하는데, 이곳에서 일부 씨앗들이 땅 속으로 떨어져 자라게 된다.

좋은 토양, 풍부한 물, 그리고 많은 양의 햇빛이 존재하는 지역으로 씨앗이 퍼져나가는 것이 이상적이다. 씨앗은 대개 환경이 생존에 적합한 경우에만 발아를 하며, 많은 씨앗들이 서리와 같이 생명을 앗아갈 수도 있는 위험 요소를 피하기 위해 휴면 상태를 유지하기도 한다. (씨앗에게는 특히 초봄이 위험한 시기로, 일부 지역에서는 이때 날씨가 갑자기 영하로 떨어질 수도 있다.) 하지만 발아를 하게 되면 이미 자라고 있는 식물들과 경쟁을 해야 한다. 빽빽한 산림, 척박한 토양, 그리고 비가 거의 내리지 않는 지역은 씨앗이 발아할 수 있는 최적의 장소가 아닐 수 있다.

대신 씨앗이 대량으로 서식하기에 이상적인 장소는 자연 재해로부터 회복하기 시작한 지역이다. 예를 들어 최근에 산불이 발생했던 곳은 식물의 군집화에 완벽한 장소이다. 불에 타 죽은 식물에서 나오는 유기 물질이 토양의 영양분 수치를 증가시킨다. 게다가 성장하는 다른 식물들이 — 특히 키가 큰 나무들이 — 없기 때문에 실제로 어린 식물들이 충분한 햇빛을 받을 수가 있다. 이로써 어린 식물들은 빠르게 성장해서 튼튼하고 건강한 식물이 될 수 있는데, 산불이나 홍수로 파괴된 지역이 일반적으로 빠르게 회복되는 하나의 이유가 바로 이러한 점 때문이다.

WORD REMINDER

propagate 번식, 증식하다 disperse 흩어지다 colonize 대량 서식하다 husk 겉껍질 vicinity 근처, 부근 aerodynamic 공기 역학적인 buoyant 물에 뜨는 defecate 배변하다 cache 은닉처

Actual Test 06

Passage 1 • History p.155

식민지 미국의 뉴스

미국의 식민지들이 영국으로부터 독립하기 위해 투쟁함에 따라 1775년부터 1783년까지 미국 독립 혁명이 일어났다. 그 당시 신문, 소책자, 그리고 우편물은 미국의 식민지 사람들이 뉴스를 접할 수 있었던 주요 수단이었다. 이러한 정보의 출처들은, 영국인이 여기에 세금을 부과함으로써 결국 영국인들과 식민지 주민 사이에 긴장이 고조되었는데, 혁명에 필수적인 것이었다. 이들은 넓은 지역에 흩어져 있던 사람들을 단합시키는데 도움이 되었으며, 혁명의 진행 상황과 관련된 뉴스를 전달해 주었다.

20세기 이전 사실상 모든 뉴스는 입에서 입으로 전파되거나, 편지, 신문, 브로드시트, 그리고 소책자에 의해 전파되었다. 영국인들이 1600년대에 북미 지역에서 식민지를 건설하기 시작했을 때 그들은 본국과 그 밖의 유럽 지역의 뉴스를 담고 있는 브로드시트를 인쇄하여 식민지에 배포했다. 당시 수송의 특성상 식민지에서 가장 고립된 지역까지 뉴스가 도달하려면 통상적으로 최소 6개월의 시간이 걸렸다. 게다가 식민지 주민들이 미국의 다른 식민지에서 일어난 사건의 뉴스를 인쇄된 형태로 받아보는 경우는 거의 없었다.

이러한 상황은 18세기 초에 변하기 시작했다. 1721년 최초의 미국 신문인 *The New-England Courant*가 메사추세츠 주 보스턴에서 벤자민 프랭클린의 형인 제임스 프랭클린에 의해 출간되었다. 불과 5년 동안만 발행되었지만, 이 신문은 이후 식민지 전역에 등장한 신문들의 본보기가 되었다. 약 50년 후 미국 독립 혁명이 시작되었을 당시 신문은 13개의 모든 미국 식민지에서 흔히 볼 수 있는 것이었다.

미국 독립 혁명 직전, 이러한 신문은 미국의 식민지 주민들이 영국의 행동과 관련하여 자신들의 의견을 표출할 수 있는 공간으로 작용했으며, 이로써 양측은 점차 군사적인 대치 상태에 놓이게 되었다. 많은 신문들이 사설을 발표했고 독자들이 보낸 편지를 실었다. 다수의 미국인들은 영국의 행동에 대해 단호한 반영 감정을 표출했고, 그 결과, 인쇄 매체를 통하여, 영국의 통치에 대한 악감정이 식민지 전역으로 퍼져 나갔다. 이러한 신문들이 교전의 시작에 어느 정도 영향을 미쳤는지는 측정하기 어렵지만, 신문의 지속적인 반영주의적 태도가 여론 형성에 일정한 역할을 했다는 점은 분명하다.

더 나아가 글을 이용해서 다른 사람들에게 영향을 끼치기 위한 방법으로 소책자 출판에 의존한 식민지인들도 있었다. *Common Sense*보다 더 큰 역할을 했던 소책자는 없었는데, 이는 토마스 페인이 쓰고 혁명의 첫 번째 총알이 발사된 이후인 1776년에 발행되었다. 글에서 페인은 미국의 독립을 강하게 주장했다. *Common Sense*는 식민지 전역에서 출판되어 읽혀졌고, 혁명 초기 혁명에 대한 사람들의 지지를 끌어 모으는데 필수적인 역할을 했다.

그럼에도 불구하고 혁명 초기에 많은 식민지인들은 폭력 사태에 대한 준비가 되어 있지 않았다. 영국인과 미국 식민지인들 간의 전투는 1775년 봄 메사추세츠 주에서 시작되었다. (첫 번째 총성이 4월 19일에 렉싱턴 콩코드 전투에서 울렸다.) 서서히 전투에 대한 뉴스가 퍼져 나갔고, *Common Sense*의 발행과 1776년 7월 5일 독립선언문의 서명과 합쳐진 무장 반란의 탄력은 막을 수 없는 것이 되었다. 그럼에도 불구하고 이러한 사건 및 이후의 전투에 대한 뉴스는 느린 속도로 식민지 전역에 퍼져 나갔다.

그 이유는 우편물과 뉴스가 주로 세 가지 방법에 의해 전파되었기 때문이다: 배, 말과 마차, 그리고 도보를 통해서였다. 배는 뉴스를 전달하는 가장 빠

른 방법이었기 때문에 보통 항구에 사는 사람들이 내륙에 사는 사람들보다 훨씬 먼저 다른 지역의 뉴스를 접할 수 있었다. 또한 전쟁 중에는 뉴스 서비스가 중단되는 경우가 잦았고, 종이의 부족과 인쇄기의 고장으로 많은 신문들이 제때에 인쇄되지 못했다. 영국인들은 자신이 통치하는 지역 내의 신문사들을 탄압하곤 했다. 결과적으로 많은 식민지인들이 입으로 전해지는 뉴스만을 들었고, 따라서 몇몇 정보들은 전적으로 신뢰될 수 없는 것이었다.

이러한 문제점에도 불구하고 미국 독립 혁명 당시, 간헐적이긴 했지만, 다양한 형태의 뉴스가 여전히 전달되었고, 사람들은 가장 중요한 사건들에 대한 정보를 얻을 수 있었다. 신문, 소책자, 그리고 기타 정보 전달의 수단들이 혁명의 성공에 끼친 영향을 측정하는 일은 쉽지 않겠지만, 이러한 수단들이 없었다면 혁명 자체가 일어나지 않았을 것이라고 해도 과언은 아니다. 어찌되었든 영국에 맞서 미국의 식민지 주민들을 통합시키는데 도움이 된 글들은 신문과 소책자에 인쇄되어 있었다.

WORD REMINDER

levy 세금을 부과하다 broadsheet 브로드시트 (한 면만 인쇄된 오늘날의 신문과 크기가 비슷한 간행물) confrontation 대치, 대결 decidedly 확실히, 단호하게 print media 인쇄 매체 resort to ~에 호소하다 integral 필수적인 momentum 탄력, 가속도 make a point of ~하곤 하다, 으레 ~하다 suppress 억압하다, 탄압하다 sporadically 드물게, 산발적으로

Passage 2 • Environmental Science p.163

빙하기의 영향

지구의 역사에 걸쳐, 약 15,000년에서 20,000년 전에 일어났던 가장 최근의 빙하기를 포함하여, 수없이 많은 빙하기가 있었다. 이러한 빙하기 동안 북극 지방과 그 밖의 산악 지역에 거대한 빙상이 형성되었다. 이러한 얼음 층은 수 킬로미터의 두께로 커져서 천천히 이동했으며, 이들의 움직임으로 육지의 형태가 점차 변형되었다. 빙하기는 육지뿐만 아니라 바다도 변화시켰는데, 과학자들은 멕시코만 해류와 같은 현재의 해류들이 빙하기 때문에 나타났다고 생각한다.

빙하기 동안 지구의 평균 기온은 급강하한다. 이로 인해 육지의 담수와 바다의 염수가 모두 서서히 얼어붙는다. 바닷물이 얼어 빙상 내부에 갇히게 되면 전 세계적으로 해수면이 낮아진다. 마지막 빙하기 당시에는 대부분의 지역에서 100-200미터 정도 해수면이 낮아졌다. 이로써 많은 지역에서 해저가 노출되었고, 넓은 바다에 의해 분리되어 있었던 지역 사이에 육교가 만들어졌다. 이는 육지의 형태와 지구에서 인간의 삶이 확산되는 과정에도 지대한 영향을 끼쳤다.

약 40,000년 전 빙하기 당시 인도네시아와 뉴기니 사이에 육교가 생겼기 때문에 사람들은 남쪽의 뉴기니로 이동했다. 훨씬 더 큰 영향을 끼친 것 중 하나는 아시아의 시베리아와 북미의 알래스카를 연결하는 육교의 등장이었다. 이 육교가 생겨나기 전에는 북미와 남미에 인간이 거주하지 않았다. 하지만 마지막 빙하기 때 사람들은 극도로 추운 날씨에도 생존하는 법을 알게 되었고, 시베리아에도 인간 부족들이 살고 있었다. 약 15,000년 전 베링해에 육교가 생기자 시베리아의 많은 부족민들이 떠돌아다니는 동물 무리를 따라 알래스카로 건너갔다.

마침내 북미 지역의 인류는 남쪽으로 향했고, 빙하 지역을 떠났으며, 인류가 이전에 결코 보지 못했던 동물들이 가득한 보다 따뜻한 육지를 발견했다. (여기에는 매머드, 검치호, 다디어울프, 그리고 땅늘보가 포함되었다.) 그들은 이러한 많은 동물들을 재빨리 도축하기 시작했다. 이러한 일은 주로 인류가 수렵-채집민이었고 농사에 대해 알지 못했기 때문에 일어났으며, 그 결과 그들은 주요 식량원으로서 동물에 의존했다. 하지만 과도한 사냥으로 많은 종의 동물들이 멸종했다. 그럼에도 불구하고, 천 년 이내에, 사람들은 남미 대륙의 최남단까지 계속해서 나아갔다.

또한 과거의 빙하기가 현재의 해류에도 막대한 영향을 끼쳤을 것이라고 생각되는데, 해류는 날씨의 형성에 중요한 역할을 한다. 빙하기 때 가끔 기온이 상승하는 짧은 시기가 있었고, 이때 일부 빙상이 녹아 내렸다. 예를 들면 이러한 온난한 시기에 유럽과 북미의 커다란 빙산들이 거대한 빙상에서 떨어져 나와 대서양으로 떠내려갔다. 이러한 빙산들이 남쪽으로 이동해 녹기 시작하면서 염수의 바다에 상당한 양의 담수가 유입되었다. 이는 대서양의 염도를 변화시켰고, 대서양에서 가장 중요한 해류인 멕시코 만류의 경로 및 세기가 결정되는데 중요한 역할을 했을 것이다. 멕시코 만류는 남쪽에서 북쪽으로 따뜻한 물을 이동시키고 유럽 인근을 통과함으로써 유럽 대륙이, 멕시코 만류가 없는 경우 그곳 북쪽 위도에서 가능할 수 있는 수준보다 더 온화한 기후를 유지하는데 도움을 준다.

이에 대한 증거에는 두 곳으로부터 나온다. 첫째, 그린란드 만년설을 시추하여 얻은 얼음 핵을 통해 다른 기간보다 얼음 층이 더 두꺼웠던 시기가 존재했다는 점을 입증할 수 있는데, 이는 얼음과 눈이 보다 적게 쌓였던, 온난화 시기가 존재했다는 점을 암시한다. 몇 번의 온난화 시기들은 수십 년 정도 지속되었던 것으로 알려져 있다. 두 번째 증거는 대서양 해저에서 채취한 암석 견본으로부터 나온다. 이 암석들은 북유럽의 특정 지역에서만 발견되는 암석들과 일치한다. 이러한 암석들이 바다 한 가운데에 있다는 사실을 통해 과학자들은 이들이 빙산에 의해서 그곳까지 운반되었다는 결론을 내렸다. 빙상이 나아가면서 육지를 파내고 암석들을 끌어 모으자 암석이 얼음 속에 파묻히게 되었다. 이러한 빙상에서 빙산이 떨어져 나와 바다에서 녹을 때 바닥으로 암석들이 떨어졌다. 이와 동시에 빙산에서 담수가 흘러나왔고, 이는 멕시코 만류의 형성에 도움을 주었다.

WORD REMINDER

plummet 급락하다 distribution 분포 subsequently 그 후에, 이어서 devoid ~이 전혀 없는 slaughter 도살하다 tremendous 상당한, 엄청난 iceberg 빙산 temperate 온화한 latitude 위도 accumulate 축적하다 consistent 일치하는

Passage 3 • Psychology p.171

유아의 모방 행동

유아가 어떻게 배우는지는 아동 심리학자 및 교육학자들이 오랫동안 해답을 찾으려고 노력해 온 문제이다. 대부분은 유아들이 주로 어른의 행동을 보고 그대로 모방함으로써 배운다는 점에 동의한다. 하지만 이러한 모방 행동이 본능적인 것인지, 혹은 유아들이 몇몇 종류의 의미와 어른들의 행동을 연결시키는 것인지에 대해서는 확신하지 못한다. 게다가 아동 교육 전문가들은 유아들이 몇 살 때 어른을 모방할 수 있는지 뿐만 아니라 몇 살 때 자신의 행동으로부터 배우기 시작하는지에 대해서도 의견이 일치하지 않는다. 유아를 대상으로 한 포괄적인 연구에도 불구하고, 아동 교육 전문가들은 아직도

유아들의 머릿속에 어떤 일이 일어나고 있는지 확실하게 말할 수 없다.

여러 해 동안, 대부분의 아동 교육 전문가들은 유아들의 어른 모방 행동이 선천적인 것이라고 확신했다. 유아들은 태어나면서부터 눈에 보이는 모든 것을 모방하려는 경향이 있다고 생각했다. 그러한 관점에서 이들 전문가들은 유아들이 자신의 행동으로부터 아무것도 배우지 못한다고 생각했다. 하지만 최근 수십 년 동안 특정한 실험 연구에 바탕을 둔 새로운 이론이 명성을 얻고 있다. 유아의 모방 행동을 보다 잘 이해하기 위해 통제된 상황 하에서 유아에 대한 폭넓은 실험이 이루어졌다. 많은 실험들은 유아로 하여금 어른의 표정을 관찰하도록 만드는 것과 관련되어 있었다. 이러한 실험들이 얼굴 표정에 초점을 둔 이유는, 유아들 앞에 계속해서 거울이 없는 한, 그들은 자신의 얼굴 표정을 볼 수 없기 때문이었다. 거울이 없기 때문에 유아들은 자신의 얼굴 표정을 머리 속에 각인시키지 못했고, 이는, 그들이 어른들의 표정을 따라 했을 때, 어른의 행동을 의식적으로 모방했다는 점을 의미했다. 대부분의 연구는 입의 움직임, 특히 입술과 혀의 위치에 초점을 맞추었다.

이러한 실험의 한 가지 결과로 유아의 모방 행동과 학습에 관한 새로운 이론이 만들어졌다. 아동 교육 분야의 최고 전문가인 앤드류 멜소프와 키스 무어는 유아들이 어른을 흉내 낼 때마다 능동적인 학습이 이루어진다는 점을 밝혀냈다. 그들의 연구에 따르면 유아들이 처음으로 어떤 동작을 보았던 때와 직접 그 동작을 할 수 있는 기회가 생긴 시기 사이에 며칠의 차이가 있더라도 유아들은 정확하게 흉내를 낼 수 있었다. 이로써 유아들이 행동을 관찰해서 그것을 기억한 후 이를 따라 했다는 결론에 도달하게 되었는데, 이는 결과적으로 유아들이 무엇인가를 배웠다는 점을 의미했다.

유아 모방과 관련된 또 다른 문제는 몇 살 때부터 유아들이 모방을 통해서 배우기 시작하는지이다. 예전에는 대다수의 아동 연구 전문가들이 1살 이상의 어린이들만 모방을 통해 능동적으로 학습을 한다고 생각했다. 하지만 멜조프와 무어의 추가적인 연구를 통해 생후 6주의 유아들도 이러한 방법으로 학습을 할 수 있다는 결론이 내려졌다. 또 다른 실험에서는 6주된 몇 명의 유아들을 대상으로 며칠 동안 실험을 했는데, 이 역시 어른의 표정을 활용한 것이었다. 그들은 유아들이 자신이 보았던 것을 — 입과 혀를 움직여야 하는 복잡한 행동일지라도 — 적극적으로 따라 하려고 노력한다는 점과, 다른 사람들이 표정 짓는 모습을 더 많이 볼수록 스스로 표정을 짓는 일을 더 잘 한다는 점을 알아냈다.

멜조프와 무어는 더 나아가 매우 어린 유아들이 일정한 얼굴 표정을 하고 있는 사람을 보고 자신이 동일한 표정을 지을 때 느끼게 되는 감정을 서로 연관 지을 수 있다고 생각했다. 기본적으로 유아들은 자신의 감정과 자신이 흉내 내는 사람의 감정이 동일하다고 생각한다. 그들 생각으로, 유아들은 자신이 본 것과 자신의 행동을 연관시키고, 더 나아가 자신의 행동과 자신의 감정을 연관시키며, 마지막으로 어른의 얼굴 표정을 관찰한 후 이를 바탕으로 자신의 감정을 타인에게 투영한다. 예를 들어 유아가 웃는 사람을 보고 따라서 웃을 때, 유아의 기분은 갑자기 좋아진다. (마찬가지로 겁먹은 얼굴을 보고 겁먹은 표정을 짓는 유아는 두려움을 느낄 수도 있다.) 동시에 유아는 웃고 있는 사람 역시 행복할 것이라고 믿는다. 따라서 멜조프와 무어는 유아가 다른 사람들의 심적인 상태를 이해하는 능력을 가지고 태어난다는 결론에 도달했다.

유아의 모방 행동에 관한 멜조프와 무어의 이론은 당시에 인정받고 있던 이론과 크게 달랐기 때문에 아동 연구 학계에서 상당한 논란 거리가 되었다. 오늘날 유아의 모방 행동에 대한 양쪽 이론 모두에 지지자들이 존재한다. 당장은 각각의 학설에 강점과 약점이 있으며, 유아의 의사 소통 능력에 한계가 있다는 점을 고려하면, 대부분의 유아들이 어른을 흉내 내기 시작하는 정확한 시기에 대해서는 확실한 결론이 나지 않을 가능성이 높다.

WORD REMINDER

exhaustive 철저한, 광범위한 be inclined to ~하는 경향이 있다 imprint 강한 인상을 주다, 각인시키다 ascertain 알아내다, 밝혀내다 correlate 밀접한 연관이 있다 radically 급진적으로 school of thought 학설, 학파

Passage 4 • Architecture p.178

그리스 및 로마 건축의 영향

그리스와 로마는 가장 위대한 고대 문명 중 두 개로, 이 둘 모두 역사와 문화에 지속적인 영향을 미쳐 왔다. 후대 문명의 사람들이 그들을 모방했던 분야 중 하나가 건축이다. 예를 들어 그리스와 로마의 건설 기술 및 건축 양식은 15세기와 16세기 유럽의 르네상스 시대에 부활했으며, 이후 18세기와 19세기 신고전주의 시대에 크게 모방되었다.

그리스 건축은 수백 년에 걸쳐 발전했다. 전성기는 그리스 고전기 때로, 이 시기는 대략 기원전 500년에서 100년까지 지속되었다. 고대 그리스의 건축 양식은 일반적으로 세 개의 시기, 즉 이오니아, 도리아, 그리고 코린트로 구분된다. 이 세 개의 양식은 본래 지역적 차이에 기반을 둔 것이었다. 도리아 양식은 그리스 본토와 밀접한 관련이 있었던 반면, 이오니아 양식은 에게 해의 그리스의 섬들 및 오늘날 터키에 해당되는 소아시아에 위치해 있던 그리스 식민지들과 보다 밀접한 관련이 있었다. 한편 코린트 양식은 이오니아 양식의 한 분파라고 생각되지만 본질상 더 정교하다. 세 양식 간의 차이는 그리스 건물에 사용되었던 기둥에서 가장 잘 찾아볼 수 있다. 도리아 양식의 기둥은 다소 단순하고, 이오니아 양식의 기둥은 화려한 꼭대기로 유명하며, 코린트 양식의 기둥은 복잡한 디자인을 지니고 있다. 또한 도리아 양식의 기둥은 짧고 두꺼운 반면에 이오니아 및 코린트 양식의 기둥은 보다 길고 가늘다.

일부 방식들이 그리스의 것과 다르기는 했지만 로마인들은 기둥의 디자인 및 활용에 있어서 그리스인들을 따라 했다. 예를 들어 주로 로마인들은 구조물의 각층에 서로 다른 스타일을 적용함으로써 같은 건물에 세 가지 양식의 기둥을 모두 사용했다. 하지만 로마인은 스스로의 노력으로 혁신가가 되었다. 로마가 건축에 기여한 가장 중요한 것 중 두 개는 아치와 돔이었다. 로마인들은 아치와 돔 덕분에 고대 그리스인들이 만든 것보다 — 보다 커다란 내부를 갖춘 — 훨씬 더 거대한 건물을 세울 수 있었다. 그리스인들은 종종 지붕이 뚫린 사원과 구조물들을 지었지만, 로마인들은 커다란 건물 위를 돔으로 덮었다. 로마의 판테온 신전은 로마식 돔 건물의 가장 좋은 사례이다. 아치의 경우, 이로 인해 로마인들은 커다란 출입구와 창문을 갖춘 벽을 만들 수 있었다. 아치는 또한 로마의 거대한 수로교에서도 매우 효과적으로 사용되었는데, 그 중 일부는 길이가 수백 킬로미터에 이르렀다. (수 세기가 지난 중세 시대에도 많은 수로교에 물이 흘렀으며, 이는 로마의 토목 기술의 우수성을 입증해 주었다.)

476년에 로마가 몰락하자 로마와 그리스 건축에 대한 지식은 점차 서구에서 사라졌다. 하지만 15세기 이탈리아에서 로마와 그리스 건축의 부활이 시작되었다. 이 시기에, 그 전에는 서유럽에서 유행한 고딕 양식에 영향을 받았던 이탈리아 건축가들이 고대 그리스와 로마의 건축 기법에 관한 정보를 얻게 되었다. 이러한 지식은, 주로 현재의 터키와 그리스에 해당하는 지역에 있었던, 비잔틴 제국의 수도인 콘스탄티노플로부터 나왔다. 당시 비잔틴 제국은 오스만 투르크에 포위당한 상태였고 서서히 세력을 잃고 있었다. 결국

패배를 직감했던 많은 비잔틴 사람들이 서쪽으로 도피를 했다. 도피를 하면서 고대 그리스와 로마에 관한 서적들과 다른 정보의 출처들을 가지고 갔다. 많은 이들이 도착했던 이탈리아에서, 그들은 배움에 목말라 있었던 학생들을 발견했다. 이탈리아의 건축가들은 이들 도피자들로부터 로마의 둥근 아치와 돔의 비밀에 대해 알게 되었다. 또한 건물 설계에 있어서 수학적인 정확성과 대칭성을 활용한 로마의 방식을 따르기 시작했으며, 무질서하고 부정확한 고딕 건축 양식은 폐기했다. 마침내 이러한 새로운 양식은 다른 유럽인들의 상상력을 사로잡았고, 르네상스 기간 동안 서구의 전 지역으로 퍼져 나갔다.

수 세기가 지난 18세기 중반, 1,700년 전 베수비우스 화산 폭발에 의해 완전히 재로 덮여 있었던 폼페이라는 로마의 도시가 발굴되었다. 이 도시가 발견되자 또 다시 고전 건축에 관심이 쏟아졌다. 이로써 신고전주의 시대가 시작되었다. 18세기와 19세기 동안, 많은 대학 건물, 도서관, 그리고 정부 건물들이 고대 그리스와 로마의 건축물들과 비슷하게 보이도록 설계되고 지어졌다. 20세기에 강철이 사용되고 고층 건물이 지어지면서 고대 그리스와 로마의 영향은 다소 감소하기는 했지만, 이들의 기법과 양식, 그리고 컨셉은 오늘날에도 여전히 유의미하다.

WORD REMINDER

realm 영역, 분야 heyday 전성기 offshoot 분파, 파생물 scrolled 장식이 있는, 화려한 intricate 복잡한 slender 날씬한 in one's own right 혼자 힘으로 doorway 출입구 aqueduct 수로교 besiege 포위하다 symmetry 좌우 대칭 haphazard 우연, 무계획 imprecise 부정확한 initiate 시작하다, 주도하다

Actual Test 07

Passage 1 • Meteorology p.189

강수의 유형

강수는 구름에서 지면으로 떨어지는 모든 형태의 물을 말한다. 구름은 수증기가 상승하여 응축된 후 대기 중의 먼지나 소금 입자에 달라붙어 결국 다른 입자들과 결합할 때 형성된다. 구름에 응축된 수분이 너무 많으면 구름에서 수분이 방출되어 액체, 착빙, 혹은 동우의 형태로 땅에 떨어진다. 낙하하는 강수의 유형은 기상 조건과 기온에 따라 차이가 있다.

액체성 강수는 기온이 섭씨 0도 이상인 대기에서 형성된다. 기본적인 두 가지 형태는 비와 이슬비이다. 비는 지구상에서 가장 흔한 형태의 강수지만, 일부 지역에서는 지속적으로 비가 내리는 반면 사막과 같은 지역에서는 수십 년 동안 비가 내리지 않기 때문에, 모든 지역에서 동일한 양의 비가 내리는 것은 아니다. 비는 일반적으로 0.5밀리미터보다 큰 물방울로서 정의된다. 구름으로부터 직접 떨어질 수도 있고, 혹은 영하의 온도에서 형성된 눈이나 얼음 결정이 대기를 통과하여 하강하는 과정에서 녹음으로써 비가 내릴 수도 있다. 이슬비의 경우, 이는 0.5밀리미터보다 작은 물방울로 이루어진다. 이슬비는 아열대 지방과 바다 위에서 흔히 볼 수 있으며, 낮게 깔리고 평평하고 거의 특색이 없는 구름으로서 종종 서로 결합하여 하늘 전체에 균일하고 커다란 회식 덩어리를 만들어 내는, 층운에서 떨어지는 경향이 있고, 보통은 안개나 박무가 낀 기상 상황에서 떨어진다.

착빙성 비는 서로 다른 층에서 다양한 온도를 나타내는 대기에서 형성된다. 여기에는 두 가지 형태가 있다. 결빙성 진눈깨비와 우빙이 그것이다. 액체성 강수와 마찬가지로 낙하하는 결빙성 강수의 종류도 물방울의 크기에 의해 결정된다. 두 종류의 착빙성 강수 모두 대기의 높은 곳에 있는 구름에서 눈이 내릴 때 발생한다. 눈이 보다 따뜻한 대기를 통과하면 완전히 녹아서 물방울로 변한다. 하지만 보다 지면과 가까운 곳에도 차가운 공기 층이 존재하는데, 이 때문에 물방울이 얼음 결정체로 변하기 시작한다. 완전히 얼어붙을 시간이 충분하지 않기 때문에 이들은 딱딱한 얼음 결정체의 형태로 땅에 떨어진다. 어떤 표면에 떨어지더라도 결빙성 진눈깨비와 우빙은 그 순간 얇은 얼음 층을 만들어낼 수 있다. (전자는 후자에 의해 만들어지는 것보다 더 작은 얼음 층을 만드는 경향이 있다.) 이들은 특히 위험한데, 그 이유는 이들로 인해 도로의 표면이 미끄러워지고 나뭇가지와 전선이 무거운 얼음 층으로 덮이기 때문이다. 그 결과 이러한 얼음은 나뭇가지와 전선을 부러뜨릴 수 있으며, 이는 도로가 차단되고 정전이 발생하는 원인이 될 수 있다.

동우의 세 가지 주요한 형태는 진눈깨비, 우박, 그리고 눈이다. 진눈깨비는 눈이 따뜻한 대기의 층을 통과하면서 일부만 녹을 때 만들어진다. 그 후 보다 차가운 공기 층에 진입하면서 다시 얼어붙지만, 이때 형성되는 것은 눈송이가 아닌 단단한 얼음 알갱이이다. 진눈깨비가 도로에 쌓이면 운전하기에 위험한 상황이 조성될 수도 있다. 우박은 커다란 층적운에서 형성되는데, 층적운은 뇌우를 발생시키는 구름이다. 뇌우의 내부에는 서로 다른 온도의 층을 통과하여 상승과 하강을 반복하는 기류가 존재한다. 뇌우가 형성될 때 물방울이 상승하여 차가운 대기에 진입하면 얼어붙어서 얼음 알갱이로 변한다. 뇌우의 상태로 인해 알갱이들은 상승과 하강을 반복한다. 이러한 과정에서 보다 많은 물방울들이 알갱이에 달라붙고, 이들은 보다 차가운 공기 층에서 얼어붙게 된다. 마침내 얼음의 층이 너무 무거워지면 알갱이들은 우박이 되어 땅으로 떨어진다. 우박은 무겁고 커서 — 직경이 최대 12센티미터에 이른다 — 보통 농작물, 차량, 그리고 건물에 피해를 입히며 사람과 동물에게

부상을 입힐 수도 있다.

눈은 과냉각된 물방울이 섭씨 영하 18도에서 31도 사이의 온도에서 얼어붙을 때 만들어진다. 결빙 온도에서 얼음 핵이 생성되며, 격자 모양으로 얼어붙은 물이 그 주변에서 눈송이를 만든다. 눈송이가 너무 무거워지면 지면으로 떨어진다. 눈은 지면의 온도가 결빙 온도보다 낮을 때 낮은 층에 있는 층운에서 내리는 경우가 많다. 이 구름이 비교적 낮은 고도에 위치하는 경우에는 눈이 다른 유형의 강수로 바뀌지 않고 지면에 도달할 가능성이 높다. 대기 높은 곳에 있는 구름에서 눈이 내리는 경우에는 지면에 도달할 때쯤 눈이 액체성 강수나 결빙성 강수로 변하는 경우가 많다.

WORD REMINDER

precipitation 강수 condense 응결되다 drizzle 보슬비 subtropical 아열대의 stratus cloud 층운 slick 미끄러운 obstruct 막다 respectively 각각 sleet 진눈깨비 hail 우박 thaw 녹다 pellet 둥글게 뭉친 것 snowflake 눈송이 treacherous 위험한 cumulonimbus cloud 층적운 spawn 야기하다 draft of air 기류 supercool 과냉각시키다 lattice 격자

Passage 2 • Economics p.196

아유타야 왕국의 경제

현재의 태국은 유럽인들이 샴이라고 불렀던 일련의 왕국으로부터 발전했다. 가장 번영했던 왕국은 아유타야라는 도시를 중심으로 삼았는데, 이 도시는 17세기와 18세기 당시 세계에서 가장 큰 도시 중 하나였다. 아유타야 왕국은 14세기 중반에서 18세기 말까지 지속되었다. 이곳의 주요 도시는, 몇몇 강이 합쳐지는 일련의 섬들에 위치한, 요새화된 지역에서 시작되었다. 시간이 흐르면서 이 도시는 강력한 왕국이 되어 동남아시아에서 상당한 영향력을 가지게 되었고, 보다 작고 힘이 약한 왕국들로부터 조공을 받았다. 아유타야 사람들은, 현재의 국가명이 여기에서 유래되었는데, 스스로를 타이라고 불렀으며 주로 불교를 믿었다. 아유타야의 경제는 농업에 기반을 두었고, 쌀을 재배하고 지역의 영주들에게 노동력을 제공했던 다수의 소작농에 의존하고 있었다.

넓은 농토와 풍부한 강수량 덕분에 오늘날 태국의 방콕 북부 지역에 위치해 있었던 아유타야의 농부들은 거의 항상 모든 사람들에게 식량을 제공하고도 잉여 농산물을 생산할 정도의 충분한 식량을 재배했다. 이러한 잉여 농산물은 영주 및 불교 사원의 수도승을 부양하는데 사용되었고, 그 밖에 남은 농산물은 다른 지역으로 판매되었다. 이러한 거래는 사실상 해상 무역이었고, 타이 사람들은 근본적으로 토지에 묶여 있었기 때문에, 이주해 온 중국인 상인들에 의해 주로 이루어졌다. 이들은 누군가에 의해 소유된 것이 아니었으므로 노예는 아니었지만, 타이의 모든 소작농들은 영주에게 귀속되어 있었다. 이러한 영주들은 자신이 소유한 토지의 넓이와 자신이 관할하는 소작농의 수로 자신의 권력을 판단했고, 이로써 소작농이 경작하는 쌀의 양이 결정되었다. 소작농들은 영주들에게 강제 노역을 제공해야만 했다. 이는 모든 소작농들로 하여금, 필요한 곳이면 어디에서라도, 영주에게 무료로 노동력을 제공할 것을 요구했던 시스템이었다. 여기에는 건설 작업이나 혹은 심지어 전투 참여도 포함될 수 있었다. 하지만 중국인 이민자들에게는 그러한 의무가 없었기 때문에 그들은 자유롭게 돌아다니면서 무역에 종사할 수 있었다.

무역의 기반은 쌀이었기 때문에 쌀은 종종 물물 교환 방식을 통해 다른 물품들과 교환되었다. 이 지역에서는 주로 두 가지 종류의 쌀이 재배되었다. 하나는 지역 품종으로, 이 쌀은 조리하면 점성이 있어서 서로 잘 달라붙었다. 오늘날 태국의 고지대에서 재배되는 주요한 품종인 이 쌀은, 관개 시스템에 의해 유입되는 물의 양이 조절되는, 깊이가 얕은 논에서 자란다. 하지만 아유타야의 토지의 상당 부분은 현재의 방콕을 가로지르는 강들이 있는 차오 프라야 범람원에 있었다. 이 넓은 지역은 50센티미터 정도 깊이의 물에 잠겨 있었으며, 이 때문에 단립도를 재배하는 것은 불가능했다. 따라서 아유타야 왕국 초기에 타이인들은 벵갈 지역으로부터 부도라는 품종의 쌀을 들여왔다. 이는 보다 긴 낟알을 가지고 있었고, 고지대에서 재배되는 쌀과 같은 점성을 지니고 있지 않았으며, 가장 중요했던 점으로, 수심이 깊은 범람원에서도 잘 자랐다.

그 결과 아유타야 지역의 농업에 커다란 변화가 일어났다. 갑자기 보다 넓은 토지에서 경작이 가능해지고 더 많은 쌀이 재배될 수 있게 되자 왕국의 부는 급격히 증가했다. 새롭게 얻은 부와 권력의 중심지로 기능했던 요새화된 도시 덕분에 타이인들은 동남아시아에서 가장 강력한 민족이 되었다. 이후 수 세기 동안 그들이 통치하는 영토는 늘어났고 많은 지역에서 아유타야 타이 지도자에게 조공을 바쳐야만 했다. (이러한 지역에는 지금의 캄보디아, 라오스, 그리고 미얀마에 위치해 있었던 왕국들이 포함된다.) 이는 유럽인들이 이해했던 것과 달리 지리적인 관점의 영토를 관할함으로써 나온 권력이 아니었다. 대신 부, 영향력, 그리고 지도자들 간의 개인적인 관계에 기반해 있었다. 때때로 반란이 일어났고, 외부 세력들, 주로 중국인들과 유럽 인들이 아유타야 왕국에 영향력을 행사하려고 했다. 하지만 4세기 이상 아유타야의 통치자들은 대규모의 쌀 생산과 무역에 힘입어 해당 지역을 지배했다.

왕국의 몰락은 18세기 후반에 이루어졌다. 외세에 의해, 특히 무역에서 이권을 차지하려는 유럽인들의 시도에 의해 지배층이 분열되기 시작했다. 연이어 발생한 내부의 반란과 함께, 단기간에 이루어진 몇몇 통치자들의 왕위 찬탈 사건들은 왕국을 약화시켰다. 1765년 버마군이 침략했을 때 타이인들은 저항할 수 없었다. 아유타야의 위대한 도시는, 그곳의 모든 부로도 도시를 구할 수는 없었으므로, 1767년 포위를 당해 불에 타버렸다.

WORD REMINDER

fortify 요새화하다 converge 모이다 tribute 조공, 공물 tract 면적, 넓이 arable 경작하는 corvee 강제 노역, 부역 glutinous 끈적끈적한 staple 주식 paddy 벼 floodplain 범람원 short-grained rice 단립도 (짧고 둥근 모양에 가까운 벼) floating rice 부도 (깊은 물속에서 자라는 벼) alteration 변화 exponentially 기하급수적으로 bolster 강화하다 hold sway ~을 지배하다 downfall 몰락 concession 이권, 허가 usurp 찬탈하다

Passage 3 • Zoology p.204

꿀벌의 의사 결정

꿀벌은 수분을 퍼뜨려서 꽃과 나무를 수정시키는 능력을 가지고 있기 때문에 생태계에서 매우 중요한 요소이다. 이들은 꿀벌 무리라고 불리는 군집 형태의 생활을 하며, 각각은 벌집이라고 불리는 둥지에서 살아간다. 전형적인 꿀벌 무리는 한 마리의 여왕벌과 수벌이라 불리는 몇 마리의 수컷 꿀벌, 그리고 일벌이라 불리는 수천 마리의 암컷 꿀벌들로 구성된다. 봄이 되면 대부분의 꿀벌 무리는 벌집에 개체수가 과도하게 많아지는 상황에 마주한다. 꿀벌 무리에게 이러한 일이 발생하면 꿀벌 무리는 둘로 갈라진다. 꿀벌들의 절반은 벌집에 남지만, 이전 여왕의 암컷 새끼인 새로운 여왕이 이들을 이끌

게 된다. 나머지 절반의 꿀벌들은 원래의 여왕을 따라 새로운 둥지로 이동한다. 꿀벌들이 벌집을 짓기 위한 새로운 장소를 찾을 때 소리를 내지 않는다는 점은 그들이 정교한 방법으로 상호 커뮤니케이션을 할 수 있다는 사실을 나타낸다.

새로운 둥지를 찾는 과정은 무리를 떠나려는 꿀벌들이 벌집 밖에서 구름떼와 같은 커다란 무리를 지을 때 시작된다. 잠시 후 이들은, 새로운 둥지를 지을 곳이 정해질 때까지 머무르게 될, 인근 장소로 — 보통은 나무로 — 일제히 날아간다. 대부분의 벌들이 기다리는 동안, 수십 마리의 정찰벌들이 수색을 시작하기 위해 사방으로 날아간다. 각각의 정찰벌은 무리로 되돌아오면 생물학자들이 벌의 춤이라고 부르는 행동을 통해 보고를 한다. 이러한 의식적인 춤에서 꿀벌은 8자 모양으로 움직이며 동작 중간에, 마치 꿀벌이 꼬리를 흔드는 것처럼 보이게 만드는, 몸을 옆으로 떠는 행동을 한다. 이러한 움직임은 자신이 발견한 것을 무리에게 알리는 정찰벌들의 방법이다. 정찰벌은 무리가 이동하기를 원하는 방향으로 벌춤을 춘다. 예를 들어 무리가 북쪽으로 이동하기를 원하는 꿀벌은 무리의 북쪽에서 벌춤을 춘다.

벌춤을 관찰하면 각각의 정찰벌이 춤을 통해 자신이 발견한 장소의 상태를 알려 주는 것처럼 보인다. 벌춤에 동작이 보다 많은 경우는 벌이 좋은 장소를 발견했다는 점을 의미한다. 되돌아온 각각의 정찰벌은 많은 벌들이 함께 춤을 출 때까지 벌춤을 추기 시작한다. 그 후 정찰벌들은 가장 적극적으로 춤을 추는 벌이 있는 곳으로 점차 이동하여 그 벌과 같은 동작의 춤을 추기 시작한다. 사실상 정찰벌들이 동의를 표시하는 것이다. 마침내 모든 정찰벌들이 같은 동작으로 춤을 추면, 꿀벌 무리는 그들을 따라 새로운 장소를 향해 떠난다.

비디오 촬영 장비를 이용하여 정찰벌의 벌춤을 면밀히 연구한 결과, 새로운 장소를 찾고 결정을 내린 후 새로운 둥지로 이동하는데 보통 3일에서 5일 정도가 걸린다는 점이 밝혀졌다. 일부 경우, 예컨대 비가 올 때와 같이, 날씨가 좋지 않은 경우에는 보통 꿀벌들이 이동을 하지 않기 때문에 이러한 과정에 시간이 더 걸릴 수도 있다. (이에 대한 한 가지 이유로 꿀벌의 날개에 묻은 수분 때문에 꿀벌이 공중으로 날아올라 떠 있는 것이 어려울 수 있다는 점을 들 수 있다.) 과학자들은 또한 정찰벌이 하루에 12시간에서 16시간 동안 벌춤을 춘다는 점에도 주목했다. 의사 결정의 첫 단계에서는 대다수의 정찰벌들이 벌집 후보지를 지정하지 않는 것으로 보인다. 예를 들어 한 연구에서는 첫째 날에 정찰벌들이 아홉 개의 서로 다른 방향으로 춤을 추었다. 하지만 벌춤이 계속되면서 중간 단계에 이르면 일부 정찰벌들이 춤을 멈추고 가장 적극적으로 춤을 추는 다른 정찰벌들과 합류한다. 마지막으로 의사 결정의 마지막 단계에는 점점 더 많은 정찰벌들이 자신의 춤을 추지 않고 다른 정찰벌들과 합류한다. 생물학자들이 관찰했던 사실상 모든 경우에서 벌의 무리가 어느 방향으로 가야 하는지에 대한 정찰벌들의 결정은 결국 만장일치로 정해졌다.

꿀벌들이 이처럼 독특한 방식으로 결정을 내리도록 만드는 메커니즘은 생물학자들에게 미스터리로 남아 있다. 몇몇 학자들은, 다른 정찰벌들이 더 큰 열정을 보이는 후보지가 있는 경우, 자신이 생각한 후보지에 대한 열의를 버리게 만드는 화학적인 과정이 정찰벌에게 일어난다고 추측한다. 결국 이것은 벌들의 무리로 하여금 벌집을 새로 지을 수 있는 장소를 찾을 수 있게 함으로써 꿀벌의 생존을 보장해 주는 자연적인 방법인 것이다.

WORD REMINDER

component 구성 요소 pollen 꽃가루 swarm 떼, 무리 overpopulated 인구 과잉인 demonstrate 입증하다 en masse 한꺼번에, 일제히 commence 시작하다 waggle 흔들다 divulge (비밀을) 누설하다, 알려 주다 inclement (춥거나 비가 와서) 좋지 못한 unanimous 만장일치의 eagerness 열의

MEMO

MEMO

MEMO

TOEFL® MAP ACTUAL TEST

New TOEFL® Edition

Reading 2